A Darker Shade of Crimson

Odyssey of a Harvard Chicano

BANTAM BOOKS

NEW YORK

TORONTO

LONDON

SYDNEY

AUCKLAND

A DARKER SHADE OF CRIMSON

ODYSSEY OF A HARVARD CHICANO

RUBEN NAVARRETTE, JR.

A DARKER SHADE OF CRIMSON

A Bantam Book/November 1993

All rights reserved.
Copyright © 1993 by Ruben Navarrette, Jr.

Grateful acknowledgment is made for permission to reprint from the follow-ing: "Stopping By Woods On a Snowy Evening." From *The Poetry of Robert Frost* edited by Edward Connery Lathem. Copyright 1951 by Robert Frost. Cop-yright 1923, © 1969 by Henry Holt and Company, Inc. Reprinted by permission of Henry Holt and Company, Inc. The lines from "being to timelessness as it's to time," are reprinted from *Complete Poems, 1904–1962*, by E. E. Cummings, Edited by George J. Firmage, by permission of Liveright Publishing Corpora-tion. Copyright © 1923, 1925, 1926, 1931, 1935, 1938, 1939, 1940, 1944, 1945, 1946, 1947, 1948, 1949, 1950, 1951, 1952, 1953, 1954, 1955, 1956, 1957, 1958, 1959, 1960, 1961, 1962 by E. E. Cummings. Copyright © 1961, 1963, 1966, 1967, 1968 by Marion Morehouse Cummings. Copyright © 1972, 1973, 1974, 1975, 1976 , 1977, 1978, 1979, 1980, 1981, 1982, 1983, 1984, 1985, 1986, 1987, 1988, 1989, 1990, 1991 by the Trustees for the E. E. Cummings Trust.

Book design by Barbara M. Bachman

Library of Congress Cataloging-in-Publication Data
Navarrette, Ruben.
A darker shade of crimson : odyssey of a Harvard chicano / by
Ruben Navarrette, Jr.
p. cm.
ISBN 0-553-08998-6
1. Mexican Americans—Education (Higher)—Massachusetts—
Cambridge—Case studies. 2. Harvard University. I. Title.
LC2683.6.N38 1993
378.1'98'0896872—dc20   93-7985
                                                                          CIP

Published simultaneously in the United States and Canada

PRINTED IN THE UNITED STATES OF AMERICA

BVG 0 9 8 7 6 5 4 3 2 1

In a speech, I once referred to them as the two best teachers that I ever had. The handsome young couple in black-and-white wedding pictures. So perfectly suited to parenthood. So completely convinced that education alone would pave the road to a better, gentler life for their children. They provided us with love and support and, when necessary, argument. They taught us our earliest lessons. They praised us incessantly, and boasted of us shamelessly. Their commitment to using education to secure something more for their children endured long after the horrible moment when they were no longer able to understand our homework assignments.

For my mother and father.

"A MAN DOES NOT SHOW HIS GREATNESS BY BEING AT ONE EXTREME,
BUT BY TOUCHING BOTH AT ONCE."

ALBERT CAMUS

"THE WORLD MUST KNOW, FROM THIS TIME FORWARD, THAT THE
MEXICAN-AMERICAN IS COMING INTO HIS OWN RIGHT. YOU ARE
WINNING A SPECIAL KIND OF CITIZENSHIP: NO ONE IS DOING IT FOR
YOU—YOU ARE WINNING IT YOURSELVES—AND THEREFORE NO ONE
CAN EVER TAKE IT AWAY."

ROBERT F. KENNEDY

HARVARD COLLEGE, CLASS OF 1948

CONTENTS

I glance at the Harvard diploma collecting dust on a shelf in my parents' living room. As months turn to years, it is getting harder and harder to remember the college experiences that I was once so sure I could never forget. Experiences that influenced my life in profound, even frightening, ways. Experiences so personal, so intimate, that many of those who have lived through similar ones would never dare embark on the introspective journey that these pages represent. That is especially true of those who have come before me, those who could have taken the journey many years ago but did not.

This year marks the twenty-fifth anniversary of the first class of Chicano students to enter Harvard College in the fall of 1968—the dismal season that followed the assassination of Martin Luther King, Jr. A gesture of healing, proponents of affirmative action called it. What was then only a small handful of students has, in a quarter century, grown inch by inch into a bigger handful. In 1985, I entered the college as one of thirty-five Mexican-American students in my freshman class and became one of the one hundred twenty-five such students on the entire campus. Today, those numbers are almost exactly the same.

Harvard is, it will tell you, proud of its recruitment efforts and its sprinkling of Mexican-Americans. From a population who number over 20 million in the United States, the admissions committee of what is perhaps the finest educational institution in the country has somehow managed to find enough "qualified" young people to make up a mediocre 2.5 percent of Harvard's student body.

Those talented few Mexican-Americans who have squeaked through a barely opened door into an ancient world of privilege are undeniably fortunate. And it is the idea of being a fortunate one, a chosen one, that has defined every aspect of my experience. That simple idea has nurtured my ambition, reassured me of my ability, and at times of distress sustained me in the belief that I would somehow endure and survive. Yet, as an unforgivable side-effect, the concept has also subjected me to horrible loneliness, alienated me from the once-familiar intimacies of my hometown and family, and gradually consumed me with guilt over the precarious nature of academic success in the American educational system.

Now, three years after my graduation from college, it is those experiences that call out for redress.

"What's this I hear?" a young friend asks. "You're writing a *book?*"

I notice the hint of surprise in her voice, the emphasis on a word that is for so much of my generation so unfamiliar. Conventional wisdom suggests that, for people my age, books are not as glamorous as trendy magazines and compact discs. Publishing executives believe, argue, swear that young adults simply do not buy books, read books, even steal books. The argument is not without merit. In the Los Angeles riots, a tide of young hooligans looted scores of record stores while nearby bookstores were left untouched.

"There are some things that happened to me in college, at Harvard, that I need to say out loud," I explain, hoping that she will drop the questioning.

Consider this ambitious effort first and foremost a catharsis promising to exorcise demons that linger in the clearest recollections of my college years. Years that are usually intended to be carefree and delicate were, in my case, neither. For the five years of my university experience, and in truth for many more years that preceded it, the separate entities of education and ethnicity—co-existing, co-operating, and at times colliding with one another—have come together, in bizarre and precarious ways, to define the character of my life.

My friend presses on with a smile, "What have you done that's worth writing a whole book about?"

As she awaits my response, I sense that she craves an answer tinged with scandal, controversy, suspenseful drama. She and I are part of a generation whose childhood bedtime story was a tantalizing movie of the week. Ask high-priced advertising executives who sell fast-food hamburgers and expensive tennis shoes to the estimated 80 million Americans who are between eleven and thirty years old, and they will tell you matter-of-factly that we understand only sound bites and sensationalism.

If my story were a film, I might envision a studio executive in Hollywood fishing for a storyline in the waters of his imagination. "Okay, a Mexican kid at Harvard. Got it. Was he a gang-banger? No, no. The son of farmworkers, right? I can see it all: Spanish-speaking family, tortillas at dinner, the whole nine yards. Real tear-jerker stuff. Right? Right?"

Wrong.

Mine is an unassuming middle-class existence, a reward for my parents' many years of hard work and sacrifice. I have soft hands and even softer experiences. Thankfully, I have not picked grapes or spent years toiling hopelessly in the packing houses that surround my hometown. I have light skin and features that harken back to Mexico's politically incorrect Spanish ancestors; ah, to have been born with a face that is more loyal to the Indian blood that flows through my veins—the credibility that would win me with my old friends and new critics from the ethnic left. And I only occasionally eat tortillas, these days feeling equally at home in a Chinese restaurant as in a Mexican one.

And, in what is, for many of the elders, the biggest disappointment of all, I—like most of my generation of Mexican-Americans—speak Spanish poorly. Horribly, in fact. The intimate, delicate words of my grandparents get stuck in my throat like a chicken bone as aunts and uncles snicker, teasing me for losing *our* language. They are wrong; I could not have lost what I never had. My language is English.

Questions of ethnic identity have, for me, never been easy. The cultural charade over which I obsessed for half my time at Harvard actually had its roots in the innocence of childhood. One day, in kindergarten, I walked home from school and confronted my mother with a fundamental question. I told her that there were some children at school whose skin was white and others whose skin was brown. Mine, I noted, was a confused shade of beige. Turning to my mother, I demanded an explanation. "What am I?" I asked her.

Nearly twenty years later, as a senior at Harvard, I woke up one morning in a dormitory along the Charles River. It was a week before my graduation from the oldest and most prestigious college in the country. I had reason to be proud, excited. I had survived a Harvard education—an exploit that had eluded several of my classmates. Still, I could not escape the unresolved questions of the past. Aware that some would anoint me a representative of the millions of Mexican-Americans who will never set foot in Harvard Yard, I questioned my fitness for the role. Methodically, critically, I studied the figure in the bathroom mirror. I remember that I found little comfort in the image of a middle class, light-skinned *pocho* who spoke Spanish poorly.

Perhaps because of what some might consider my dubious authenticity, the skepticism of others is an old friend. An aunt of mine, much more well educated than her siblings, recently floated a snide remark through the river of family gossip. Something about how I shouldn't be writing a book at my age, so young and so lacking in the wisdom that comes with age. In her mind, such endeavors were more properly the folly of older people.

And, what do I have to say anyway? The autobiography of a twenty-five-year-old? Imagine!

Others will surely be proud of the accomplishment. I envision the smile on one uncle's face, his proud boast to neighbors. "Be sure to read my nephew's book." Undoubtedly, some of the pride will be based on something over which I have no control: my ethnicity. No one concedes the vicarious bond of a shared background as readily as my father, the man who has always understood that my experience belongs to others. My father still marvels, proudly, at the Latino politician heading a government agency, or at the young Chicano with an Olympic gold medal, or at the young Mexican-American woman walking down the run-way of a national beauty pageant. Having swallowed fifty years of absence—of Latinos not being on television, not attending college and graduate school, not writing books or making movies—he is a boy again with each new discovery of a brown face in a high place.

"Look, a *mexicano*," he says as he points to the television set. With the surprised smile on his face, one might think that he had just seen a leprechaun.

Latinos, like the ones who eight years ago praised the Harvard acceptance letter in my hand, may now extol the published manuscript in theirs. In the past, I have not bathed in such attention but have typically recoiled into a private embarrassment. Years ago, a few months after my graduation from college, the one major newspaper in the San Joaquin Valley ran a story about me in its Sunday edition. In the space

of two full pages, the story lauded my accomplishments, cul-
minating in my graduation from Harvard. I remember the story's pompous headline, so full of itself introducing a young
man, so full of himself: "Bound For Glory." In the days and
weeks after the article appeared, my father was routinely approached by dozens of people—good and kind people, many of
them Latino—who congratulated him for my success.

I remember the Mexican-American woman, a stranger to me,
who called my parents' home on the same day that the article
appeared. She called to thank me, she said. A graduate of my
old high school some thirty years ago, in the bleak days when
my parents attended it, she told me that she was proud of my
accomplishments. She implored me to realize that, given generations of educational neglect of Latino students, my achievement takes on a life of its own. It is bigger than me, she said.
It transcends my individual distinctions, the assortment of academic awards on the shelf in my parents' living room, and
becomes a symbol for others. A faint beacon in the dark mine
shaft of low expectations.

"You don't understand," she said. "What you've done . . . you
don't know what it means, what it means to all of us, here in
this town." Suddenly there is a sniffle. "You don't know"—by
the time she finishes her sentence, she is in tears—"how they
treated us back then."

Instantly, I am convinced that her story is infinitely more interesting than mine. I thank her for her kind words, and I wish
her well. As I hang up the phone and hide for a moment in
silence, I realize that she is right. I do not know.

Because I want to know, I have attempted a reconciliation of
sorts. I have begun a second education. I have asked the elders
to tell me their stories. I have traveled throughout the San Joaquin Valley, listening to the concerns of elementary and secondary school students. I have delivered motivational speeches
to those who do not consider themselves worthy of attending a
school like Harvard. I have attempted to change that horrible
notion, and to change it early. John F. Kennedy once recited a
story about a French marshal who asked his gardener to plant
a tree, but the gardener maintained that the effort was pointless since it would not bloom for a hundred years. "In that
case," the marshal replied, "plant it this afternoon."

It is in that spirit that I find myself speaking to a third-grade class in a poor rural town. The young Mexican faces before me seem tired and lost. Still, today there is excitement about their guest speaker. As my contribution to the traditions of show and tell, my Harvard diploma is passed throughout the room by tiny hands. As it returns to me, I see in the tiny fingerprints smudged against the framed glass the flickering hope of a future generation.

For now, though, I am consumed most by the challenges facing my generation, in all its shades. Invariably, from campus activism to book buying to voting, the elders are disappointed in us. "Twenty-nothings," someone called us. We have inherited not only debt, but also despair and division. We have learned, from our parents, not to trust one another. But I am tired of old battles, of the labeling, of the assessing of ethnic authenticity, and of the American tendency to discriminate against one human being in favor of another. It is my hope that my contemporaries will learn from the mistakes of those who have come before us.

At the brink of the twenty-first century, a young man settling into adulthood knows at least two things. One is that the American educational system is badly in need of repair, particularly with regard to its treatment of minority students. Only if our country can honor its educational promise with regard to all its citizens will it be able to live up to its true spirit. The other is that our society is coming apart at the racial seams and must launch an honest, and perhaps painful, national dialogue on the racial division that has steadily worsened to an alarming level. These are the challenges left over for the leaders of tomorrow, those who have overcome the constraints of their parents' racial prejudices, inhibitions, and insecurities. It is left to the youngsters to create, in a new century, what Robert Kennedy called "a better world."

And so, in these pages is written a story for this generation.

Ruben Navarrette, Jr.

Sanger, CA

February 1993

A young man finds himself gradually abandoning a boy's words. Angry, confining words.

In this text, I have most frequently used the term *Mexican-American* to refer to an American citizen of Mexican ancestry. At times, I use the word *Mexican*—not to describe a citizen of Mexico but, rather as a relaxed substitute for the hyphenated term; some may take exception to this, but that is precisely the way in which I heard it used in my childhood and adolescence.

I have refrained from using the term *people of color*, which I find offensive, preferring instead the more relative term *minority*. I have not often used the word *chicano*—a political remnant of an earlier time. I have also been reluctant to use the more contemporary term *Hispanic*, choosing *Latino* instead, though not for the same reasons that the ethnic left finds the label *Hispanic* objectionable. Not because of the term's implicit reference to Spain—the conquering father of Latin America— or the fact that it was, a decade ago, introduced into the public vocabulary by government bureaucrats. But simply because the word attempts, too conveniently, to lump together too many people who are, in reality, too different.

Still, the reader may find some of these terms indiscreetly intermixed. I am tired of answering questions, however well-intentioned, from non-Latinos about which labels are preferred and which are off-limits. "So, what should we call you . . . your people, I mean?"

These are inquiries best asked of the elders, those whose wrinkled scars have—for fifty years—cried out for what they assume to be the soothing ointment of respect. My generation, so numerous and so troubled, has more urgent matters to address.

CHAPTER 1

"IF YOU HADN'T BEEN MEXICAN..."

"I YIELD TO NO ONE IN MY EARNEST HOPE THAT THE TIME
WILL COME WHEN AN AFFIRMATIVE ACTION PROGRAM IS
UNNECESSARY AND IS, IN TRUTH, ONLY A RELIC OF THE
PAST. . . .
BUT IN ORDER TO GET BEYOND RACISM, WE MUST FIRST
TAKE ACCOUNT OF RACE. THERE IS NO OTHER WAY."

HON. HARRY BLACKMUN

   HARVARD LAW SCHOOL, CLASS OF 1932
   UNIVERSITY OF CALIFORNIA V. BAKKE: DISSENT

"THE EXPERIENCE OF OTHER UNIVERSITY ADMISSIONS
PROGRAMS, WHICH TAKE RACE INTO ACCOUNT IN
ACHIEVING EDUCATIONAL DIVERSITY, DEMONSTRATES THAT
THE ASSIGNMENT OF A FIXED NUMBER OF PLACES TO A
MINORITY GROUP IS NOT A NECESSARY MEANS TOWARD
THAT END. . . . AN ILLUMINATING EXAMPLE IS FOUND IN
THE HARVARD COLLEGE PROGRAM."

HON. LEWIS POWELL

   HARVARD LAW SCHOOL, CLASS OF 1932
   UNIVERSITY OF CALIFORNIA V. BAKKE: MAJORITY

The adventure begins with an overstuffed manila envelope in my parents' mailbox.

It was one of five parcels that I received in those warm April days, the kind that invoke the gentle serenity of springtime in the San Joaquin Valley. This place called home. The return address of each bundle alluded seductively to forbidden places of privilege and affluence far away from a small farming town in the center of California. Despite stiff competition for spots in the entering classes of elite universities, an arrogant high school senior was playing the college admissions game for high stakes. Without a net, if you will. I had applied to only five schools, each of them extremely competitive.

These were schools that, a generation earlier, my parents would never have dreamed of attending. More historically honest, schools that, before the late 1960s, Mexican-Americans were simply not allowed to attend. For those colleges and universities generally considered the most exclusive—if not the best—in the country, the criteria for admission was once quite clear. Qualified candidates were from private preparatory academies in the East. They were wealthy, male, and Protestant. And, of no small importance, they were white.

Now, several generations of protest and petition and sit-ins later, five letters of acceptance beckoned a Mexican-American boy who knew nothing of racism. Of denial of privilege because of one's skin color. The concept was almost foreign to me, locked away at a safe distance in dusty history books about the American South. It was certainly nothing that had affected me—a light-skinned, middle-class child of progress who spoke Spanish poorly, four embarrassing years of high school instruction in the native language of my grandparents notwithstanding.

A naive seventeen-year-old took as a final, bold reaffirmation of his legitimate place in white America five letters congratulating his academic success and offering him a highly coveted space in their private world. These were, after all, schools of high reputation with student bodies and faculty lists that were overwhelmingly white. Berkeley. Stanford. Princeton. Yale.

But it was the letter from Cambridge, Massachusetts, that my parents and I awaited with the most anticipation. It began: "I am delighted to report that the Committee on Admissions and Financial Aid has voted to admit you to the Harvard College Class of 1989." My eyes left the page and I read no further. To this day, I have never read in its entirety the one piece of paper that has completely changed my life.

The choice of which offer to accept was one I took seriously. A diligent, yet unimaginative student, I left nothing to chance. Since my sophomore year, I had collected bits of information that filled five bulging manila folders. I spoke by phone with admissions officers and current undergraduates. I knew which schools had the best resources and happiest students. I knew about the surrounding college towns in which students lived. Should I be accepted to more than one, I was determined to be a selective buyer. After all, I reasoned, I would suffer the immediate consequences of my decision for four years and feel its full effect for many more years after that.

It both amused and irritated me that, for my parents, the choice was much clearer. Student recruiters from colleges competing with Harvard for bright high school seniors routinely complain about the international name recognition afforded the oldest, most prestigious university in the country. "You've got the name, that's all . . . ," a dear friend at Yale once told me in frustration after a Mexican-American prospect from El Paso told her of his intention to study in Cambridge and not New Haven. Like it or not, almost everyone has heard of Harvard and, around the country and world, many who hear the name equate it with great intelligence and academic quality.

Perhaps the assumed quality of the institution was half the reason my parents believed that I would choose Harvard over the others. I hear my father's voice: "If you can have the best, then why not take the best?" The best—an elusive term! Image, what people think, has always been more important to my father than it is to his oldest son. The way he saw it, if you were going to a dance, why not take the prettiest girl that you could find? And Harvard was, everyone said, the prettiest girl of all.

Pretty was fine, but personality was becoming more important to a skeptical young man who was far more concerned with having a good time at the dance than looking good on the way there.

The other half of Harvard's allure for my parents, the part that I shared, is more cynical. It was the school's exclusivity, the fact that there were, I knew, fewer acceptance letters like mine to Harvard floating across the country and world than to the other four schools. "Not everyone can go to a school like that," my mother said matter-of-factly at breakfast one morning as she placed a plate of *huevos con chorizo* in front of me.

Given the tiny percentage of Latino students in the United States who will one day be in a position to excel in high school and to attend a predominantly white college like Harvard, its exclusivity has special meaning for my people. I remember wondering to myself, as dark-skinned Mexican parents listened intently to a College Night presentation about Harvard, if they would be as interested in the school if its student body was, say, 80 or 90 percent Latino. I suspect not. Would they be as impressed with a school in which the vast majority of students and faculty looked not like the President of the United States, or the majority of the Congress, or most of the country's lawyers and businessmen, but like *them*? And if not, what awful meaning should I attach to that? Is our image of ourselves so damaged and degraded?

It may be that Mexican-American parents anxious for their children to attend exclusive schools such as Harvard or Yale feel that way precisely because only a few of the millions of Mexican-American students who graduate from high schools in the United States are deemed capable of attending the traditional bastions of white male privilege. This sad logic dictates that, as the number of minority students on campus increases (as with public universities), the perceived quality of the institution suffers.

An official from the University of California at Berkeley, where white students are a numerical minority, tells me that in the most recent round of admissions, over 70 percent of Chicano applicants were accepted—a rate twice that of white applicants. I remember my father's snobby distaste for the school, the assumption that "*anyone* with a Spanish surname can get into Berkeley." That sentiment quieted only after my brother began study at the East Bay campus.

Harvard was not nearly as racially integrated as Berkeley. In the early 1990s, over 20 percent of the student population at Berkeley was Mexican-American; at Harvard during the same years the figure was a dismal, almost laughable, 2.5 percent. For my parents, and perhaps too many more like them, that meant that Harvard was more exclusive, more selective. Better. At very least, *whiter.* What awful meaning...

There was, I would learn, an overall significance to my acceptance to Harvard that went well beyond my being a determined and studious seventeen-year-old.

As I began my junior year, the student body of Sanger High School was over 60 percent Mexican-American. The school served a small community of less than 20,000 people that was nearly 70 percent Latino. Still, until the warm April day on which I received my letter of acceptance, there had never been a Chicano graduate of my predominantly Mexican high school who had been accepted to Harvard. I would be the first. For me, therein lay much of the attraction—and also, I would soon learn, an odd sense of responsibility.

Along downtown Seventh Street, a Mexican housewife gives congratulations. With warm words in Spanish, an old man offers his hand, calloused by decades of field work. Strangers. "We did it!" *We.* It seemed odd to me at the time that people whom I did not know could somehow feel vicariously enriched, even empowered, by a piece of paper in *my* hand.

The boy did not know then what the man knows now: A shared ethnicity provided a link between them and me, allowing them to share in my accomplishments. My father understood much better than me, claiming that those who would approach him in the years to come and routinely ask about my progress somehow "claimed a piece" of me. They owned a part of any success that I might enjoy, my father explained. People like me. Different than me. Not until much later would I appreciate fully, and eventually even resent, the weight of their claim.

In spite of the statistical dominance of Latinos, my hometown resembled a sociological experiment in minority rule in which positions of power, prestige, and influence invariably belonged to white people. For instance, in the one hundred year history of the district there had never been a Mexican-American principal of its high school or superintendent of schools. Ambitious Latino administrators would stay a few years before leaving with bumps on the top of their heads from hitting ceilings of glass. In the high school's main office there was a long row of framed photographs of former principals. Was I the only one to notice that all the faces were of white males?

It was perhaps because of this shortage of Latino representation that my private life was washed away in a stream of acceptance letters to elite colleges and replaced, almost immediately, by a more unnerving public one. A Mexican writer for the local newspaper mentioned my name in a column, along with the names of all the colleges to which I had been accepted. The column was written in Spanish, a language that I had some difficulty reading, by a man whom I did not know. A man who, in his lifetime, knew discrimination that I did not know.

I went from being the subtle boast of my parents to a symbol of hope, a beacon for other Hispanic parents who wanted desperately to believe that our country's promise of equal educational opportunity would not go unfulfilled for their children. As unfulfilled as it had been for them, dating back scores of horrid school years past.

In a new age when some, albeit too few, Latino students are graduating at the top of their high school classes and attending elite universities such as Stanford, Yale, and Princeton, I was tempted to dismiss the injustices of the past with a hopeless sigh. "That was then, this is now." In fact, much of my generation has no knowledge whatsoever of the forms of educational malpractice inflicted upon Mexican-Americans in just this century.

Because most history textbooks conspicuously ignore such matters, it falls to a new generation to ask the elders to tell us their stories. As I prepared to graduate from a public school system that had treated me well, I asked, and was told.

My grandfather tells me in Spanish of a memory now over sixty summers old—a memory of two separate schoolhouses in Goliad, Texas, a small town near San Antonio, where he and his Mexican classmates were placed in one school and his white classmates in another. The Anglo teacher spent the entire day in the white school teaching the white students, leaving the Mexicans to draw and doodle with inferior supplies that had been discarded by the others. In fact, the only time she turned her attention to the Mexican students was to dole out punishment. For sixty years, he has carried with him the impression that *los gringos* consider themselves better than non-white people and are inclined to use societal institutions to support that prejudice. The thing I find most amazing is, that a general distrust of white America notwithstanding, he speaks with no bitterness for the injustice that he and countless others suffered. There is not much *coraje* here. Yet as I stare into his eyes and see immediately the pain in the life lived by this hard-working man with hard hands, I cannot be as gracious.

In my own hometown, the historical march of Mexican-Americans toward the mythical land of equal educational opportunity has been a slow but deliberate one. Fifty years ago, in the years before and after World War II, most Mexican-American children were not enrolled in public schools. In many cases they were not allowed to enter, and in other cases, they were prevented from attending by factors beyond their control. Even if born in the United States, they spoke Spanish as their first language and traveled the state during the school year working alongside their immigrant parents in the peach orchards, lettuce patches, and grape fields of the San Joaquin Valley.

For those tempted to heap blame on parents for a life of migratory fieldwork that made school attendance impossible, it is important to remember that at the time the idea of public schooling was, for many Latino parents, simply beyond their frame of reference. Imagine the suspicion and uncertainty of today's parents if they were asked to send their children through courses preparing them for space travel. Perhaps Mexican parents were afraid that their children would be mistreated in an institution that was controlled by people who looked nothing like them. The events of the next five decades suggest that their fear was a reasonable one.

In the 1950s, those Mexican-American children who were finally incorporated into the Sanger Unified School District were assigned to attend elementary schools that were still racially segregated. An uncle of mine, an earlier graduate of Sanger High School, remembers two elementary schools at separate ends of town. The students at one were exclusively white; those at the other, exclusively Mexican. He remembers asking a school official about the two schools. He was told that they existed because students were "different," and that he should not ask again. The official said "different" but could have just as honestly said "better."

I pressed my uncle: "How did you know, as a ten-year-old, that the white school was better than the Mexican school? Different, yeah, but *better?*" He replied with ease. "Simple. The equipment, the baseball diamonds, the classrooms, the books that students had with them were all newer, better than ours." The hurtful lesson passed on to a ten-year-old Mexican boy was that those in power, school officials who "knew best," considered white students in the same school district to be better than him.

Another uncle, and yet another graduate of Sanger High School, remembers a series of more subtle, but no less obvious, efforts by white elementary school officials to maintain what they must have believed to be the natural order of things. Once, his mouth was literally taped shut by a teacher. My uncle remembers that when the class drank its milk and ate its graham crackers, that he was—as the only Mexican boy in his class— each day assigned to pick up the empty milk bottles. At the time, he naturally thought it a privilege; since then, he has come to appreciate a more sinister motive. He also remembers clearly that, in the lunch line, he and the other Mexican children were placed at the end of the line, while the white students assumed their "natural" place at the front. At least the Mexican children were allowed into the cafeteria, he admits. "There was another group that they hated more than us and they ate outside," he recalls over his coffee. The time period was post–World War II, and the boys and girls who suffered such indignities were Japanese-Americans.

Most of all, he remembers one afternoon when his teacher discovered a few dollars missing from her desk drawer. Incredibly, she sent the white students out to recess and kept the Mexican children in their seats, asking over and over which one of them had taken the money. The students denied any wrongdoing and yet the police were called. Later, the culprit was eventually discovered to be a white student. The teacher never apologized for her prejudiced assumption that the thief must be Mexican, and may never have realized that she did anything wrong.

I see my uncle's hurt and feel guilty for asking questions that required answers buried deep in safe pockets of memory. He admits that, though not often discussed, such things are never really forgotten. Not only are these sorts of lessons not usually forgotten, they likely manifest themselves in years of lingering anger and insecurity. When children grew into adolescence, that anger erupted on junior high school and high school campuses into numerous interracial fistfights and even a few all-out racial brawls involving dozens of white and brown students. Without exception, gray-haired Mexican-American men—some of them now policemen, firemen, lawyers, or even a priest or two—who participated in such frustrated displays claim their racial group victorious. At least in that arena, they explain, they were allowed to excel.

Thirty years ago, in the revolutionary time of the 1960s, even as college campuses were timidly opening themselves up to nonwhite students in an attempt to be progressive, Sanger Unified seemed more intent on stifling the progress of Mexican-Americans than encouraging it. According to most accounts, such students were rarely sought out for career advice by guidance counselors; in fact, when I asked one person about career counselors, his puzzled look suggested that, in four years of high school, he had never met such people. Those Chicanos who were counseled usually received condescending advice that seemed to lower expectations rather than raise them.

One day during her senior year, my mother remembers being asked to complete a test designed to measure hand-to-eye coordination; the test consisted of having to put small beads into a small cup within a certain time frame. Conditioned by years of work in local fruit packing houses, my mother quickly mastered the task and scored the highest of the group. The white instructor who supervised the test intended to pay her a compliment, no doubt. Unfortunately, she chose entirely the wrong words: "That's great! You're good with your hands! You can work in a cannery . . . or a packing house," the woman said, unaware that she was yielding not a compliment, but an insult.

Even today, my mother still remembers the sick feeling in her stomach when, expecting to be rewarded for finishing the test first, she was instead made to feel that she was "qualified" for only a certain type of work. She was, in fact, "good with her hands" (and her mind) like a bank teller, telephone operator, or secretary should be good with their hands (and their minds). But in the 1960s world of possibility as defined by that white instructor, those jobs were reserved for someone else. Someone of another color.

For that educator and for countless others at the time, my mother and her Mexican classmates belonged in the grape fields, canneries, and packing houses. And, if that point was lost in its own subtlety, then it was accentuated through two separate field trips for seniors on Career Day. One bus, loaded with white students, toured the downtown businesses including the banks, post office, and shops. The other bus, loaded with Mexican-American students, appropriately toured the packing houses and local canneries. Apparently not worried about overstatement, the school officials had consciously taken different groups of students to different employment sites because they assumed that they were destined for different career paths. At one cannery my mother noticed an older Mexican woman with swollen and cut hands from canning peaches. My mother remembers the gruesome sight of bones in one of the woman's hands coming through her skin. This horrid place was, they said, where she belonged.

After graduation and in spite of such bad advice, my mother did go to college and later worked at a bank and at various government agencies—no thanks to career counselors at Sanger High School and the ethnic prejudices that stifled their sense of possibility.

Twenty years ago, in the years before and after the Vietnam War, despite the fact that some Sanger High graduates had discovered colleges like the University of California, the overwhelming majority of Mexican-American graduates still went off to attend either local community colleges or California State University, Fresno. There, they worked their way through school and spent five or six years collecting a four-year degree.

Ten years ago, during the Reagan Revolution, even as some Mexican-American students used outreach programs to gain access to the campuses of the University of California, there still never had been a case where one had graduated from Sanger High and attended Harvard.

In 1985, despite the all-too-familiar skepticism of educators, one Mexican-American student would be the first—a walking symbol of social change that some would still maintain had come too quickly.

After all, not everyone was pleased with the events of that spring.

A few months earlier, Ronald Reagan had been re-elected by a landslide, sporting a Republican Party platform that included a clear indictment of affirmative action programs in education and employment. Affirmative action, newspaper columnists said, was unfair to white men. Affirmative action, right-wing politicians claimed, was responsible for the hiring and promotion of unqualified women and minorities over more qualified white male co-workers. Most important to a seventeen-year-old in a small town, affirmative action, it was assumed by some, was solely responsible for my admission into schools like Harvard. I was Mexican-American. I had been accepted to Harvard. In the minds of some (it seemed like many) the two had to be connected in the most insidious of ways. $A + B = C$ Affirmative action for minorities + Bypassing standards of merit = Conspiracy to keep white people out of college. Simple.

In a senior class in which the academic elite relished cutthroat competition, my letters of acceptance to five top universities would, under normal circumstances, have been a juicy plum ripe for sharing with classmates. "Look what I've got!" Still, these circumstances were, I knew, far from normal.

Rather than a well-deserved opportunity for shameless show and tell, I suspected that my news would put me on the defensive in angry debates about the propriety of race-conscious decision-making in college admissions. Not political debates with a mere office to be won, but personal ones with the stakes being much, much higher.

I was not disappointed. In those especially warm spring days, insensitive remarks flew freely and adolescent friendships wore thin. At stake: a boy's self-esteem, honor, and dignity.

Also at stake: that boy's idealism about the rewards of hard work. The American spirit dictates that those who achieve and excel because of talent and hard work expect, perhaps deserve, to have their effort praised and not questioned. When praised, we are happy and productive. When attacked, we become embittered and cynical of the work ethic.

The first spear of the impending attack had actually come months earlier and from an unlikely source. As with much of the world's bigotry and ignorance, the most frequent culprits are not children, but grown-ups who should know better.

My high school principal had apparently heard faculty rumors about the extraordinary caliber of colleges to which I was applying. One autumn day, months before my trip to the mailbox, he took it upon himself to counsel me not to "bite off more than I could chew," so to speak. As I read Conrad in an advanced placement English class, he approached. Unannounced. Uninvited. He squeezed his six-foot frame into the uncomfortably small desk next to me. After a few moments of polite small talk about some obscure topic, he gently broached the sensitive subject that he felt compelled to discuss with me.

"Ruben, I understand that you're applying to some pretty competitive colleges. Harvard, Yale, Stanford?"

I shrugged and smiled, then nodded.

"Well, that's fine. But you should consider applying to . . . uh, well to Fresno State, too. Just in case."

I stopped smiling. *State college?* Here I was, class valedictorian with straight As and scattered A+s on my transcript, high SATs, strong recommendations, the works . . . and the man wanted me to apply to a state school, anyone-with-high-school-diploma-and-four-hundred-bucks-accepted state school!

There were classmates of mine, white classmates, who were also rumored to be applying to highly competitive colleges. Stanford. Cornell. The Naval Academy. And Harvard. As I struggled with my composure, I wondered why he had chosen me as the lucky recipient of his little speech sprung of low expectation. The sort of low expectation that his predecessors had for decades heaped upon people like me. A speech, I suspected, that he would not have dared repeat to one of my white friends with credentials like mine. Someone who would go home and tell his mother who played bridge with a school board member,

"Do you know what my principal told me?" Oh, there would be none of that, I knew. What he recognized as an insult that he dare not launch at them, he apparently gave little thought in voicing to me. I knew and, as he awaited my reply, I was sure he knew that I knew.

Biting off my words, I politely, if disingenuously, thanked him for his advice and unusual concern. I told him that I was confident I could hold my own in the admissions process, and so I would disregard his advice.

Rebuffed, the principal cast his spear. "You may be right," he said with a faint grin. "After all . . . your race should help you a lot."

In five short seconds, my high school's top administrator had casually dismissed four long years of hard work and sacrifice and the perfect grades they had produced in the toughest courses that the place had to offer. He opted instead for a more simplistic, more race-conscious explanation of why he presumed I might be accepted to an elite college. My classmates had their qualifications, Navarrette had his race on his side. And, oh yeah, a near-perfect high school record.

To his last remark, I said nothing. Maybe a polite, insincere smile to end the awkward episode. I looked away, afraid of his scornful glare. I resumed reading Conrad. *Blindfolded bearers of light destroy what they profess to enlighten. . .*

His work done, the principal lifted himself from the tiny wooden desk and walked from the classroom. He was most likely completely unaware of the sting in his words and the damage that they had done to the self-image of a young man whose talent and arrogance was supposed to make him immune to such pain. Supposed to.

And so came my nervous anticipation of spring and the storm that was brewing in its wake. Spring should mean warm San Joaquin Valley days reserved for lush walnut trees alive in the sunshine, and for baseballs whizzing through the air. It should mean young children screaming in exuberance as they scamper through high grass in search of Easter eggs, wonderfully oblivious to things like racial differences between them. A poison not yet administered them by their parents.

Yet the spring of my senior year in high school was ushered in not by sunshine or baseball, but by delicate tension, whispered innuendo, and vicious accusations by white classmates that I was simply "not qualified" to have been (legitimately) accepted into a school like Harvard. The fix was in, they said. It had to be, they reasoned.

Over years of dinner-table conversation, some of them had likely heard from their parents about "dumb and lazy Mexicans." They saw caricatures that immortalized the popular stereotype. A childhood memory of the docile "Frito Bandito." A serape-clad Mexican asleep underneath a cactus. Dumb, lazy Mexican. Mexican-Americans, they assumed, were people of the field, not of the classroom. Now, as they entered adulthood, they were confronted by an alarming contradiction. A Chicano admitted to Harvard and Yale and Princeton and . . . They searched for a plausibility that would allow them to keep their prejudice.

Compounding their confusion was the sting of rejection by some of the schools that had accepted me. They were haunted by the pain of the unwanted, something that we all struggle with sooner or later in life. When our time comes, if we are lucky, we are able to blame our shortcomings on someone else. When a pretty young girl is dumped by her boyfriend, we understand if she chooses to blame a prettier rival for her rejection.

Misunderstanding what they heard on a newscast or read in an editorial, they launched a tantrum of accusation. There was, it seemed, only one plausible answer.

"Now, you know if you hadn't been Mexican . . . ," someone said in chemistry class. . . . *you would not have been accepted*, I presumed to be the rhetorical ending never added. One girl argued in calculus that it was unfair, that she had been "turned down because (she) was white." Someone else nodded agreement, chiming in, "This is reverse discrimination!"

Reverse discrimination—that was the phrase from the evening news being carelessly bandied around by young people claiming themselves as America's newest victims. For them, my acceptance letters were the direct result not of hard work but of affirmative action. And for them, affirmative action was wrong. They were entirely unswayed by the contentions of government, the private sector, and universities that changing demographics called for race-conscious hiring and admissions. In their minds it amounted, simply, to hurting "qualified" white people to help "unqualified" minorities.

Suddenly, the admission of minority students from my high school into competitive colleges, far from being a private matter between those students and admissions committees, became a public issue open to debate by anyone with an opinion. In fact, even though the exchange was taking place in an election year, affirmative action seemed to be the only issue that apathetic young people cared about. This time, the skin was coming off their noses. The result was a self-centered debate guided not by reason but fueled by passion. Anger. Resentment.

Equal educational opportunity and the sort of historical exclusion recalled by my parents meant nothing to them. They were outraged because the beast seemed to hamper *their* chance at success. It was the 1980s, after all, and Ronald Reagan had removed the stigma of selfishness. It was okay, a new generation had been told, to look out for number one. And so they did.

They seemed not to care that, in many cases, the Mexican-American students who were beating them so badly, so embarrassingly if you will, in the admissions game were numerically more qualified than they were. In my senior class four Mexican-Americans, including me, were admitted to Stanford. All four had perfect grades, a 4.0 in advanced placement courses. All had above-average scores on the Scholastic Aptitude Test. A few were athletes; a few more were student body officers. They were, by the standards conventionally employed by the Stanford undergraduate admissions committee, "qualified." No matter. Still the charge. Whispers became shouts. Arguments that began in a morning English class might be carried over to afternoon government. Reverse discrimination! Unqualified! *If you hadn't been Mexican. . .*

There are, I would learn in subsequent years, endless stories of angry white Americans searching for whipping boys and girls on which to vent their frustration at Johnny and Jessica having been rejected by the school of their dreams. College friends from Yale, Columbia, Brown, Princeton, UT Austin, and countless other schools of high reputation would remember, with a twist of a beer bottle cap, the hurt of being accused of illegitimately usurping the admissions' places of other white, presumably qualified, classmates.

One young woman of incredibly high ability remembers a friend's father being visibly upset at the injustice of any system that would allow her—a Mexican-American girl—access to Harvard but deny it to his son. He may have professed anger at the system, but it was toward her that his eyes directed their anger.

Sadly, in spite of all that these high-powered, well-educated Latino students would achieve in lives full of promise, it would be many subsequent springs before they could overcome the stigma attached to them when their acceptance letters arrived in their parents' mailboxes. Because others thought less of them in high school, they thought less of themselves in college. After all, like awkwardness in one's physical appearance, when you feel something at seventeen, you feel it forever.

"When you got in," the young Harvard freshman would ask with a beery slur, "did they say . . ."

Yeah, they did.

Affirmative action tantrums, although often unfair, are understandable. We start with the presumption that all parents deem their offspring immensely qualified to attend any college they choose. Inevitably, there are some who are confronted by the unpleasant April reality that—after years of compassionate child rearing, private tutorials, family reading time, and expensive SAT prep courses—their child is simply not able to pull that off.

For them, minority students perform an invaluable service. Disappointed parents loyally reject the very real possibility that Johnny and Jessica were, in the sterile file room of some admissions office littered with empty coffee cups, simply outgunned by another more qualified, more interesting candidate of the same color. Instead, they trumpet to golf partners that their children are the victims of a chic, new kind of discrimination. Reverse discrimination. It seems to them particularly insidious because it affects those who are not accustomed to being hampered by the color of their skin.

So messy is the issue of affirmative action that it blurs the usual lines separating those who label themselves "liberal" or "conservative." Even those teachers who were usually supportive of Latino students, in this case, only compounded our discomfort.

One day a teacher, a self-professed liberal and voting Democrat with whom I had agreed on numerous political issues during the recent election, approached me in his European History class. He had heard through the gossip that permeated the teachers' lounge that I had been accepted to high-caliber schools. He intended to support my achievements. He chose entirely the wrong words. Instead of reminding me, as he could have, that I had earned one of the highest grades in his class and that I had consistently impressed him and my classmates with my work in it, he said only one thing.

"You know, I'm in favor of affirmative action..."

As he returned to his desk, as proud of himself as if he had just sent a check to the American Civil Liberties Union, I realized that I had not mentioned affirmative action. It was he who had invoked the term and he who had instinctively, even if approvingly, linked the concept to my admission to these various colleges. As with the principal's careless quip which heralded the storm, I knew that any congratulatory remarks to my white classmates would conspicuously lack any reference to affirmative action.

The teachers' lounge gossip persisted, and my ears burned. "Did you hear about Ruben Navarrette? Well, I guess they need their minority." At one point, a teacher of mine came to my defense. Fed up with innuendo from his colleagues—ironically people paid to build kids up and not tear them down—he lost his temper one morning and snapped back.

"Look, you wanna compare Ruben with your favorites . . . let's do it. Let's go to the registrar, get the transcripts and scores, and lay it all out. Then, we'll see who's qualified!"

His colleagues relented and shifted their gossip back to local affairs and divorces and the like.

A man is embarrassed to admit the petty torments of a boy. Still, those were lonely and hurtful days for me. Especially lonely and extra hurtful for one simple reason: Those white students doing the accusing were my friends. We were close. We had grown up together, met each other's parents, confided in one another our schoolyard crushes on pretty girls. We trusted one another, in the kind of fragile trust that exists between children and adolescents. That trust was shattered in the spring of our senior year in high school by a wave of innuendo and slander. Children parroting adults. My friends' affirmative action tantrums left me with an acute sense of isolation, even betrayal. I was alone. Not knowing in whom to confide. To trust.

April became May, and the days were longer. I remember that at that crucial window in time, the one thing that I wanted was for someone, anyone, to put their hand on my shoulder, to hug me and tell me what I already knew: I was qualified, more than qualified, to be accepted by a school like Harvard. Each morning, as I reluctantly pulled my tired young body from its resting place, I hoped that this would be the day without innuendo, accusation, or insults disguised as compliments. I hoped that this would be the day that teachers, principals, and classmates would swallow their prejudice and own up to the truth: I had excelled according to their own standards of excellence and had done my modest part to bankrupt their sacred myth that Mexican-Americans were somehow not as good as whites. But that day would not come for me. And even as I write this, I know that it has not come for hundreds of thousands of bright Latino students across the country.

There was a harsh irony to all this. If I found myself alone in those few months, it was because for many years before that I had painted myself into such a corner through my academic achievement. Since elementary school, I had done my homework, obeyed my teachers, strived for As instead of Bs, and through it all, distanced myself from my fellow Mexican-American classmates. It was no accident, then, that as I sat in calculus class or physics or a variety of advanced placement courses, I was surrounded by white faces.

There were other Latinos, of course, but Latinos like me— smart, ambitious, with no trace of an accent. We were presumably immune to discrimination; low expectation was a foreign concept. We dated white girls. We considered ourselves acceptable to white America, and so we expected to be accepted by white America. Imagine our profound disillusionment after April's accusations.

Not so privileged were the others. Young men with dark skin, dark hair sprayed stiff and motionless, dark eyes. Hollow eyes devoid of hope. Knowing things that a valedictorian did not. I knew them, once. We played kickball during recess in a dusty elementary school. Five or six of us gathered routinely in the bathroom in sixth grade and gawked at pictures from forbidden magazines, played poker, talked about girls' developing anatomy, and gingerly toyed with tools of vice. There was intimacy. We felt at ease with one another. Each of us, Mexican. Each of us, headed down a different road.

In junior high school—a crucial point for students labeled "at risk" by educators—we lost one. One day, he dressed differently. Acted differently. He cut class, then classes, then the school day, then the school week. A thirteen-year-old was getting tougher, harder before my eyes. He cared about sex, alcohol, intimidation, money, and most of all being *cool.* We acknowledged each other with a wave, then a nod, then not at all. He gave up on education; education reciprocated. His vices became more serious. Later, it was juvenile hall and then county jail, maybe prison. I don't know.

The others remained in school, struggling to graduate. School was to be endured, not enjoyed. In our senior year, they leaned neatly against the wall of a high school corridor in between classes, single file, side by side. Dressed impeccably in clean white T-shirts, khaki pants, and patent leather shoes. Hard bodies, hard faces. Hollow eyes. The *pachucos* of the 1940s, immortalized in Luis Valdez's play *Zoot Suit*, had gracefully evolved into the *cholos* of the 1980s. Hands in pockets, perhaps caressing a switchblade or even a gun. Certainly not a pencil. I didn't know. Because I didn't know them anymore. I walked their gauntlet on my way to some stuffy, high-browed class where I would study abstraction with people like me. Unlike me. I smiled to an old friend from kindergarten. We didn't talk. What would we talk about? What would my five acceptance letters mean to him? Nothing. Absolutely nothing.

Still, there was a respect between us, and perhaps mutual admiration. Maybe they liked that I was engaged daily in academic battle with the *gringos*, the sons and daughters of those who had treated our parents so badly. And, unnerving to some, in the competition for grades, I was winning. Taking the same tests, reading the same books, *Good with your hands . . .* Hands full of acceptance letters to places that have rejected you.

In return, I admired my old friends' strength, their strong sense of self. They would not later write editorials in national newspapers with headlines like: "How Mexican Am I?" They knew. They also knew discrimination. They might have snickered at my disillusionment and said that, of course, white people think themselves superior. Of course. "Where have you been for seventeen years?" they might have said to me, shaking their heads mockingly that someone who knew so much could know so little.

The intimacy of our youth was gone. It had been sacrificed years before at the altar of academic success. We were no longer close. The American educational system's first and most thorough lesson is one of division. Remedial students. Honors students. Gifted students. *Better* students.

And so, when I was beseiged by the insults of white classmates, my old friends were not there for me. Could not be there for me. I was in another world. What would they have done to defend me, anyway? They likely would not have been able to debate reflectively citing newspaper articles defending affirmative action.

I dreamed of a confrontation. An old friend would come to my rescue against the pack. He would enter the high-browed classroom for better students. He would approach the student body president, and tell him that his homeboy had beaten him out not because of some improper system but because he was simply smarter than him. He would point the finger at the end of his muscular, brown arm at the terrified young white man turning paler each second, and expose him as a child of privilege. He would mock the young man's contention that things should be "equal" in the admissions process by reminding him that the two of them lead lives that are anything but equal. He would invite him home to see the squalor and the neglect and the hardworking parents who had been told by guidance counselors to work in the canneries. And so they had, providing for their children an existence that compared more closely to those in Third World countries than it did to that of the privileged young man who trembled before him. He would argue finally that for Latinos, the ticket out of the American underclass was in the hands of ambitious and successful Latinos like his old friend, and how dare he or anyone else get in the way of that progress with their snide, childish, self-centered remarks.

In my splendid fantasy, the *cholo* would win the debate with the student body president because the victor knew something that the loser did not. He knew what it was like to be considered less intelligent, less capable, less, less, less by a system that was grooming others to succeed in his place. He knew what it was like to be Mexican-American in public school. But the student body president, surrounded by friends, would not concede. My old friend would lose his temper, and strike out in a more primitive, though more effective, way. Like our fathers had done at the same school three decades before, he would resort to knocking the shit out of his opponent before being hauled away to face punishment.

But reality was not so comforting. There was no rescue. The *cholos* stayed in their world. I was alone in mine. In that tiny school, as in life, they were separated from me (and from those whom the educational system expected more of than a life of dropping out, pregnancy, and crime) by a wall much higher, much more formidable than the one that they leaned on in between classes. This was my fight, and mine alone. At stake, I realized for the first time, was not only my own pride and self-image but also the dignity and progress of a whole race of people.

Should the reader tire of my complaining or see it as mere whining, I offer here a true story of an academic casualty in this battle for respect. As a college student and recruiter for Harvard, I spoke one day to a high school class in the San Joaquin Valley about the admissions process at Ivy League schools. A young man confronted me about what he considered to be the impropriety of race-conscious admissions. He spoke with passion and anger. Surprising to me at the time, he was Mexican-American. He was angry because he claimed that, no matter what his accomplishments, he would never be taken seriously by his white classmates. We argued. We resolved nothing.

Three months later, I received a phone call from a friend in the admissions office. Had I heard? The same young man, an outstanding student, had been accepted into both our incoming class and that of Yale. He had decided, the caller continued, to reject both offers of admission and instead attend a small, less assuming college in New England. My friend was baffled. For the young man to stay in California was one thing. Yet to be willing to travel 3,000 miles but not to accept what were clearly more highly coveted spots in schools like Harvard or Yale seemed not to make much sense. For me, given the frustration, and perhaps embarrassment, that I saw in the young man's eyes during our heated exchange months earlier, I understood at once his desire to pick a less conspicuous apple from the tree.

"Tell me," I asked my friend. "If you're invited to a party, but don't feel that you deserve the invitation, would you go?"

"You don't mean . . . ," the voice fell off to a whisper. "Shit!"

Ultimately, the young man in question was not spared, as he had hoped he would be, the ribbing of his high school classmates even though he had chosen to attend the small, less assuming college in New England at which he never felt comfortable and from which he eventually withdrew. A statistic in a government study, he and his nearly 1400 SATs now went on to attend a community college in Fresno. There, he was no longer subjected to ribbing by classmates and instructors, who finally considered him to be exactly where he was "qualified" to be. He became one of the hundreds of thousands of Mexican-American students who attend community college in California, and not one of the just over one hundred such students who at any given time attend Harvard, apparently those who constitute a more controversial and threatening entity.

In high school, the weapon that I finally chose in my own self-defense was justly academic, my senior term paper in American Government: "Affirmative Action and Preferential Treatment in College Admissions." The paper was clearly a young man's effort; its real strength lay in the direct and thorough treatment of a thorny and personal issue. It was in researching that seemingly insignificant high school term paper that I first discovered Allan Bakke.

Somewhere deep in the stacks of library books and magazine articles, I encountered the spirit of the thirty-three-year-old NASA engineer who one day decided to become a doctor. After being rejected for admission by twelve different medical schools in two successive school years, Bakke hired a lawyer and challenged the admissions policy of the medical school at the University of California, Davis. Bakke claimed that the school's special admissions program, whereby 16 of 100 seats in the entering class had been set aside for "economically and educationally disadvantaged" applicants who were usually minorities, violated his federal right to equal protection under the Fourteenth Amendment.

Despite solid grades and high test scores, Bakke had his liabilities. A Davis official who interviewed Bakke during the admission process sensed that much of Bakke's view of the world was narrow and self-centered. Like my high school classmates, what upset him about affirmative action was that it hurt *him* by hampering *his* chances to become a doctor. Aside from the question of race, Bakke's age was apparently viewed as a negative factor in the committee's decision. Once the committee admitted a student to the study of medicine, it expected from the applicant a return of several decades of medical service. At thirty-three, Bakke's years of return were in question.

Bakke complained about what he termed "quotas" for racial minorities, which he considered an attempt by government to "atone for past discrimination." He charged that Davis was perpetuating a new racial bias and asserted that successful applicants should simply be the most *qualified*.

Qualified. Qualified. Qualified. The word haunted me in those painful spring days. With 96 As on my transcript, and many of them followed by a "+" sign, I wasn't sure how much more qualified my white friends expected me to be. Still, the tantrums. Still, the whispers from those not as qualified as me. No less troubling was my developing awareness that the term *qualified* is perhaps the most subjective in American history. Since this country's founding, those in power have assessed qualifications for jobs, school attendance, land grants, and a variety of social programs, according to their own prejudices and beliefs.

I heard Jesse Jackson quip that twenty years ago, he and people like him were deemed not "qualified" to use a toilet in the American South. And I understood. It was no coincidence that for the first two hundred years of the American Republic, those individuals who were considered most qualified to be a doctor, a policeman, or a Harvard student were wealthy, white males. Qualified.

In 1978, the United States Supreme Court handed down its decision in the *Bakke* case. It decided that racial quotas did indeed violate the Fourteenth Amendment and ordered Bakke's admission to the medical school. Yet significantly, it also allowed, even encouraged, universities to continue considering the race and gender of applicants in order to bring diversity and racial parity to American higher education.

Though Bakke won his battle, proponents of race-conscious admissions seemed to have won the war. The United States Supreme Court had ruled that race could be, should be, considered a factor in college admissions as, I was beginning to realize, it might have been in mine. I drew comfort from the decision of nine men, eight white and one black.

Even more comforting to me was the fact that Justice Lewis Powell, the author of the opinion, had taken the unusual step of specifically making reference to the admissions process at Harvard College as being an ideal for other schools to follow. Justice Powell, a Harvard man himself, seemed to welcome me to the family with his approval of the proper and just way that the folks who worked at the return address on my manila envelope did business. Suddenly, it was a little easier to pull myself from bed each morning. The air was clearer. I was less alone. Less unsure of myself.

Meanwhile, taking his precarious place in history beside Linda Brown and James Meredith, Bakke was catapulted to the dubious position of poster boy for a new kind of racial injustice. For the opponents of affirmative action, Allan Bakke was the blond, blue-eyed victim of a new kind of racial discrimination— one with a catchy name. *Reverse discrimination.* A term with which I was by then quite familiar.

Still, the seventeen-year-old knew what grown men would not admit. Allan Bakke was never, and could never be, comparable to Linda Brown or James Meredith. Ms. Brown had been denied a place in the public school system of Topeka, Kansas, specifically because she was African-American and in deference to a historical assumption that her race was an inferior one. The same was true of Mr. Meredith and the University of Mississippi. On the other hand, Mr. Bakke was not denied access to the medical school at UC Davis because he was white, or because white people were considered inferior to African-American, Hispanics, or Native Americans. The presence in the incoming class of eighty-four younger and presumably more qualified white medical school aspirants makes that claim ludicrous.

Nonetheless, even as I dismissed Bakke's case in the private tribunal of my own conscience, I recognized his spirit as it appeared before me. It strolled the corridors of my high school, finding comfort in the broken hearts and bruised egos of the young people there. It was there in heated debates with once dear friends, who held in clutched fists letters of rejection from universities that had accepted me. It was there in their snickers, whispers, and innuendos. And it was there in their fresh, young faces—all twisted in hate for a concept, idea, theory that they despised but did not understand. It thrived in the warmth of those difficult days of spring. *Hello, Allan.*

May finally yielded to June. Graduation came. Friends signed one another's yearbooks and shared teary good-byes. For me, the race issue would not go away and there was, in those final days, one battle left to fight.

I had chosen as the theme of my valedictory address, an impassioned plea that our generation resist the aura of intolerance and self-interest that was crippling the nation's spirit in the 1980s. I had included in my speech a brief reference to a controversy that was brewing quietly at that moment in the town's junior high school.

At the junior high, another valedictorian, a thirteen-year-old girl, had decided to say a portion of her speech in Spanish. She had done so, she said, out of respect for her maternal grand-mother who spoke no English. The group of junior high school teachers assigned to monitor, and if need be censor, what was said by student speakers had denied her request, claiming that the gesture might cause disruption. There would be some in the audience, they reasoned, who would not understand what was being said. They relented only after being confronted by the young girl's mother, someone who, like my own parents, knew discrimination.

Upon hearing all this and learning, by talking with people who had attended Sanger High School a decade earlier, that this drama of language had been played out before when a similar incident occurred in the 1970s, I was outraged. How dare they! In a town whose population was nearly 70 percent Latino, why had they not been similarly concerned over the years about those, like my grandparents, who had not under-stood what had been said by *English* speakers?

I resolved to include in my speech mention of the young girl's story. Yet not long after I submitted the final draft to the group of high school teachers that had been assigned to monitor, and if need be censor, what was said by student speakers, I was told that the principal wanted to see me in his office. I walked in with a confidence and ease that had been missing in our earlier meeting, months before. The sort of confidence that comes from struggling in battle, and surviving.

As I sat down, he explained gingerly that there was a "prob-lem" with what I intended to say to the five thousand parents and family members who were expected to crowd into Tom Flores Stadium on Friday night. He wanted me to remove the reference to the young girl's speech. I suspect that he was wary of embarrassing the junior high principal who had allowed the episode to progress as far as it had.

After listening to his concerns, I explained that I did not share them. I *was* concerned, however, about the First Amend-ment. I assured him that, if he denied me the right to say my speech as I wanted to say it—aware, of course, of legal restric-tions that prohibit obscene or offensive language—I would ob-tain legal counsel and, within twenty-four hours, sue him, the school, and the district to secure my right to free speech. With a frown (or was it a scowl?) he relented. I left his office and returned to class. Later that week, I delivered my speech as I had written it, urging my generation to reject the intolerance of the past and recognize that an injustice is no less wrong just because it affects someone else. As I looked out into the audience of listeners, I spotted my old friends from elementary school, those who had made it through high school. One of them smiled at me. I knew that I could not have realized the full importance of my speech and its message before the tantrums of spring, and the lessons they taught me about the resilience of racism and low racial expectation.

After graduation, friends followed different paths in life. Some went on to four-year universities. Many more settled for community college where they spent three or four years pursuing a valueless two-year degree. Some went into a floundering job market, armed only with a high school degree.

The adolescent pain of high school, the universal sense of not fitting in, remains safely tucked away in memory. My last and hardest lesson in public school taught a protected child of privilege something that my parents and grandparents already knew, something that they learned through segregated classrooms and horrible speeches of low expectation and field trips to canneries. Simply: It is sometimes the case that a race of people progresses faster than are abandoned the prejudices of others.

Some ask when I became so concerned with issues that affect Mexican-Americans. I tell them that I can do them one better; I can tell them exactly when I began thinking of myself as even *being* Mexican-American. It was somewhere in the anger and loneliness of those merciless spring days.

I was a statistic, albeit a positive one. In the year that I graduated from high school, 50 percent of Latino students in American public schools did not. I was an exception, some said. A bright star in a black hole. And when my pursuit of excellence yielded accusation, I endured it. As I walked away from the football field on graduation night, I realized Webster himself could provide no better definition of the word *qualified.*

Ironically, if my letter of acceptance to Harvard could have solidified my belief that I was so very different from the dark-skinned young men with hollow eyes who idled against high school walls, then the vicious and insensitive response to my news from white friends shattered that belief. There was no running away from past or from prejudice. In the minds of some, I knew, I would always be defined by my ethnicity. I would continually be judged by the color of my skin and not, as Martin Luther King, Jr. had dreamed before I was born, by the content of my character. A Mexican-American scholar. A Mexican-American valedictorian. And now, I was beginning to suspect—like it or not—a Mexican-American student at Harvard.

CHAPTER 2

ENTER TO GROW IN WISDOM

"GREAT GOD, I ASK THEE FOR NO MEANER PELF
THAN THAT I MAY NOT DISAPPOINT MYSELF,
THAT IN MY ACTION I MAY SOAR AS HIGH
AS I CAN NOW DISCERN WITH THIS CLEAR EYE."

HENRY DAVID THOREAU

HARVARD COLLEGE, CLASS OF 1837

The old woman shook her head, as if to remind her son, my father, of exactly where in the gene pool he and I had received much of our tenacity. In the weeks before I was to leave for Cambridge, my father had tried valiantly to win my grandmother's approval for my decision to attend college three thousand miles from home. At first, he had little luck in convincing her. He persisted because he considered her blessing to be no small matter. My grandfather's death a few years earlier had left her with an unchallenged aura of authority in a family of five sons and five daughters-in-law and fifteen grandchildren. It had also left her alone. Alone in a house that once burst with the laughter of children and the familiar banging of pots and pans cooking dinner for a dozen or so family members.

Now, at a stage in her life when she most wanted to be surrounded by her grandchildren, one of them was leaving. And worse, as some of my cousins might have mumbled under their breath, this one was her favorite. Perhaps familiarity had bred affection.

When I first came home from the hospital as a tiny wrinkled bundle, it was to her house on the ranch that she and my grandfather had worked all of their lives to afford. My mother remembers that my grandfather would sneak into the guest bedroom in the early morning hours and, while she and my father slept, wake me with a tickle from his strong, calloused hands. He would lift me from the crib and take me to the kitchen table. We would play together in our smiles until he left for work. He would leave me with my grandmother and begin his long, hot days of supervising the operation of a local packing house. Years later, as I breathed anxiously for speech, I would await his return from work at the end of the day and call out to my grandmother when I heard the familiar sound of the old red truck. *Mamá, chiki . . . chiki.* My earliest, and perhaps most pleasant, childhood memories are of my grandparents' ranch in the country. I still remember the noisy tractor, the sunlight coming through cracks in the walls of the barn, and long, infinite rows of grape vines. These images come to me willingly whenever I smell the crisp Valley scent of a cool, moist field in the first minutes after dawn. The smell of dirt.

The matriarch's strong, dark eyes dissected him through her spectacles. Why, she asked my father. *Por qué?* Why did her grandson, so young, have to go so far away? Somehow she reasoned in the odd but foolproof logic of grandmothers that less horrible, terrible, unspeakable things could happen to me if I stayed close to home. Well, at least, an old woman would worry less.

"*Hay colegios aquí en California, qué no? Porqué no se queda aquí, cerca de su familia?*" she asked.

The Ivy League—the images in my head of snowy evenings and well-endowed Irish girls from Boston in tight wool sweaters who neglected to pronounce their *r*s ("Hahvahd")—meant nothing special to her. College was college.

Meanwhile, my father was running out of wonderful things to say about Harvard, this awful kidnapper of grandchildren. Finally, as his last ploy, he played his ace.

"Mamá," he said with a sigh of authority, *"Rubencito quiere ir a la escuela adónde fueron los Kennedys."*

My grandmother stopped shaking her head. *"Oh, sí?"* she replied with renewed interest. She listened intently. Respectfully.

She understood the reference to the Kennedys and she yielded to it. It was with a distinct pride that, in the months and years to come, she would shamelessly tell sisters, neighbors, and complete strangers that her grandson was attending the university that schooled the Kennedys. *"Sabes que mijo está estudiando con los Kennedys . . ."* After all, Mexican grandmothers love to keep their families intact, but they also love the Kennedys.

I tell that story here to remind myself of the earliest, and weakest, link between the life I was eagerly leaving behind in the San Joaquin Valley and the one that I was so anxious to begin so far away. True enough, Harvard was *la escuela de los Kennedys.* I knew that.

Harvard had trained several members of the prominent Irish-American family from Hyannis Port, Massachusetts, that in the 1960s came to represent for Mexican-Americans the personification of those honorable ideals for which one labored and endured and protested. The Kennedys were fighters, we said to one another in Spanish. They devoted their lives to the eternal fight for justice and righteousness, compassion and courage. They cared about Mexican-Americans.

And we cared about them. From the first "Viva Kennedy" campaign for JFK in 1960, to Robert Kennedy's allegiance to United Farm Workers' leader Cesar Chavez in 1968, to the continued support of Ted Kennedy by Latinos in his 1980 presidential bid, the family has enjoyed, for three decades now, a kind of adopted status in the Chicano community. Cesar Chavez once said of Bobby Kennedy: "It was like he was ours." For Mexican-Americans, the same could be said of the entire family.

Meanwhile Harvard and the Kennedys were also linked, in

folklore. There were those charmingly nostalgic stories passed
on by amateur historians like the old, gray-haired man who
checked books at Widener Library for fifty years. About Jack
nearly failing American history and dating most of the girls at
Wellesley before going off to war. About Bobby going to parties
with a book under his arm and quietly reading alone in a corner of the room. About Ted paying a fellow student to take his
Spanish exam for him and getting caught only when he got
hungry, went to Elsie's for a roast beef sandwich, and ran into
his professor there. Anyone who wonders why Teddy would
risk expulsion so trivially has never tasted the roast beef at
Elsie's.

In an odd way, Harvard's association with the Kennedys, or
rather, their association with it, made my decision to attend
that much easier. The fable and the folklore suggested to a
hungry eighteen-year-old that he follow his dreams by following in the footsteps of heroes.

There was more. The alumni list of six presidents and scores
of Supreme Court justices. The Marshall Plan as a Harvard
commencement address. The embarrassingly-well-staffed-
with-graduates ranks of *The New York Times, The Washington
Post*, and *The Wall Street Journal.* A reputation of not merely
national but international proportion.

I knew a bit more about the place. I knew that it was the
oldest college in the country, founded in 1636 to train young
men for the ministry. I knew that, as such, it was older than
the Declaration of Independence or the Constitution. I knew
that it was the most prestigious in an elite fraternity of universities, the name of which even sounded exclusive: *Ivy League.*
I knew that it had an age-old rivalry with a school named Yale,
and that a prized dimension of that ancient competition was
the great-grandfather of all collegiate football feuds. I knew
that the school had on its faculty a large crop of nationally
known scholars; when Dan Rather needed a source of *assumed*
authority on any matter, he called Harvard. The school was, as
one university president put it, "the standard-bearer of excellence." It was the measure to which others compared themselves, as when Duke called itself "The Harvard of the South."

Had I known more about Harvard's reputation, I may have
had second thoughts about attending, perhaps feeling as un-

worthy as a commoner in a king's palace. A wise man defers to immensity, never engages it. Yet at the start of September, I was neither wise, nor yet fully a man. I did not yield. Instead I pressed on.

My father's voice bellowed through the house, an irritably predictable steam whistle telling his sons or daughter to come to dinner or to move a car from the driveway. This time, it was fulfilling a familiar role, that of hustling his oldest son through the front door with warnings of how late it was and how I would "never make the plane." My father would likely claim credit for each of the countless flights for which, over the years, I have been on time; he would attribute the one instance where I did miss a flight, from Los Angeles to Albuquerque, as a consequence of my own irresponsibility.

I struggled through the hallway with my father's army green duffel bag, stuffed with fall and spring clothes; the Harvard students that I had spoken to by phone all agreed that I should buy my winter clothes once I arrived in Cambridge since they claimed that California tailors simply "did not understand New England winters." I remember not liking the way that sounded.

The drive to the airport seemed longer than usual. My younger brother and sister fidgeted in the backseat of the family car, a reminder that all three of us were outgrowing the limiting constraints of childhood.

We had grown up separately. Two boys and a girl in the middle. The oldest, I remember feeding my infant sister from the Gerber's jar when I was three or four. But in childhood, years seem decades; our experiences were distinguished by age. My brother and sister were only a year apart, but the intimacy of their relationship was likewise inhibited by gender. We might have taken care of one another, but instead learned to take care of ourselves. Intimacy became a natural casualty of independence.

My sister is gifted not only with intelligence but with the sense of responsibility and discipline I lack; my brother with a quick mind that attacks projects with a creativity and boldness that I envy. We all went to the same elementary, intermediate, and secondary schools. I do not doubt that following in the footsteps of their obsessively competitive older brother was difficult at times. They must have dreaded being assigned to teachers who had had me in class years earlier and had grown accustomed to high quality, if unimaginative, work from a student with the surname Navarrette. On the first day of school, there was the inevitable question during roll call: "Is Ruben your brother?" Still, they excelled at their own pace.

And if they ever resented me, or the life they felt I had indirectly prescribed for them, they never showed it. Only pride at their brother's accomplishments. In our twenties, as in childhood, our parents have actively cultivated in us a sense of camaraderie that has eluded them in their own familial ties. In our immediate family, at least, it has always been understood by all that there is no greater sin than fraternal attack.

As my father drove anxiously, my mother asked repeatedly if I had forgotten anything.

"Did you pack enough clothes, *mijo?*" she asked.

"Yes," I replied without looking at her.

I stared out the window and into the peach trees that rushed by the roadside in the blur of speed. Months earlier, Mexican farm workers had been in those fields at six in the morning, standing on wooden ladders and picking fruit in one hundred degree heat for minimum wage. Boys my age, living my grandfathers' life. Now the season was over and the field was empty.

"Do you have your plane ticket?" she asked for the fourth time, as if to ignore that I was ignoring her.

"Yes," I snapped back.

I was losing patience with all of it. With the claustrophobia of being confined to a small space with family members, if only for a twenty-minute drive. A family of independents, and those who struggled to be.

After eighteen years, I had reached the critical point of wanting freedom, of needing liberation from my parents' lives and the place in which they lived them. The responsible, predictable life of a small town. The life that high school friends who stayed in that town would surely lead. I was developing a certain contempt for the place, for its limited world view. The sting of my final few months in high school had only made matters worse.

I was convinced that I was going to a better place. A more

enlightened place with less prejudice, where excellence determined success. I went eagerly.

Once at the airport, my parents helped check in my bags as
the pretty Latina behind the American Airlines counter asked
for my destination.

"Boston," I said.

Two years earlier, the town meant nothing more to me
than the setting for a few pages in a history book. Now it was
stamped on my airline ticket. A one-way ticket. I planned to
return to Fresno for Christmas, of course. I would have to
buy the return ticket in Cambridge, once I knew my finals
schedule.

I heard once of Mexican parents having a son who was leaving for Harvard blessed by a priest. For me, there was only my
parents trying to conceal their sadness. Although my mother
was proud to be sending her son to Harvard, she had initially
wanted me to go to college in California; there is something
oddly reassuring about the possibility of weekend trips home.
When I was accepted to Harvard, she cried an unnerving cry
that I had not heard before, or since. Still, she loved her children enough to want only the best for us, and eventually
watched helplessly as all three of us left the San Joaquin Valley
for colleges in other parts of the state and country. Once I was
accepted, my father, though he never said it aloud, expected
that I would attend Harvard. Given his own lifetime of closed
doors, elusive invitations, and denied opportunity, settling for
a less elite school would have been illogical.

My father's eyes are tired as he recalls his ten-year struggle
to attain a bachelor's degree at Fresno State. As a police officer,
he worked an eight-hour shift to help my mother support the
three of us. He attended class at night, slept for a few hours,
and then got up and did it all over again. For ten years. My
childhood memories are full of my mother's afternoon whispers for me to keep quiet so as not to wake my father. *Shh* . . .
I remember him asleep as I walked to the elementary school
around the corner. I remember the red cardboard boxes in
which McDonald's used to pack its hot apple pies. I remember
finding one of those pies waiting for me on the kitchen counter
on many a morning—a reminder that the young, old man

asleep in the master bedroom had, among his countless other concerns the night before, remembered his young son.

My mother's ancestors are *tejanos,* people of Texas. As children, her parents both endured neglect in segregated public schools and learned early not to trust *los gringos.* Instead, they trusted hard work, long days, and a pain in the small of your back. My mother remembers an instance where, after having the entire family complete a week of fieldwork, her father (my grandfather) discovered that the labor contractor had disappeared and reneged on paying them the wages due them. There is likely no comfort on earth for a man who has seen his family deprived of the food, shelter, and medicine they need by individuals who act with impunity toward those they consider inferior.

Like my father, my mother struggled in the same high school that would later educate all three of their children. She remembers herself as an average student. She somehow managed to graduate exactly in the middle of her senior class, as if to solidify the level of mediocrity dictated to her by educators and guidance counselors and stupid tests of hand skills. She may never forget the faces of the young girls in her high school, exclusively white, who were encouraged by teachers and counselors to go on, not to packing houses and canneries but to colleges and universities. It is with a special pride that, still today, she sees them along Seventh Street and notes to herself that I have done so much better in school than have their sons and daughters. Through me, she finally is able to exorcise old demons.

As I paced around the Fresno airport, I remembered that my parents had themselves been to Harvard. In the autumn of my senior year in high school, they went into debt to accompany me on a campus visit. After arriving in Cambridge in late morning, we got lost. I had scheduled an interview at the admissions office, Byerly Hall, for early afternoon, and I was worried that I would miss it.

Instinctively, as he has done so many times in so many cities, my father had sought out a trusted source of help. He approached a Cambridge police car parked in Harvard Square and "badged" the police sergeant inside, an imposing Irish cop with a thick mustache. My father explained the situation, telling this complete stranger but fellow peace officer that I was applying to Harvard and that we were looking for the admissions office. The sergeant nodded calmly and instructed us to follow him. He led us to Byerly Hall and wished me good luck in my interview. "Get through here, young man," he said through his mustache, "and you can write your own ticket." Later, after my interview was over, the sergeant was even more helpful. We had not yet found a hotel at which to spend the night; he escorted us to one on Massachusetts Avenue, a few blocks from the Square. The desk clerk told us that there was no vacancy, until our new friend explained to the clerk in a thick Boston accent that we were "old friends [of his] from out of state" and asked if he was sure that there were no rooms left. I was more surprised than was my father when the clerk nodded and slid a bronze room key across the hardwood counter.

That story, an innocent memory of my first visit to Harvard, illustrates the universal code of courtesy among the national fraternity of law enforcement officers. My father would eventually make similar contacts with such officers in Santa Barbara and Berkeley, where his other two children attended college. More than that, it reminds me of my father's uncanny resourcefulness, his ability, as he might say, to "make chicken salad out of chicken shit." I admire that quality in him; still, that day in that foreign place, it was, for him, not enough. Not nearly enough.

There is another memory from that afternoon that is not as pleasant to recall. Still, it is one that I know my father will never forget. Once we entered Byerly Hall, my parents and I waited in the reception area with two or three other prospective applicants and their parents. I studied the young man flipping through a magazine across the room. He was white, with a nice suit and tie, and a shorter haircut than mine. He must have been my age but seemed older somehow. He was confident. He sat next to his father, who was wearing an expensive suit and a gold class ring of some sort on his finger. When he approached the table of magazines next to which I was sitting, I noticed that the ring bore the Harvard insignia. He twisted the band conspicuously as he searched for the latest issue of *Fortune* magazine and then returned to his seat. An alumnus, he was even more confident than his son. Father and son smiled and joked with each other. I marveled at their ease. They were relaxed and at home. It was like they were visiting grandma's house for Sunday dinner. Meanwhile, nervous and apprehensive, I felt as though I was visiting a foreign planet.

Then the defining moment. An admissions officer approached and introduced himself to the father and son. They all smiled.

"Does John Taylor still work here?" the father asked. "I'd like to say hello to him before I go." It was no secret to anyone listening that he was employing, with very little subtlety, the time-honored Harvard tradition of name-dropping. They all smiled and left the room together.

My father had been watching the scene as closely as I had. Minute by minute, he seemed to lose his composure. I was not used to seeing him in an environment in which he lacked confidence. It made me uneasy. He knew that I would be competing with that young man, and perhaps 16,000 others like him, for a coveted space in Harvard's entering class. Furthermore, if an article that appeared years later in the *Harvard Crimson* is any indication, that young man, as the son of an alumnus, stood to benefit from his kind of affirmative action.

My father wanted to help me. He felt he couldn't. He did not have a Harvard ring on his finger, only a band reminding him of a decade of study and sacrifice at Fresno State. He did not have a name to drop; the only person he knew in Cambridge, an Irish cop, would not carry much weight with the bluebloods about to pass judgment on his son's intellectual worthiness. At that moment, a boy knew for the first time what every father hopes that he will never discover—the limits of paternal power. For all the love and support and apple pies in little red boxes, my father was ill-equipped to help his oldest son. He felt powerless. Inadequate. And it hurt him.

Perhaps that is why, once I was accepted to Harvard and awarded enough financial aid to attend, my father seemed so impressed by the feat. He has still not forgotten the faces of that father and son. I doubt that he ever will.

Though Harvard's scholarship offer was intended to alleviate any financial burden that might be placed on my family by my attending, those of us gathered at the airport that September day were thinking in terms of another kind of sacrifice. I knew that my leaving would take an emotional toll on my family. We knew that there would be no weekend trips home. Since Harvard was three thousand miles away, my going meant that I would be connected to my parents and family by only telephone wire and see them only twice a year. For four years! Still, all the books they bought for me, all the chores they excused me from so that I could study, and all the sacrifice had been for something like this. Despite the likely toll on my family, I had no real choice. Expectation prodded and hunger burned in my gut. I had to go. Harvard would be not only an intellectual challenge, but a psychological one as well. It seemed only right. I had chosen the school precisely because it posed the greatest challenge. As my flight number was called, I hugged my brother and sister. "See ya . . ." I hugged and kissed my mother, who was struggling with her composure. My father slipped two twenty dollar bills into my coat pocket, hugged me, and hurried me along. I had only seen my father cry twice in my lifetime; once after arguing viciously with my mother and again on the day of my grandfather's fatal heart attack. "Call us when you get there." It was not until their images disappeared behind the closing door that, alone in the concourse, I began to appreciate the full significance of the adventure on which I was so readily embarking. The last image I saw was my father's eyes welled up with tears.

The airplane bumped through an air pocket and I was awakened by the sharp jab of a neighboring passenger's elbow at my side. I had enjoyed the chance to sleep, however uncomfortably, and to dream, if only for a few minutes, about a new world that seemed ripe for conquest by the young and the brave. As the captain announced descent into Logan International Airport, my stomach quivered with uncertainty. The elbow belonged to a young man in his late twenties—a new friend. Upon learning that I was about to begin my first year at Harvard, he had insisted on buying me one, then two congratulatory beers. Taking full advantage of my liberation from California's legal drinking age and my parents' stringent house rules against underage drinking, I accepted. Now, as the seat belt sign lit up, I was not sure whether it was altitude or alcohol that was responsible for the nervous rumblings in my stomach.

Below I could see, with my nose pressed against the window, the lights of an immense city winking seductively to a boy stiffened by excitement and terror. What unknown challenges awaited him in this strange place so far away from home and family and friends?

Once on the ground I remember that, at the time, it was still a strange, new experience for me to land at an airport—any airport—amid a sea of strangers with no one there to greet me. To struggle alone with one's luggage—careful to keep all your belongings in sight—while those around you are hugging and kissing loved ones who are telling them with broad smiles how fit they look and that mother has supper ready, is at once frightening and liberating.

At such moments, abundant in four years of school away from home, you have only yourself on which to depend. There is no nagging parent directing you to a waiting taxi, and no friend to help with your bags. There is no one but you. A boy of eighteen had wished for that feeling. Now, on an autumn evening in New England, it was his.

Outside the airport, the wind was crisp and the city streets dark but alive with car horns and screeching tires. At the curb, I tossed my luggage into the trunk of a yellow cab and climbed into the backseat.

"Where to?" the driver asked.

"Harvard," I replied. "Harvard Yard, I guess."

As the taxi moved precariously through the madness of Boston traffic, I hungrily soaked up the bright images passing before me. One building after another, each with a story to tell to a boy eager to listen. The architecture of the Boston skyline captures the essence of a city of the future in respectful appreciation of its past. The tall, mirrored exterior of John Hancock Tower coexists peacefully just a few miles from Bunker Hill and the Old North Church. The taxi passed between two skyscrapers and we were momentarily swallowed by the city. We drove along Storrow Drive, following the Charles River which separates Boston and Cambridge.

Across the river, I soon noticed a row of colonial-style buildings that I assumed to be part of Harvard. As we crossed the Charles and entered Cambridge at John F. Kennedy Drive, I noticed that my surroundings were suddenly more subdued, sprouting reflection for the oldest college town in the United States. Gazing out the taxi window, I saw the crooked sidewalks paved of old brick and the narrow streets designed for carriages, not cars. I saw the ancient buildings with white trim, precolonial Georgian red brick harkening back to an earlier time. I saw young people talking vigorously as they walked briskly to ice cream shops and bars which, along with bookstores, thrive in Harvard Square, the area immediately surrounding the oldest university in the country.

I remember noticing the timelessness of the place, the sense that I was suddenly only an insignificant part of a much greater, much more complicated drama. I would learn, gradually and painfully, that I was no longer the academic superstar who walked high school halls exuding confidence, cut classes in my senior year, and blew away tests. For thirteen years in the public schools of Sanger, California, education had been my playground. I always impressed my teachers. I always knew the answers.

Now, I suspected, in this place, I would not always know the answers. Maybe I wouldn't even understand the questions. Would I fail, and could I even handle a concept as foreign as *failing*? Always, I had only one objective in education, and in life: to be the best. Absolutely, indisputably, the best. In a high school class of thirty or thirty-five, it was important to me not to get a certain grade, but to get the best grade. At Harvard, I knew, that would stop. It was unrealistic for me to think that I could be the smartest person in such a place. The best of the best, as it were. I know no one with whom I went to college who would have dared make that claim.

One reason was that I was, by no fault of my own, trained in public school—a fine school system, yes, but hardly comparable to the sort of stringently academic private academies that, I knew, would be represented in my freshman class. In a few days, I would be competing *mano a mano* with people who read one hundred books a year at schools with six sections of calculus, expensive computers, and scores of National Merit

Scholars. The standards of excellence were fundamentally different. I remember, for instance, an administrator at Sanger High School boasting on graduation night that 60 percent of graduates were going off to some form of college, including two-year community colleges. At that exact moment, three thousand miles away, a headmaster of a private academy was telling another set of parents that their hefty educational investment had paid off and boasting that 60 percent of their graduates were destined for the Ivy League.

The names of such schools struck fear in the hearts of those of us ready to compete, expected to compete, with their graduates. Stuyvesant. Bronx Science. Andover. Milton. Exeter. A Chicano friend from South Texas would later joke nervously about such schools, "Man, those *gente* don't play games. Go to Exeter, check it out up in New Hampshire. Ain't no Mexicans up there . . . not even the gardeners. Those *gente* don't play."

As all this passed through my head, so did a question. Should I tell the taxi driver to take me back to Logan, board a return flight, and fly away from this awful place? I could probably still kiss and make up with Stanford, I thought. I hadn't been that unkind in my rejection of their offer. No. No. If I left, I would never know what I was really made of, what I could really do.

We pulled up at a stop sign, across from Harvard Yard. Out the window, past the gate, I could see some sort of foliage growing along the sides of some of the buildings. Growing up in the agriculturally rich San Joaquin Valley, I assumed that I had seen every kind of bush, scrub, and vine known to man. Still, this was new to me. I'll be damned, I thought to myself. Ivy. Not just an advertising gimmick, it really existed after all. Maybe the rest of the brochure was true, too. I hoped.

The threshold through which students enter the Yard from Harvard Square is marked with an inscription that had likely been there for hundreds of years. In four years, I would pass through that entryway perhaps thousands of times. Reading a newspaper as I walked, running to an exam, or sporting dark Ray•Bans mercifully shielding a hangover from sunlight. Rarely would I look up at the handful of words inscribed in granite overhead. Still, though I never gave much thought to the first line of the inscription, its overall significance never escaped me.

Enter To Grow In Wisdom.

As we entered the driveway at Johnston Gate, the driver stopped the cab and poked at the meter.

"Seventeen fifty," he said into the rear-view window.

I passed one of my father's twenty dollar bills over the seat. "Keep it."

The driver nodded a thank you, and put the bill into his pocket.

I got out of the cab and removed my bags from the trunk, placing them on the ground next to me.

"Good luck to you, young man," the driver said, as he shifted back into drive.

I waved to him as the cab disappeared from sight. Then I wandered off in search of the building to which I had been assigned to report. As I walked awkwardly with too many bags and not enough hands through the darkness of Harvard Yard, the driver's words echoed. *Good luck.* Odd. It seemed a wish that might be bestowed on someone who might bungee-jump from the top of Longfellow Bridge or run the Boston Marathon.

I was, after all, merely going to college. As so many of my classmates from high school—60 percent of them, to be exact—were doing and as others had done for generations before me. Good luck? I didn't need luck, I thought to myself. Public school or not, I was *bad.*

Harvard arrogance, huh? I'll show them arrogance. I had seen my press clippings, and I believed every one of them.

Still, even in my confidence, I was beginning to suspect that my classmates and I would share no ordinary experience. After all, the first lesson is immediate and unmistakable: Harvard is no ordinary place.

Actually, I had arrived ten days earlier than most of my classmates. I had volunteered for a special work detail, through which a group of us would clean and ready the dormitory rooms of arriving undergraduates. Being part of the dorm crew gave us a valuable head start on our classmates. We had ten days to familiarize ourselves with the campus, uncover good restaurants in Cambridge, visit Boston, and set about the impossible task of buying underage beer in the Square. The humility of menial labor was for me, at that moment of life, a bonus. When asked of all that Harvard taught me, I sometimes joke that my very first lesson was how to scrub a toilet. Appropriately so, perhaps.

Dorm crew also allowed us to practice what is, for incoming freshmen, a necessary ritual. We were able to ask one another various sorts of probing questions, all intended to get to know one another, to break the ice, and to make friends of strangers. Slowly, we approached one another. We smiled. We introduced ourselves. And then we started.

"What's your name?"

"Where are you from?"

"What's it like there?"

"Do you have brothers and sisters?"

"What do you think you might want to study here?"

Blah, blah, blah. They were the most sterile of questions designed to make light conversation and practice early a Harvard tradition of mindless, not to mention pointless, cocktail party chatter.

We would have been better served by asking what we *really* wanted to know.

"Are you scared, too?"

"Do you think we'll make it through here?"

"What do you think they'll do to us?"

"I'm thinking of busting out after dark. You wanna come along?"

My temporary roommate during those first ten days was a tall, stocky young man from Chicago, a Russian Jew who had immigrated to the United States when he was a young boy. I asked him many questions. "Tell me about the Soviet Union and living in a closed society. Tell me about politics and religion and winter in Moscow and how they view Americans. Tell me."

My brief relationship with the young man eventually faded away, but not before giving me my first taste of the immensely valuable geographic, religious, and racial diversity that I would continually encounter in the Harvard student body. There may well be a two-billion-dollar endowment and ten-million books in the library system, but anyone who has attended Harvard can tell you that it has only one truly priceless treasure: its students.

The end of my stint with the crew also provided me with the memory of a special night. Her name is not important, although I will never forget it. We met early in the week, exchanged nervous smiles, and stole glances at each other. She had creamy, white skin, and a pretty face and a well-developed, curved body. She talked of going to graduate school, and she impressed me with her words as well as her looks. During our first and last night together, we held hands through the Square and nibbled on ice cream. Unexpectedly, it started to rain. We returned to my room, which by then had been graciously evacuated by my roommate. We talked some more and then stopped talking altogether.

She waited impatiently for me to do something, say something. I didn't, at first. I only smiled and gently rubbed the back of my hand against the curve of her face. Maybe I was afraid of being too forward, too aggressive, too predictable. Too much like the football players I knew in high school who reduced girls to mere conquests.

Though I was attracted to her, and she to me, I had not brought her to this room with two empty beds, a locked door, and an aura of sexual tension with any specific motive. Perhaps if I had, she would have been more guarded. As it was, she was at ease. Waiting, and I sensed, wanting.

Gently, awkwardly, I leaned over and kissed her lips. Her eyes closed and her moist mouth cupped to fit mine. She wrapped her arms around my neck. I moved over to the bed, pulling her toward me. She came willingly. Slowly, I began to undress her. As if by instinct, because I was supposed to undress her, I thought. Boy meets girl, boy kisses girl, boy undresses girl . . . That was stupid, I think now. What sense did that make? But then again, what sense was served by leaving a beautiful woman's soft and firm body covered by denim? I remember that, as I gently removed each piece of clothing, I expected her to stop me. "No, no. . ." I imagined she would say as beads of sweat gathered along her hairline and her lips moistened. "We can't." But, listening for objection, I heard none, and only saw her smile. She removed my shirt and pulled me close. I felt her abdominal muscles quiver under mine. Suddenly, with a single movement, I was part of her.

We were clumsy and embarrassingly unprofessional through it all, owing perhaps to our youth and inexperience. Still, we were gentle in our affection. Her body pressed against mine. Afterward, we held each other tight and talked intimately. The intimacy of lonely strangers enduring a common ordeal. The intimacy of fear.

We were alone, not only alone in a literal sense, in that ancient dorm room with wood floors but also, in a wider sense, *alone*—away from home, adrift toward some unknown destination at which we were completely unsure we would ever arrive. We were scared, and we reached out for one another. It was pure. My first time, and it was pure. It would be some years before I knew that purity again. We treated each other tenderly that night. We did not know if, later, when similarly exposed and vulnerable, John Harvard would be as tender with our fragile young hearts.

Then the tranquillity broke. My God! Oh, my God! Protection, putting something on . . . Uh. Shit. The voice in my head was loud and relentless: *Hey, you, smart guy with all the hormones and no brains. Remember that biology class you aced in high school? People do get pregnant, you idiot!*

Nervously, I asked my new friend if, well . . . she was worried about anything. No, she said with a smile as she squeezed me tighter and placed her head back down on my chest. What I meant, I explained as I squirmed further, was whether she might get pregnant. She smiled again and, with a sigh, graciously let me off the hook. "It's okay," she said. "We're fine." She explained that nothing was going to get in the way of "that piece of paper," and an eventual career as a lawyer.

What struck me immediately about the response of this eighteen-year-old girl, uh . . . young woman, was her mature decision that sex would not interfere with her responsibility to herself and to her future. Back home, I knew girls the same age who were still approaching sex and pregnancy like a game of Russian roulette. The result are dire headlines for the evening news: one million teenage pregnancies each year; most abortions in the United States performed on young women, ages 16 to 25. This woman here with me, this Harvard woman, was determined not to be a statistic. Indeed she was more together, responsible, and careful in our little experiment than I had been.

No matter, I realized that I was still an idiot. I should say that, in the month and year that I recall here, less than a year into Ronald Reagan's second term as president, there was still no real public attention given to AIDS. The Surgeon General had not yet issued his controversial report, in which he concluded that the most effective weapon against contracting AIDS, barring abstinence, was the use of a condom. The president himself had for two terms lacked the moral courage, if it meant angering his supporters on the religious right, to even say the word *AIDS*. As a result, eighteen-year-olds knew very little about a disease that some still believed, at the time, only gay men could contract and spread.

A whole generation began experimenting with sex at the threshold of an international epidemic, blissful in our own ignorance. Young people reading this, and learning from a boy's insensitivity, should remember that now there are deadly consequences to not being together, responsible, and careful.

Eventually we left the room, and I walked her home. Once school started, we would see each other in the bookstore or at the twenty-four-hour market where we all went to buy junk food at three in the morning. Usually we would smile to each other. We never really spoke again. I blew her off as well as could any high school football player who had satisfied himself. Eventually my immature reluctance to confront past indiscretions faded away in my own emotional growth. Now I am ashamed for acting as reprehensibly as have so many other men in similar situations, something that I soon thereafter resolved never to do again.

As I left her that night, it was raining harder than it had been earlier. Harvard Yard was quiet. I spent the early morning hours moving, piece by piece, all of my belongings from my temporary dorm room to what would be my permanent room in Canaday, a newer residence building across campus. My roommates, along with a flood of other students, were getting in the next day and I wanted to be settled when they arrived. Under the weight of boxes and suitcases, a walk that normally took just five minutes lapsed into twenty. Two hours later, on my final trip, I stopped for a breather in front of University Hall.

Sitting in front of the building of old, gray cinderblock, an ancient statue of John Harvard himself sits atop a pedestal, watching solemnly as over the years, hundreds of thousands of young men and women passed before him en route to class or work or dinner. Staring at the statue, I was struck again, as I had been ten days earlier, by the inescapable aura of tradition. During the school year and tourist season, student guides for the Crimson Key Society take tradition quite seriously as they explain to the couple from Topeka and the family visiting from Portland that, as is said shamelessly in the history department: "Much of the history we teach was made by people we taught."

True. The school boasts a distinguished list of alumni spread across three centuries; Eugene O'Neill, T. S. Eliot, Ralph Waldo Emerson, Henry David Thoreau, Leonard Bernstein, Norman Mailer, and W. E. B. Du Bois are all Harvard men. *Are* and not *were*, because as they say with unapologetic pretension: "Once a Harvard man, always a Harvard man." Even in death.

Still, I sensed even before I arrived there was more to the place than heroes and history. Harvard had been breaking hearts and building character for three hundred and fifty years before I arrived in Harvard Yard with my parents' Samsonites, so full of myself. And now my entire future was completely, hopelessly, wrapped up in a school that hardly seemed to notice my presence. Splendid, I thought to myself.

I should have realized earlier my own irrelevance. I should have seen myself as occupying nothing more than a blink of an eye in a complicated, timeless drama. The story is that, during a campus protest in the 1960s, an angry student protester was told matter-of-factly by a dean: "Young man, you lack perspective on all this. You see, you will be here for four years. I will be here for a lifetime. But Harvard, my boy, will be here forever." Instantly, you sense that the place is much larger than you are, greater than you could ever hope to be. Instantly, you recognize the inequity of the relationship; Harvard needs you far less than you need it. That simple idea, a frightening one.

The literature from the admissions office that cluttered my rolltop desk back home spoke of tradition. Tradition? "100 Men of Harvard," The Hasty Pudding Club, sculling the Charles, and shit like that. Who were they kidding? Tradition? Tradition was for alumni newsletters. After all, even before I attended my first class at Harvard, I knew at least two things. I was an intellectually starved Mexican-American boy from a small, stifling farm town in central California. And as my once-trusted white friends in high school had been good enough to point out, my brown behind being at Harvard had absolutely nothing to do with tradition.

I was standing in Harvard Yard, occupying with the soles of my brand-new white Reeboks a tiny piece of holy ground that scores of parents with children in diapers would kill for, not because of any beloved Harvard tradition but in *spite* of it. I was there because of pickets and petitions and protest. I was there *not* because John Harvard was a great humanitarian who had converted from centuries of sinful exclusion and institutional racism but because some agitated white student had thrown a brick through a window in University Hall on a spring day before I was even born. He had screamed for change, for an end to normalcy, and for the inclusion of people who looked like me. To shut him up, they sent out for *minority students*, as if they were ordering a pizza. A pizza, of course, being an inanimate object, without needs, fears, or concerns.

And I would learn later, I was there because of unspeakable tragedy. I was there because in the cool evening air of Memphis in April, James Earl Ray had aimed a rifle at a hotel balcony and killed Reverend Martin Luther King, Jr. Cities burned, people were killed, advocates called for inclusion, and after the ashes cleared, a handful of African-Americans and other "disadvantaged" minority groups were invited to John Harvard's secret clubhouse, as if to say that whether or not the systematic exclusion of our parents was justified, it was at least no longer prudent. Perhaps they reasoned that if they did not allow at least token access to their books, the mob in the street would burn down their libraries. So they opened the door, albeit halfheartedly and halfway.

I guessed that, in their concession, those proud men of Harvard never envisioned or intended to allow subsequent internal disruption from those privileged few who had been admitted. I presume that in the first few years of their tenure, minority students were expected to be, above all else, well-behaved. Now, twenty years later, standing in John Harvard's exclusive playground, I wondered if those rules still applied to the school's second generation of Mexican-Americans. Were we expected to be well-behaved? And if not, would we be asked to leave? Thrown out? I could not escape the thought that other Chicanos and I were on silent probation in this strange land.

I was most of all aware that, until very recently in the school's history, the vast majority of the hundreds of thousands of young people who passed before John Harvard's statue had been white. Few had looked like me. Few had mothers who sent handmade *tortillas de harina* parcel post to Cambridge. Few had Spanish-speaking grandfathers from Chihuahua or Native American great-grandparents. The Jew from Brooklyn, the Italian-American from Chicago, and the African-American from Atlanta could, in those merciless moments of self-doubt, search through the history of Harvard and find comfort in a role-model who had survived. *Will I make it . . . ? Yes, I will because others have before me . . .*

But what comfort was allowed a Mexican-American boy from a small farming town in the San Joaquin Valley?

This was it, I sensed. That solitary moment alone in the pouring rain captured and held the essence of what I felt was the uniqueness of my Harvard experience.

My grandfather worked with his hands all his life, his skin burned a dark bronze by years of grueling fieldwork in the unforgiving sun of places like the San Joaquin Valley. His body ached in old age. Roaming through my grandparents' house as a boy, I remember the smell of ointment coming from the bathroom medicine cabinet. There was no golf, no country club for this senior citizen. We played gin-rummy while he sat in his armchair. He died knowing only a few words of English, but seven decades of hard work, this hard-working, proud man of Mexico.

My father resolved early in his own life that he would not dwell in fields devoid of hope. He was reared speaking Spanish. He struggled in school, assigned ultimately by white guidance counselors to classes with nicknames like "bonehead English."

Ignored, abused, neglected, and forgotten. Left content merely to graduate near the bottom of his class from a high school that, thirty years later, would graduate his oldest son with top honors.

"You don't understand how proud I am," he would tell a young boy for whom A's had always come easy.

"School was hard for me. When I graduated from high school, I was ranked number three from the bottom of the class. There were just two Okies dumber than me," he would say as his voice tapered off to a milder, humbler tone. An unsettling voice. "Now you're at the top!" I thought I noticed a restrained moistening of his eyes, as he switched the talk to less solemn matters.

I should say that I have never liked hearing either of my parents refer to themselves as "dumb," although they are only parroting what they were told so often by so many for so long. What I like even less, though, is subtle, well-intentioned reminders of how I am smarter than they are. I feel a piercing sense of guilt in my stomach at those moments, one that returns on occasion.

That is my own personal, unsettling, rendition of the American Dream. Each generation doing better than the next. Maybe, as a Harvard man, I was at the top. But as I stood in the rain and studied the contours of John Harvard's face, I was consumed by nothing as much as the events of the past.

Inexplicably, I drew an inner strength from the injustice, racism, and poverty endured by generations of my family, and countless other Mexican-Americans like them. I was strong because the survival of past indignities by those who had come before me made me that way. I knew my capability, and damn it, I resolved, before I left this strange place, John Harvard would know it too. As they say on the playground, we were gonna get it on. And may the best man win. That settled, I pulled away from the statue's hypnotic gaze, strutted off to bed, and fell into deep sleep moments before dawn.

Yet it would be much easier in the months to come to feel confident rather than comfortable. The "Harvard Mystique" constantly hung overhead, relentlessly reminding me that I was but a negligible part of an institution that at times seemed more like a museum than a college. And in subsequent years when

I entered museums in Montreal, New York, or Los Angeles, I was always instantly inhibited, restrained in movement, and afraid of breaking anything. Yet on one late September night before the floodgates opened and the madness began, mine had been a solitary figure moving confidently through Harvard Yard and selfishly soaking up the generous silence of a museum in the hours before its opening.

A Harvard man from an earlier, simpler time, Robert Frost, wrote of two paths diverging in the woods, and how taking the one less traveled had "made all the difference." An eighteen-year-old had thumbed his nose at low expectation and resisted the very real temptation to simply attend good colleges in California—*cerca de su familia*. By not doing what many of my high school classmates had done, I had chosen my less traveled path. Now I eagerly awaited my reward.

I was awakened in early afternoon by the sound of jostling suitcases and muffled whispers. My two roommates had arrived, separately, from their homes in Connecticut and Pennsylvania. At the time, those states meant nothing to me. What did they look like in autumn? What kind of people lived there? I would eventually have my answers through visits to each of my roommates' hometowns—a warm pleasantry that, logistically, I could not offer either of them. What I found there in Ridgefield, Connecticut, and West Chester, Pennsylvania, were kind, good-hearted and hospitable people. I learned early that small town values were not limited to small towns in central California.

What I did not find in either of those charming northeastern towns, however, or in all of New England for that matter, were large populations of Latinos. There were a few neighborhoods like that of Villa Victoria in Boston, but not whole towns or cities where Latinos constituted the majority of the populace. And those Latinos concentrated in northeastern neighborhoods were not Mexican-American, anyway. Or even first generation Mexican. They were Puerto Rican, or Central American. The reality was that these two well-educated, well-mannered boys from the suburbs had, in their eighteen years, likely never seen a Mexican-American up close before. And they had certainly never lived with one. So as the adventure began, I was not the only resident of freshman dorm room, Canaday F-31, visiting a different world.

I pulled myself from bed and opened my bedroom door. Standing a few feet in front of me, telling one another to be quiet ("Shhh . . ."), were two young men, my roommates. We exchanged smiles, introductions, and a few pleasantries. I offered help with their bags; they smiled and accepted. Later that evening, and for many more evenings in the next several weeks, we sat in our common room and asked one another intrusive questions about where we were from and where we were going. I was impressed by their confidence. They seemed to belong here. If they were at all afraid or unsure of what awaited them at Harvard, they hid it well. I wondered if I did.

Though we attended the same school, lived in the same room, and were even enrolled in a shared class, I expected the Harvard experiences of each of my two roommates to be fundamentally different from mine. Both were white. One had attended a private preparatory school; the other, although a public school graduate like me, lived in a neighboring state. The personal, geographic, and sociological changes that they might undergo as a result of their time in Cambridge, I suspected, would not compare to the ones that awaited me. Neither better nor worse. Just different.

On the night before classes began there was a mass, spontaneous gathering of freshmen students in Harvard Yard. How it began was never known and unimportant. Maybe a group of ten freshmen started talking with one another in front of John Harvard's statue, and then called out to a few friends. Before long, others joined them. Minutes later, word reached Canaday. My roommates and I, brimming with curiosity, wasted no time in joining the fray of what was, by the time we arrived, possibly over one thousand young people occupying the space of half a football field. We mingled into the crowd, and were engulfed in what was a massive mixer. The introductions were brief and tedious. And numerous. I must have shaken two hundred hands in an hour and a half. The questions were mindless samplings of stale repetition.

"What's your name?"

"Where are you from?"

"What's your major?"

Yawn. No matter. There was an excitement in the September air, the excitement of newness and unknown possibility. And anyway, the place carried its own freshness. It was new and fresh and frightening and unknown all at once.

Then suddenly, I felt a tap on my shoulder and turned around. In front of me stood a thin, dark-skinned young man with dark brown eyes and straight black hair. There was a childlike quality to his presence. And a familiar one. I knew this stranger, though we had never met.

"Hey, you a Mexican . . . ?" he asked bluntly with a hopeful, vulnerable look on his face.

At first I hesitated. Then something inside me prompted the answer. "Yeah," I said with a smile of relief. "You?"

He smiled back, nodded, and introduced himself. We shook hands, not as country club tennis players reaching over a net, but as brothers. A circular, relaxed grip of the palm and a curled tug on fingertips. A Chicano handshake.

CHAPTER 3

OTHER ISLANDS

"I THOUGHT THE SPARROW'S NOTE FROM HEAVEN
SITTING AT DAWN ON THE ALDER BOUGH:
I BROUGHT HIM HOME, AT HIS NEST, AT EVEN;
HE SINGS THE SONG BUT IT CHEERS NOT NOW.
FOR I DID NOT BRING HOME THE RIVER AND THE SKY."

RALPH WALDO EMERSON

HARVARD COLLEGE, CLASS OF 1821

The young man and I bonded instantly. He said that he was from a small town outside of Houston, but that his family was originally from the Rio Grande Valley. I delighted in telling him that my mother, too, was from *El Valle*. We paired off into a corner of the Yard and talked for hours, oblivious to the mass of students around us. We skipped the trite, unimportant questions about majors and the like and focused immediately on more interesting and substantive matters. Personal things, not often shared with someone whom one has just met.

"How many in your family?"

"Are you scared?"

"Are you the oldest?"

"Are you scared?"

"Did your parents want you to stay closer to home?"

"Are you scared?"

"When you got in here, did your classmates say . . . ?"

"Have you seen any more of us?"

Us. By us, I meant other Mexican-American students. Other Chicanos. He understood and shook his head. Looking around the Yard that night, into the giggling masses of young people babbling to strangers about majors and hometowns, we saw almost all white faces. Maybe one face out of ten was black, one of twenty was brown. After one considered Puerto Ricans, Dominicans, Cubans, and Mexican nationals, only about one face in forty resembled ours.

Given all that I had heard from high school classmates and teachers about how Mexican-Americans were much more likely to be admitted to Harvard than white students, I half-expected to be greeted at Johnston Gate by smiling hordes of brown-skinned young men and women. A red carpet. Nachos, *piñatas*, and mariachis at the president's welcoming luncheon.

Reality was not so generous. Of an entering class of just over 1,600 freshmen, I was one of only 35 Mexican-Americans. On the campus as a whole, we numbered 125 of 6,000 undergraduates—a percentage of 2.5 percent. Was this the browning of the academy that affirmative action critics on Sunday morning talk shows foretold so ominously? Furthermore, aside from the low numbers, it was impossible not to notice the "quality" of those who had made it through Harvard's half-opened door. We had been carefully chosen it seemed. We were valedictorians, star athletes, class presidents, and National Merit Scholars. We were, in short, the *crema* of the Mexican crop.

Invited to attend an elite university that, just one generation earlier, had excluded people such as their parents, Mexican-American students at Harvard are a strange lot. An enigma born of protest. A mysterious paradox of progress that escapes simple definition. A freak of nature. Two concepts, as distinct as oil and water, delicately fused together as walking examples of educational and social progress.

Who were these people?

Much of who we were was tied up in what we represented to others. An admissions officer's model minority, a stellar candidate who made the implementation of affirmative action efforts easier through excellence. A teacher's pet, at every turn raising an extended arm with the right answer. A high school counselor's overachiever, needing little guidance. An educationally starved community's role-model, an example of what other young people should aspire to become. A tearful parent's pride and joy, proof of the American ethic that, with hard work, anything is possible. Most of all, a scared and lonely eighteen-year-old with too many people to please and too much baggage to carry in a foreign place that is too, too far away from home.

I met them, my fellow Chicanos, one by one. In the first few days of school, I searched them out like colored eggs in high grass on Easter morning. I spotted them at the gym or in the dining hall, and I was drawn to them as a distant relative. We smiled at one another, gaining some comfort from a small lifeboat of familiarity in a foreign sea. We came from throughout the country, including midwestern cities such as Chicago, Detroit, and Kansas City. But predominantly we came from the West and the Southwest. El Paso. Los Angeles. Phoenix. Albuquerque. Fresno.

We had all lived in, and had become accustomed to, communities in which the majority of people were Latino. For much of our young, impressionable lives, we had been surrounded by the familiar sight of other brown faces, the hint of Spanish in the warm air, and the taste of Mexican food. In the small, predominantly Mexican farm towns of the San Joaquin Valley, Cinco de Mayo and the Diez y Seis de Septiembre meant city-wide fiestas with *campesinos* in their best western shirts coming in from their labor camps to drink beer and hear *música* amid red, white, and green crepe paper. The populations of Texas, California, and Arizona, each of which bordering Mexico, were over 30 percent Latino. The population of Los Angeles was 40 percent Latino, a percentage that easily outnumbered that of both whites and African-Americans. My own hometown, nestled unassumingly in the center of California, was nearly 75 percent Latino. Those images were comforting. Still, before leaving home for Harvard, I had no idea just how comforting.

Geographically, the places that Chicano students called home were incredibly far removed from that of Cambridge, Massachusetts, and indeed all of New England. If we had grown accustomed to seeing people with skin like ours at the supermarket, post office, and local movie theater, simple demographics dictated that we would see them no more. Certainly the place had its own ethnicity. There were the Irish in South Boston, and the Italians in the North End. There were Jews in the garment district, Germans, and immigrants from Russia. The richness of their ethnic experience was obvious. There were African-Americans in Roxbury, who certainly knew about race and racism. There were even other types of Latinos, recent immigrants from Central America and Puerto Ricans in Villa Victoria.

Among Latinos, too, there were obvious differences. Differences often obscured by activists invoking the perceived strength in that elusive political fiction, Latino unity. Among Harvard undergraduates, Byerly Hall may have been content to lump all of us together in a single bar graph under the government term, "Hispanic." But as Hispanics, Latinos, or whatever, we were not convinced of our similarities so easily. We recognized that we were different within the traditional Harvard student body. And so we saw mainly the differences in ourselves. It was the uniqueness of our individual experiences that impressed us most. Puerto Ricans were from Northeastern cities such as New York, Philadelphia, and Trenton. They had darker skin, kinkier hair, and drank rum instead of tequila. Even our food was different: their rice much spicier, their beans much darker, and deep-fried bread instead of tortillas. Cubans were from Florida and voted Republican. I remember, during my political awakening in high school, that I had assumed that all Latinos were Democrats like me; it was not until much later, in college, that I realized my own naïveté. Mexican citizens seemed almost aristocratic; we knew enough about the socioeconomic structure in Mexico to know that often only the light-skinned children of the rich and powerful were in a position to receive a letter of acceptance to Harvard.

We all spoke the same language, Spanish, but Puerto Ricans and Cubans spoke it much faster than we did. For much of my time at Harvard, I hesitated at speaking my grandfather's native tongue. When I braved the chore, I could hear my awful mangling of words. Never, though, was I more conscientious of my inability to speak Spanish smoothly than when I encountered Mexicans, those citizen children of Mexico who roamed confidently through Harvard Yard. Thus, even among portions of an ethnic group that seemed similar, cultural entities like language, food, and drink provided no real link of intimacy. Maybe that is why the geographic presence of other sorts of Latinos in the Northeast did not matter much to me. What did matter to me, and perhaps to others, was that the nearest concentration of Mexican-Americans was a thousand miles away in Chicago, two thousand miles away in San Antonio, or three thousand miles away in Los Angeles.

At Harvard, for the first time in our lives, my Chicano classmates and I were suddenly part of a racial and cultural minority. And naturally, we were as disoriented as Dorothy upon her arrival in Oz. "*Gee, ése, I don't think we're in the Southwest, anymore.*" All at once, the face of our immediate world had changed radically. It was a white face, with blue and green eyes; one that we did not recognize or trust. The experience was frightening. Poetically we were indeed minority students.

A friend once scribbled on a postcard mailed from Europe the line of a poem: "What I love most is to visit other islands..." As I would in subsequent years tell the wide-eyed young people who gathered in their high school cafeteria to hear my recruitment pitch for Harvard, the opportunity for one to be totally uprooted and undergo a completely different set of human experiences is a frightening and valuable one that allows for immeasurable personal growth. What I did not know quite how to tell them was that visiting "other islands" is seldom easy to do. And, as I could painfully attest to, it can be especially difficult when minority students are involved.

Among those who have endured it, the psychological phenomenon that awaits some of those Mexican-Americans who attend colleges and universities in the frigid, largely white-populated states of the Northeast is referred to, rather matter-of-factly, as *culture shock*.

It begins appropriately, as it does with students of all color, with a distinct element of self-doubt. For generations, bright young adults have wandered through Harvard Square in the first few weeks feeling like frauds. We are convinced that the admissions office must have made a dreadful mistake. This is Harvard, we tell ourselves. The school of Emerson, Thoreau, and Kennedy. What am I doing here?

For Latinos and other minority students who may see themselves—indeed, have been encouraged by hometown insults to see themselves—as the winners of a dubious affirmative action lottery, the question of unworthiness endures like a stale odor. You begin to believe old critics, assuming that you have come to this bizarre place not by your own merit but by the grace of a government handout.

I saw among my Chicano classmates two different reactions to their own self-doubt. There were a few who undertook their academic program with a sense of low expectation. At the beginning of freshman year, in a course on Latin America, I asked an upperclassman from Santa Fe for advice on academic strategy. I realize now that I was fishing for what was expected of me and what sort of grades I should expect. He gave me well-meaning but harmful advice, suggesting that we would be "okay" to graduate in four years with B's. I took that to mean that while A's were, for all Harvard students, unlikely, they were, for Harvard Chicanos, also unexpected. I had not lived my life settling for "okay"; since elementary school, excellence had been my only goal and obsession its price. But now, for my Chicano classmates and I, the emphasis seemed to be on simply graduating one day. I am embarrassed to admit that even before I entered my first freshman class at Harvard, eventual distinctions like graduating summa cum laude or Rhodes scholarships seemed, because of my cultural bloodline, out of reach. They should not have, but they did.

On the other hand, there were those who seized the initiative and shamelessly exploited the valuable opportunity that they had been given. Like weight lifters yelling out for more weight, I saw some Chicano classmates overburden themselves with the most demanding of course loads, map out strategies for magna cum laude four years in advance, and plot for themselves multidisciplined careers like double doctorates or triple stints in law, politics, and business. One person majored in English, she said, because it was rumored to be the most demanding of majors. After the humiliation of failing to place out of my foreign language requirement in Spanish—my grandparents' mother tongue no less—I rejected a friend's advice to take Spanish during freshman year, opting instead for what would prove to be a much more frustrating and difficult course in Italian. All year I chased the phonetics. Always the words were similar to the Spanish that I had grown up hearing when my parents spoke with their parents, and yet just different enough to madden me. As my professor floated through the room testing our pronunciation, I felt a nervous pain in my stomach. *"Como estai?"* he asked me with a sympathetic glare. *I'm going to be sick, thank you very much.* My friends taking Spanish wondered why I punished myself so.

The preoccupation with overachievement was not in and of itself disturbing. I believed then, and now, that members of educationally neglected groups should aspire to the highest level of competition. What is distressing though is that, at Harvard, I always suspected that high-powered minority students were too often motivated not purely by an intellectual thirst for knowledge but instead by desperate compulsion to disprove their critics and convince themselves finally that they deserved all that they had already achieved. Whether the prize is high marks, the praise of professors, or acceptance to graduate school, proving oneself is the order of the day at a place like Harvard. It is especially so when Harvard Chicanos are involved.

Along with academic doubt, there are other, more tangible dimensions to the culture shock suffered by some, though likely not all, Mexican-American students in elite, Northeastern colleges such as Harvard. As I remember the similar experiences of friends at other Ivy League colleges, I remember also my own relief when I first realized that my difficulty in acclimating to strange, new surroundings was not unique. Strangely, over the years I developed an affinity with Mexican-American students at places like Princeton, Yale, or Columbia (who formed a kind of Chicano network) that was stronger than the bond I shared with white, Asian, or African-American students at Harvard. Their experiences were mine, and mine theirs.

I remember, for instance, that in the Northeast, the weather acts as a major force in the cultural alienation of Mexican-Americans. As September yielded to October, I bathed in the magnificent colors of autumn in New England. The bright celebration of orange, red, and yellow leaves and the passing of Halloween foretold the coming of winter. The first snowfall came a few days before Thanksgiving. I looked out my bedroom window and saw the unsettling sight of a white blanket covering the Yard. I had seen snow before, on trips to the Sierras back home. But, I had never awakened to it. I had never lived in it. That first winter seemed to drag on indefinitely. Days were long and dreary. Months seemed never-ending. Temperatures hung in single digits for weeks on end. The windchill factor, a term with which I was happily unfamiliar with before my arrival in New England, was frequently ten or twenty degrees below zero.

"Today's gonna be another cold one, folks," the voice on the morning radio warned. "Expect it to reach a high of four degrees this afternoon."

As I hit the snooze button and remained in my warm bed for a few minutes longer, I mumbled to myself that a number as low as four should not even qualify as a degree, seeming better-suited to be the winning score at a hockey game. Making matters worse, there were those memorable mornings when the Harvard plumbing system—a relic from the days of Adams, no doubt—could muster only cold water. As expletives flew, one had to appreciate the humility in a cold shower and the concession that even for Harvard's chosen few, there were those things that were simply beyond one's control.

Once outside, appropriate dress was a matter of survival. I wore thermal underwear, thick woolen sweaters, gloves, scarves, hiking boots for traction on New England ice patches and a long, wool overcoat to shield me from the wind and cold. As I walked into a heated classroom, I joined my classmates in the ritual of stripping away layers of clothing and placing the discarded wardrobe in piles on the floor.

On one November day, described by some of the young people who experienced it as "the coldest day of my life," several hundred Harvard undergraduates drove two hundred miles south to New Haven, Connecticut. We had come to sit on hard wooden seats bundled in blankets, drink hot chocolate and peppermint schnapps, and watch a football game. The announcer told us over the loudspeaker that the windchill in the Yale Bowl was a record fifty degrees below zero; those of us who endured it would argue that it never got that warm. Somewhere in the third quarter, I looked over at one friend's pale and wind-chapped face; tiny ice-crystals had literally formed from the moisture on the rims of his sunglasses. I managed a smile and joked that if we had chosen to go to Stanford, we could be getting a tan at that moment. He nodded and bundling up again, asked for more chocolate.

Certainly New England weather has a universal drudgery. People of all races, colors, and ethnicities suffer through its depression and gloom. Yet it is no exaggeration to admit that for Mexican-American students transplanted for four years to the Northeast, the ordeal of a New England winter can be especially severe. Even with recent immigration to the midwest, most Mexican-Americans still live in the warm weather region of the American Southwest. Acclimation is gradual and difficult.

I knew a Mexican-American girl from Tuscon who each year experienced both a New England winter with windchill of fifty below and then, back home, a summer day of one hundred twenty degrees; her body would, in just a few months, adjust to a drastic environmental change encompassing one hundred seventy degrees. Coming back and forth from Cambridge to Sanger, I was never at ease with temperature. On the east coast, it felt colder each year while in the west it seemed to be getting warmer. It was always too hot or too cold; my friends who lived in one part of the country and did not cross borders thought I was going mad.

For Mexicans, raised in sunlight, home is desert and lush valleys bathed in warm sunshine for most of the year, with summer temperatures hovering mercilessly over one hundred degrees for days at a time. The Aztecs, I learned in elementary school, prayed to the Sun God, not the Snow God. During Cambridge winters, my friends and I would stare in horror at the image in the bathroom mirror and watch ourselves, literally, fade in color. From September to December, one's pigmentation might go from brown to beige, from beige to white. For those of us who were already feeling culturally insecure and those who were concerned with being considered "white" in a figurative sense, the gradual changing of our complexion in cold weather only compounded our worry. I felt like Casper the Friendly Ghost. If I was brown in September, beige in October, and white in November, then would I be transparent by December?

The mind has its own psychology. As our skin paled, many of us seemed to lose much of our vitality. We were depressed. Our vibrance would be replenished only months later with the melting of snow and the coming of spring. Above all, as we trudged off to class in our bundle of clothing and with the frosty air pasting our Ray•Bans to our wind-chapped faces, we convinced ourselves that, clearly, this was not normal. A Chicano from Albuquerque spotted me in the Yard one day and joined in my walk to the library. As we hung our heads to cover our chins underneath our scarves, he mumbled without looking at me that it was so cold, that it was "not even funny." There were, we thought, places where certain people simply did *not* belong. On frosty Cambridge mornings the likes of which he and I had never seen in the cities and towns of the sun-bathed Southwest, we could not help but wonder if people like us really belonged in a place like that.

I remember also that language can have a role in alienating Mexican-American students from their New England surroundings. As I have admitted, Spanish was never my language in the first place. I spoke it poorly and with embarrassment. I spoke a frustrated linguistic mixture, Spanglish, and I spoke it slowly. I searched memory for words long ago misplaced. I fought with words until a kind uncle at a family dinner might rescue me by speaking English. Four years of high school instruction had not provided me with any more confidence in my Spanish-speaking ability. Still, I heard it at home. It was never far. I heard it when my parents spoke to their parents. It was not my language but I recognized it as belonging to what might be loosely termed "my people."

At Harvard, those of us from California would hear about the legislative campaign in our home state to make English its official language. At a newsstand in the Square, I read a headline in a California newspaper saying that Chicano activists felt that Spanish, a valuable cornerstone of their culture, was being taken from them. I doubted that a culture that had endured five hundred years was endangered by a group of nativist zealots. No matter. For me, the English-only argument was moot; I had already given away Spanish years earlier in what my parents determined would be a mainstream childhood. Both my mother and father had been raised speaking Spanish at home and they had struggled in school in great measure because of their inability to master the English language. They resolved early in their marriage that their children would be spared that obstacle. They were scolded by my grandparents for allowing us to lose *nuestro idioma*, but they took pride in our public speaking awards. They considered the certificates to be a subtle reassurance that they had made the right decision so long ago.

In Cambridge, where I found myself immersed for the first time in surroundings where Spanish was considered as much a foreign language as French or German, my personal shame intensified with the realization that the language had a natural, almost sacred, affinity with Mexican-Americans. The opponents of English-only claimed that language was culture. To abandon one would be to abandon the other. If speaking Spanish was, as the activists implied, an issue of loyalty to culture, then wasn't my broken Spanish evidence of disloyalty? Worse, the logic suggested I was being disloyal behind enemy lines, in a foreign environment where Mexican culture, if not protected, could melt away as easily as a New England snowfall.

For Harvard Chicanos, maintaining and, if necessary, exaggerating our proficiency in Spanish became a game of sorts. We felt compelled to speak Spanish in one another's company. We would pronounce one another's name with the appropriate Spanish emphasis. I was no longer *Rooo-ben*, the smooth-sounding name that I had carried through elementary school; my father's name, as it was pronounced by my mother. Suddenly, I was *Rrrrubén*, with heavy accent on the final syllable; my father's name, as I had only heard it pronounced by my grandmother. Years later, at Berkeley, my brother Roman would become to his Chicano classmates *Row-mánn*, the name of my grandfather as the same old woman, his wife, pronounced it. But this was not my grandmother's voice in the air above Harvard. The new pronunciation seemed contrived. Forced. Insincere. A pronunciation that carried respect with one generation somehow seemed cheapened as it was tossed around carelessly by youngsters on an elite college campus, a place that neither the first Ruben nor the first Roman had been allowed to enter.

Our trips to Mexican restaurants in Boston became impromptu opportunities to show off our faint grip on a language that we felt called upon to speak. More than practicing, we were showing off. As if to show one another than our individual ties to culture through language had not been weakened by our time at Harvard, we would proudly spring our phrases on the bewildered Mexican waitress taking our order or the dark-skinned busboy. I would watch as the waitress approached our table. It would fall to one of us, perhaps the one nearest her, to begin the game. I would await my turn and, when it arrived, feel my palms moisten. Afraid, no *terrified*, of the embarrassment of tripping over my words in front of fellow Chicanos, I intentionally would seek out and order the entrée whose name was least difficult to pronounce.

"Dame dos tacos, arroz y frijoles con tortillas de harina, por favor."

I was intrigued by, although I did not completely trust, the romantic notion that language somehow conveyed intimacy. At the Mexican restaurant, did my friends and I have another reason for playing our language game? I have seen others, professionals uneasy with their success, strain to prove an affinity with the working poor. Did we, as Harvard Chicanos, intend to claim a kind of solidarity with these Latino workers? If so, it was a foolish effort. There was no real allegiance to be forged. They were, after all, serving us. That single fact did more to define our relationship than the shared language of Spanish. Today, I all but laugh out loud when the Chicano lawyer at lunch leaves our conversation in English to make small talk with the waiter in Spanish. Does he really believe that he can escape class distinctions so easily?

I am part of an entire generation that hears our grandmothers' questions in Spanish, but answers them in English. Nonetheless, like all grandchildren, we are drawn to the warmth in Grandma's voice. Her words speak to us in ways that transcend simple communication. Here, there *is* intimacy.

Mijo, this is our language. Your mistakes are forgiven. We trust you with our words. You are a child again. Innocent.

And, despite my skepticism at a manufactured solidarity that ignores important class and educational differences, I admit that I am still likely to smile when the pretty Latina teller at the Bank of America on Olvera Street addresses me with exact pronunciation. "And how do you want your money, Mr. *Navarrrre-tte?*"

Of course, along with demographics, weather, and the absence of Spanish, there was also a natural homesickness. A longing for family. Though I am careful not to make assertions about one group of people having closer family ties than another and I would never presume that any ethnic group has a monopoly on the closeness of relatives, I will say that, for Latinos, the institution of family is perhaps the most sacred of all. Owing to our Catholic tradition, we consider the entity to be the center of our strength and the most likely source of weakness. Mine is a close-knit family, in which I occupy the special place of being the oldest child and, on one side of the extended family, the oldest grandchild. We were never far from one another. Squeezed into a town of less than fifteen thousand people, I had, within arms reach, my parents, my brother and sister, all three living grandparents, five aunts and uncles, a number of great-aunts and uncles, and a sizable assortment of *primos*, first- and second-cousins. My cousins became my older brothers. I deferred to my uncles as fathers. Incredibly, although they are now approaching their own old age, each night my mother and father still discuss the day's events by phone with their respective mothers. It is a family joke, this tucking-in of parents by grandparents. The idea of leaving town for a weekend without first informing *mamá* is unthinkable. Not all is jest. Mama lives alone, things happen. On the phone, there is never a raised voice, always humility and respect. "*Mande...*" In English, literally, command me.

Then suddenly, at eighteen, I boarded an airplane in Fresno, and five hours and three thousand miles later, I was alone. Completely alone. No family, no friends, no nothing.

Freshman year, I ran up incredible phone bills calling home every other night. Breathlessly, I would share my new experiences. Desperately, I would collect the most mundane and insignificant pieces of family gossip. I saw it all as a way of struggling to stay connected with the world that I had left behind so readily. I would write letters to friends after, and too often in lieu of, homework. I anxiously awaited weekly coast-to-coast phone calls. We talked for hours and hours. The telephone receiver burned warm on my ear and I tried not to think of how much of my monthly paycheck from my library job would have to go to the phone company. I bathed in the intimacy that is remarkably possible via a telephone line. Once an old friend, then a student at Berkeley, talked with me until dawn. As I watched the sun come up over the Charles, I thought about how much I missed them all and about the incredible geographic distance that separated us. I dreaded hanging up the phone. All not to be forgotten. Abandoned in this awful place.

It is perhaps the depth of my homesickness during freshman year that allows me to remember so fondly the excitement surrounding my family's trip to Cambridge to visit me. As with their first trip with me a year earlier, they could hardly afford the expense. Still, the sight of their three children united once again seemed to more than compensate them. As a close family, we took such a gesture for granted. I myself did not realize the full significance of my family's trip until I noticed my roommates' amazement. One was from a state that was much closer to Massachusetts than was California; his parents did not come to visit him as mine had. I had not been abandoned, after all.

Throughout the year, I hurried into the mail room searching for letters from home, or most prized of all, a care package. Well-stocked parcels from California brightened otherwise tedious, dreary New England days. Once a dear friend from Chicago sent ten pounds of assorted candy and a card wishing me good luck in my studies.

A favorite treat was a *Mexican* care package, which served the dual purpose of providing both physical and cultural nourishment. It might contain some sort of Mexican food or some other reminder of the millions of dark-skinned, Spanish-speaking strangers in the Southwest who we assumed we were at Harvard to represent but whose lives continued on completely unaltered by our absence. Cautiously, we shared with our white roommates homemade flour tortillas mailed overnight express from San Antonio, Tucson, or Fresno. Usually, a story was included in the deal, perhaps about how tortillas themselves have become more acceptable in American life. My father remembers from elementary school embarrassed Mexican classmates hiding their tacos made of flour tortillas. They ate them inconspicuously, fearing the likelihood that white children would tease them as mercilessly as children do. My grandmother, clearly aware of the realities of life in the San Joaquin Valley of the 1950s, was careful to pack sandwiches in my father's sack lunch. Now, as an adult, my father marvels that his co-workers at office potlucks devour nothing as rapidly as the stack of flour tortillas on the table.

Thirty years later, a friend from Yale tells an amusing story about how she and a handful of Latino classmates stood in front of a hot plate that was heating a tamal. Her white roommate asked, with all sincerity, whether they were participating in some sort of religious ritual. Another friend was amazed that white Harvard students who had never seen a tamal—or a Mexican for that matter—up close before had to be reminded not to bite into it without first removing the paper husk.

"Yeah, *ése*, 1600 SATs and the *bato* wanted to eat the wrapper..."

The absence of what we considered authentic Mexican food was, for Harvard Chicanos, nothing short of yet another ordeal to be endured. We hardly knew whether to laugh or cry when we discovered the Harvard cafeteria system serving baked chicken and Spanish rice and calling it *arroz con pollo*. We explained, to no avail, to those who served us that *con* meant *with*, after all, and that the tasteless substance sitting on our plate in separate portions was hardly what great-great-Grandma envisioned in that Mexican village generations ago. When friends at Princeton relayed stories of supermarkets in New Jersey that carried tortillas in an air-tight can, we were of course duly horrified.

"Wait a minute," I asked them in disbelief. "You're telling me that they had *canned* tortillas? Canned like peanuts? My God, that should be a sin!"

We would venture into the city in search of real Mexican. Invariably, our mission would fail. Sometimes miserably. In one restaurant, we marveled at refried beans that were black instead of chocolate brown. We drew little comfort from the fact that black beans were the norm in central Mexico; we trusted only the exactness of our own culinary tradition. We agreed that the rice was too spicy, or not flavored enough. Never like home.

In such horrid places, the margaritas, the Dos Equis, and the sangria we consumed before and after dinner were our only saving grace. They facilitated the delicate process of digestion. One night in New Haven, our digestion was facilitated all the way to a bar tab of over two hundred dollars. "How much?" the drunken chorus rang out in unison.

Alcohol was, for many Harvard Chicanos as it is for college students in general, a close friend. Confronted immediately with each of the various dimensions of culture shock and with the overwhelming feeling that you are suddenly in an environment in which no one cares if you succeed, or even survive, young people sometimes opt for immediate, if temporary, measures of relief. On every college campus in America, there are too many young people drinking too much to change too many things about the lives they live.

Harvard is no exception. On the contrary, given the extraordinary pressure and stress that the place puts squarely on the shoulders of an eighteen-year-old, it has more than its share of five-keg parties, drinking games, fake IDs, and students stumbling home through the Yard throwing up in the bushes along the way. The long-distance relationship of a girlfriend back home or a lingering doubt about whether you can make it through this museum without breaking anything or breaking down provided an excellent excuse to get lit, toasted, trashed, hammered, or wasted—the gift of forgetting, if only for a moment, just where you were.

I personally never drank in high school, and so, as with sex, I may have been subconsciously determined to use college to catch up. I did. As my drinking habits progressed and my tolerance for alcohol increased, I moved from an occasional beer at parties to beer with a hamburger in the Square to beer just for the sake of a beverage. Before long, I was experimenting with any kind of liquor I could find. I was curious about the taste, the effect. Whiskey. Gin. Rum. Vodka. A sip of peppermint schnapps seemed an appropriate morning breath freshener. Though I am not certain, I may have toyed with alcoholism. By summer vacation, I was drinking beer like water and resolved to quit only after I noticed myself on one occasion actually slurring my words. Even for a curious eighteen-year-old, the seduction was never complete. Perhaps I was bored with vice too easily.

Meanwhile, Harvard was already claiming its victims. I remember a Chicano classmate who quietly disappeared. One day, he was there eating lunch with us in the Freshman Union under the ugly moose antlers donated by Teddy Roosevelt. The next, he was gone. Someone said he had given up, turned his back on the whole scene, and gone back to Texas. Instantly, we believed it. Privately, we wondered if we would be next.

At the other extreme, among students of all colors, there were tragic, not often publicized tales of suicides that formed morbid headlines for the morning *Crimson*. A member of our freshman class who was home for Christmas in upstate New York went into the woods with a hunting rifle and shot himself in the head. A young woman slit her wrists in the shower and was saved only after friends found her and took her to the infirmary. And there were those gruesome stories about someone throwing himself off the top of Mather Tower. I saw the poor victims of such tragedy to be young people who took themselves much too seriously and wanted out of Harvard much too desperately.

Like tens of thousands of Harvard undergraduates before me, I was developing a distinct distaste for my school. As I walked through the Yard one peaceful night, I remember shocking a friend who accompanied me with an odd remark. As we passed in front of University Hall and the familiar statue of our school's founder, I whispered to my companion with total resolution, "If I die here," I said, "make sure that they bury me right here, standing up, in front of University Hall."

"Why?" my friend asked with a restrained smile.

"So John Harvard can kiss my ass!"

He stopped in his step, eased up his smile, and looked at me not knowing whether to laugh. He was not sure if I was joking. Neither was I.

CHAPTER 4

PLAYING THE ROLE

"NO! I AM NOT PRINCE HAMLET, NOR WAS MEANT TO BE;
AM AN ATTENDANT LORD, ONE THAT WILL DO
TO SWELL A PROGRESS, START A SCENE OR TWO,
ADVISE THE PRINCE; NO DOUBT, AN EASY TOOL,
DEFERENTIAL, GLAD TO BE OF USE,
POLITIC, CAUTIOUS, AND METICULOUS;
FULL OF HIGH SENTENCE, BUT A BIT OBTUSE.
AT TIMES, INDEED, RIDICULOUS.
ALMOST, AT TIMES, THE FOOL."

T. S. ELIOT

HARVARD COLLEGE, CLASS OF 1910

A s the bizarre drama that defined their lives unfolded around them, Mexican-Americans at Harvard—these strange entities—drank and danced and tried not to think of it all. Of course, the compulsion toward maintaining ethnic purity, even in drink, mandated shots of tequila. For me, the word conjured up images of old Mexican westerns. A round-bellied bandido with a long mustache and belts of bullets across his chest would stagger into the cantina and order a bottle. *"Tequila!"* My father does not drink and never has. Yet, even if he did, I doubt that his preference would be tequila. Back home, my Chicano friends, if they drank at all, were more partial to beer and wine coolers.

No matter. A world away, an elite group of young Chicanos would honor tradition, even if they first had to reinvent it. It was at those moments, as the shot glass bearing the Harvard insignia made its way around the circle of new close friends huddled in the warm intimacy of a shared ordeal, that inhibitions were shed like layers of heavy clothing. I sprinkled a dash of salt on my hand underneath my thumb. Trust passed freely from person to person before finally settling in the air like a lustful stare. A trust in brotherhood and sisterhood, born of our shared conviction that no one else on earth could understand as well the psychological trials of our experience. The liquid burned as it passed down my throat. I coughed and, oddly, remembered why Indian ancestors had referred to alcohol as "firewater." Biting into a lime wedge, one might confess insecurity, loneliness, doubt, fear.

The whispered worry, "Man, what if we don't make it through this fucking place? What if we get kicked out?"

The response, in muffled tones, "You just make sure you catch me if I fall, *ése.*"

Three months had passed since I had first walked through Johnston Gate and still I searched in the winter snowfall for some sense of reaffirmation. The accusations of high school lingered. I felt illegitimate. My scrutiny of the abrupt changes in my surroundings heightened. I felt misplaced. I had been admitted to this old and pristine institution. I had accepted. I had arrived. Now all I needed was some degree of proof that I belonged there, that the rewards of Harvard were rightfully mine to claim. More than approval, more than a red ink "A" on a freshman paper, I wanted reassurance that I was entitled to even sit in the classroom—an old, stuffy room with high ceilings, a portrait of a dead white man, and five dozen high-powered undergraduates with color-coded notebooks. Never was I able to forget that it was a room that, over the years, had been entered by relatively few people who looked like me.

Instinctively, I took refuge in familiarity. I hid behind those like me.

At Harvard, the organization of Mexican-American students is called RAZA. It was founded the year after I was born by a loose handful of ethnic pioneers. Literally, a handful. They came to Cambridge through concession. In response to the assassination of Martin Luther King, Jr. and the overwhelming sense that the United States was coming apart at the racial seams, America's powerful—including those in the nation's universities—conceded that the status quo had to be altered a bit. One alteration took the form of six Mexican-Americans—all of them male, who were quietly recruited from high schools in the Southwest to attend Harvard in the 1968–1969 school year.

It is likely that the experience of those first few young men which was, after all, unfolding at a time in our history when Jim Crow still ruled some parts of the country, would make any "culture shock" that I and my colleagues seemed to be experiencing twenty years later appear inconsequential by comparison. Maybe they thought that there was strength in numbers. Maybe the issue was not one of strength at all, but of mere survival. Whatever the reason, they united. They linked arms in a shared destiny and formed an organization. They gave it a charter, a budget, a ruling body, and a name. RAZA. Not an acronym, but a Spanish word that translates loosely to "race," by which was meant the Mexican-American race.

At its inception, the organization had, above all, one simple mission: It was to act, first and foremost, as a "support group" for Chicano students at Harvard. It was cloaked in a delicate, sacred trust among students based on the commonality of color.

A Chicano alumnus from the 1970s would tell me later, with a nostalgic puff of his cigar, that he remembered, one year, spending Thanksgiving Day with a fellow RAZA member. They huddled around a can of spaghetti on a hot plate in a drafty room and tried not to think about how alone they really were.

Years later, I leafed through the overstuffed manila envelope that crowded my parents' mailbox. I was surprised to discover in the pile of papers a second letter, different from my acceptance letter. More than simply accepting me to Harvard, this other letter was *welcoming* me to Harvard. It was less sterile than the first. The type was less neat, more human. It tried to make the world that I was being invited to enter seem somehow less foreign. Less threatening. It made promises.

It began: "On behalf of RAZA, the Chicano students' organization at Harvard-Radcliffe, we would like to extend our congratulations on your acceptance. RAZA is a support group whose aim is to address issues of concern to Chicanos at Harvard. It is a strong and unified group of undergraduates with a common culture who are in close contact with one another."

And so RAZA spelled out its reassurances. A strong and unified group. A common culture. Close contact with one another.

When I arrived in Cambridge for the first time, as a high school senior late for an interview, I was greeted by a pretty Mexican-American woman. A senior, she offered a tour of campus. I accepted. But why would she befriend me, a stranger? An adolescent from a farming town in California. Why would I do the same in later years? It was because she trusted in our common color. During the tour, she talked not about student life at Harvard as much as about *Mexican-American* student life at Harvard. She told me about the most popular majors for Chicano students. She pointed out the nightspots where Chicanos most often partied. She talked about the admissions efforts of Chicano students to recruit more Chicano students. She boasted about RAZA and its role in allowing Chicano students a graceful transition from one world to another.

I suppose that I should have been suspicious of the limited scope of her comments. How could race, that single factor, provide the filter for her entire college experience? I remember that, up to that point—five months before my classmates' affirmative action tantrums—I did not even really consider myself Mexican-American. No matter. I was too captivated by her confidence, her strong sense of self. I wanted to be like her, and I assumed that Harvard would make me like her. I was in love. Forget Yale. I would come here, I resolved, because she is here. Never mind that she will have graduated by the time that I arrive. She is here now. I marveled at the beauty in her eyes. Yet I somehow missed in their reflection the insecurity that I now suspect must have been buried deep in her soul.

When I arrived in Cambridge for the second time, as a college freshman weighted down by my parents' suitcases, I searched for RAZA. One of the questions that I asked the young man from Houston that night in the Yard was whether he too had received such a letter. He had. We wondered when those who had signed it would show themselves. Then one day at dinner a small group of upperclassmen marched confidently into the Union and with a tinkle of glassware won a roomful of silence.

"We're part of RAZA, the organization for Chicano students on campus," a handsome young man in a turtleneck said as if he were speaking to thin air.

"We just wanted to invite those of you who might be interested in learning more about RAZA to dinner," the young woman standing next to him joined in. "This Friday in the private dining room at Adams House. Thanks."

Then they were gone, disappearing quietly through the glass door that snapped shut quickly behind them. My white friends at the table seemed completely unmoved, resuming their conversation with me about some obscure facet of national politics. "Now, where was I? Oh yeah, health care..." someone said. But I wasn't listening. I was too busy relishing the possibility that I might not be as alone as I thought. Friday night. Adams House. Yes, I would be there.

As I walked into Adams, considered the "artsy house," or the "gay house" because of the large number of gay and lesbian students who choose to live there when Harvard students select permanent residences at the end of freshman year, I remembered that an upperclassman had told me about the flamboyant parties that had won the place infamy in what he called, "the ol' days." Off to one side, I noticed the private dining room. Inside was a long row of tables that had been spliced together as if for a banquet. On both sides sat a spattering of students. We introduced ourselves, and then excused ourselves as we went into the kitchen to get our trays before returning. The upperclassmen, well-dressed and at ease with one another, were curious, concerned about the mundane details of our lives.

"What classes are you taking? I have a book that you'll need; you can borrow it."

"What professors do you have? Oh shit, she's tough."

"Where do you live in the Yard? No kidding, I lived there!"

This weekly gathering was referred to simply as *mesa*, or table. It had history. Unknown to us at the time, African-American students at predominantly white colleges across the country in predominantly white towns, where they were unable even to get a haircut, were gathering at separate tables in dining halls. Just to "hang" with people like themselves for a change, they said.

As with the young man from Houston, who eventually wandered into the room himself, my connection with RAZA members was instant. It was easy. Its ease lived in all that was unsaid, all that did not need to be said. We were old friends who had just met. More than that, I assumed. We would care for one another in times of crisis. We would kneel with one another as we vomited into the toilet where the best and brightest had lost more than composure after too much drink. We would hold each others' hands and keep one another from losing our minds. We were family.

Truthfully, RAZA members had two, and sometimes only two, things in common. We were Harvard undergraduates. And we were Mexican-American. When Harvard and I first met, there were only about 125 young people in Cambridge who could make that claim. There were a few others at the various graduate schools. Still, they were different. They stumbled through their world while we stumbled through ours. When we did meet, some of them, especially the law students, seemed irritated by our cockiness. Had they not had to wait until after college to enter a world that we had entered after high school?

No, our only real camaraderie lay within RAZA. It was, for me, during all but my final year, the centerpiece of my very existence at Harvard. I drank RAZA. I dated RAZA. I argued politics and shared secrets with RAZA. Above all, I trusted RAZA. My relationship with RAZA was bathed in intimacy, and, as I would learn only later, vulnerability.

Yet as with the young Mexican-American woman who had unintentionally seduced me when I had been a visiting high school senior, I should have been suspicious. Staring across the gathering at *mesa* of no more than twenty-five Harvard Chicanos lining both sides of the spliced-together oak tables, the best question would have been to ask: "Where are the others?" Walking into monthly RAZA meetings of thirty or so in the dusty common room of Leverett House, the right question would have been: "Where are the others?"

There were, after all, according to admissions office statistics, a hundred or so other Mexican-Americans on campus who, for one reason or another, wanted no part of RAZA. They were too numerous to ignore. They represented, in fact, the majority of the entire Chicano student population.

At public campuses in the west that enrolled much higher numbers of Chicano students than did Harvard, the absence of such students from the roll sheets of ethnic organizations was even more conspicuous. My friend at UC Berkeley would tell me by phone that monthly meetings for *MEChA* (Movimiento Estudiantil Chicano de Aztlán), the school's equivalent of RAZA, would net about the same number of students that RAZA did. This despite the fact that the existing pool of total Chicano undergraduates at Berkeley was nearly thirty times greater than it was at Harvard. The omission of Chicano students from the ranks of groups intended to serve them prompted, for those brave enough to address it, an embarrassing set of questions.

Why do the vast majority of Mexican-American students on college campuses choose *not* to participate in ethnic organizations that were created in their name to address (what the RAZA letter called) issues of concern to them? And should the membership breakdown be blamed, if blame is called for, on individual students or on the organizations themselves?

I remembered meeting those other Mexican-Americans. I disliked them without knowing them. I resented the ease with which they passed from one world to another. They seemed to trivialize cultural differences, like a girl I knew back home who had used one last name throughout our schooling together and found her true Spanish surname only in time to apply to college as a high school senior. They were not like me, I told myself. I despised them, these coconuts. White on the inside. Though now, years later, I realize that I may have confused dislike with envy. They seemed not to be troubled by the sorts of insecurities that were growing stronger in me each day. I watched them suspiciously.

There was the fair-skinned, dark-haired girl from San Antonio who walked through campus with her white boyfriend. She evaded our stares, as we walked past her. She took pains to pronounce her very Mexican-sounding surname without a hint of Spanish. There was the young man from Los Angeles who refused our invitation to *mesa* saying that he "knew who [he] was." He criticized RAZA and groups like it for being an outdated haven for militant and angry Chicano student radicals. There was the young Mexican-American woman from Chicago who found a RAZA newsletter in her mailbox, cornered a member, and tossed the paper in his face. She issued a stern warning, "Don't ever send me this shit again!" And then there was the young man from the small town near Santa Barbara who believed that groups like RAZA do "much more harm than good" by further segregating disadvantaged minorities and hindering racial assimilation, which he considered a wonderful river of opportunity from which all good things flow. They were all so sure of themselves, so confident of their rightful place in an environment that seemed poised to swallow me.

I imagined myself climbing to the top of Memorial Church and letting lose a self-righteous scream from its steeple.

"Okay, *gente*, enough! You all checked the box, same as me! But now, you don't even acknowledge what color you are. You hypocrites! Do you think for one minute that if it wasn't for protest and advocacy, that John Harvard would have ever let your brown ass in here?"

At the brink of what I considered to be the enlightening exuberance of my freshman year, a time when I was becoming "ethnically aware," I was sure I knew the answer to difficult questions. *Who was to blame for the absence of the vast majority of Mexican-American students from RAZA?* The students themselves, of course. *Why didn't they participate in RAZA functions, meetings, or gatherings?* It was because they simply didn't "identify." They had forgotten their responsibilities to their culture and their people. They had forgotten who they really were. They had lost themselves in Harvard's promises. And so I judged them. I judged them to have committed an unspeakable sin. It was not until years later, when I had learned more about these RAZA refugees, about the nature of RAZA, and indeed about judgment itself, that I would realize that it was I who had committed the sin.

* * *

For groups like RAZA at schools like Harvard, the charge of separatism is a familiar one. Even *mesa*—the seemingly innocuous concept of people eating together, had its detractors. I was told by upperclassmen that, a few years before I arrived at Harvard, a small group of African-American students were sitting in one of the dining halls, talking and laughing together. A dean approached. Uninvited. Unannounced. Disappointed, he said something like, "Now, we didn't bring you all the way out here for you to sit off by yourselves. . ." The laughter stopped. The dean walked away, no doubt unaware that his listeners might never forget his condescending remark.

But more than condescension, I recognized in the story the concept of obligation. I do not actually remember when the perceived responsibility to be a cultural ambassador of sorts was initially conceived. Still, I heard it crying to me constantly during my first months in Cambridge. Faithfully, I nursed it in the night. Perhaps it was conceived with my decision to attend, perhaps earlier at the mailbox, or earlier still three thousand miles away in a dusty file room in Byerly Hall. What did they— the liberal bureaucrats who nibbled doughnuts and spilled coffee over a manila file folder summarizing my life—expect from me in return for the coveted spot that they granted me?

Yes, we'll take this one. How many does that make?

You get nothing for nothing, my parents have warned me a thousand times. So then what did Harvard expect from me in exchange for this grand gift, this coveted, if uncomfortable, seat at its private banquet?

I thought I knew. I took my answer from that story about the Harvard dean and the African-American students whose lunch he ruined. *"We didn't bring you all the way out here to sit off by yourselves . . ."* That is to say, we expect you not to segregate but to infiltrate. Mingle, obligation pleaded with me. Discover those who are different from you, and like your Indian ancestors, let them discover you. Educate our students, our *white* students, about life in the barrio or on the farm, won't you? Share with them the taste of your tortillas and show them how to remove tamale husks. Argue politics with them, give them the "Hispanic perspective" on the issues of the day. Date them, obligation winked, sacrifice your virginity to them so that you both might confront and conquer the prejudices of earlier generations.

I remember sitting in a large lecture hall for a course in moral theory; the professor sought out the sprinkling of black and Latino students most emphatically on the one day that the discussion turned to affirmative action. "What do they think?" he must have wondered. When the topic at hand was not Rousseau's *Social Contract* or Plato's *Republic* but rather racial discrimination in America, his Ph.D. from Oxford could not give him the eyes of the victim.

What did the African-American or Latino students in the front row think of affirmative action, anyway? It is a cruel pun that only affirmative action itself could provide him with the answer. He called on us. We stood up, cleared our throat, and answered. He listened, deferred to our experience. Thereby we met our obligation to the assumptions of northeastern liberalism.

Teach them, obligation screamed. Our students are one day to be elected to Congress and to the presidency and to the editorial board of *The New York Times* and the governing board of Fortune 500 companies. The nation's population is changing rapidly and graduates that we produce, like automobiles off the assembly line, must meet those changes. Demographics demand concession, and you are it. Our students must be well-rounded, familiar with ethnicity when the questioner at the last debate asks them about their perspective on racial issues. How have they themselves been affected by race. "Well, in college, I had a Mexican roommate. He helped me confront my prejudices. We ate tortillas. The experience made me more sensitive to discrimination, really." They will smile broadly into the camera and then be rewarded with a share of the Hispanic vote or the Hispanic market. Teach them. And we will, in return, teach you.

By sitting off by themselves at lunch, the African-American students who were approached by the Harvard dean were, in essence, reneging on a bargain. And Harvard wanted none of that. Never mind that the students never knew of their obligation or of a bargain that had been struck by strangers in their name.

It sounds strange, even degrading to admit, but I was not

really bothered by the implied expectation that I serve as a cultural ambassador to sheltered white people. I enjoyed sharing tortillas. I did not mind providing the academic perspective of at least one Hispanic, me. What's more, what Harvard seemed to be dangling in front of me like a ripe, juicy carrot was, in fact, acceptance. I hungered for it and I was willing to pull the cart of obligation to inch toward it. I was also flattered by the attention and was relieved to be asked questions that I could answer. My responses were creative. I somehow turned abstract discussions on nineteenth century social theory into more relevant discourse on issues that defined a new century. Everything was connected to race, I argued. Everything. My opinions mattered. I spoke with authority. I spoke well. I owned the words, the ideas. I spoke of issues that I considered important to the Latino community like immigration and language. After all, who among them could dispute my perspective? I savored their deference. Exploited it. People listened. Once, in a classroom, someone actually applauded. Yes, I enjoyed that. And I was learning as well. I was gathering up facts and arguments and contacts like apples from a tree to be digested later, at my leisure.

Still, there was a problem—a major one. Just as I was beginning to realize my contribution to the Harvard mosaic and overcome adolescent insecurities, I felt within me a new sense of illegitimacy. I worried about my ability, indeed about the ability of all Mexican-Americans on campus, to honor our obligation. I felt I was being asked to produce something that, at the time, I myself barely understood. What insight did I really have into a culture that I had been linked up with upon entering Johnston Gate, like an adhesive name tag at a convention? Not my culture, really, but my Mexican grandfather's.

My culture mirrored that of my roommate from Connecticut. I ate hamburgers, not tacos. I watched MTV and CNN, not *Univisión*. My cultural icon was Bruce Springsteen, not Vicente Fernandez. After all, like the Boss, I was born in the USA. My culture was shaped not by Mexico, the old country that invoked only images of dust, but by a middle-class upbringing in the United States. Experience? My experience had been straight A's, Little League, white girlfriends, and apple pie. I was confused by what was demanded of me.

Ah, but my grandfather was authentic. My grandfather could pull this off, I told myself. If only he were here. He would tell them about discrimination and the life of an immigrant and boyhood sunsets in Mexico. He could tell them about the day in Chihuahua when Pancho Villa rode up to his father Jose's *casita* and drafted him into the army without the nuisance of paperwork. He could tell them about restaurants in the American southwest during the 1940s with signs in their windows that read, "No dogs or Mexicans allowed!" He could tell them about picking cotton for a dollar a day in the scorching heat of the San Joaquin Valley in the years before Cesar Chavez brought clean water, toilets, and above all, dignity to the fields. He could tell them about living for most of his life with a distrust of white people and their compulsion to assert their control over those who were not white.

Yes *Papá-Man*, as I called him, could tell them all that. He could pay my cultural debt to Harvard. But wait, what would my grandfather be doing here in the first place? Perhaps gardening. Would they allow him to do even that?

The insane irony behind the cultural riddle stuffed in the fortune cookie of affirmative action was that the light-skinned, English-proficient grandson who was acceptable to Harvard because he was most American and least Mexican was then oddly expected, upon arrival, to be less American and more Mexican. And I knew, in the figurative sense, it took more than overexposure to sunlight to make one browner.

Teach us.

I cannot. I wish I could. But I can't. I don't know about fieldwork; my hands are soft. I have not suffered, with my parents, the indignities of discrimination so prevalent before I was born. No, I don't know how to pronounce that word in Spanish.

I felt like a fraud. I could not honor my obligation. I was culturally impotent. Oddly, I feared that when the admissions committee realized that they had admitted an ethnic imposter, they would comically rescind their invitation. "Oh, we're so sorry. You'll have to leave. You are no good to us. We thought you were a real Mexican . . . and where is your sombrero, might we ask?" I had no sombrero, only a Red Sox cap I had bought at Fenway Park weeks earlier.

I remember, in one class, being called upon specifically by a section leader to explain the reasons why Hispanics might drop out of high school.

Well, as a Hispanic valedictorian, I'd have to say . . . that I have no fucking idea. How 'bout you?

My guilt mandated action. If I did not have culture then I would manufacture it. If I did not have a truly ethnic persona, then I would create one. I exaggerated my ethnicity, like a baker stretching a small amount of dough to cover every inch of a cookie sheet. I walked a certain way, a defiant strut like the one I remembered little *cholos* using in junior high school. I talked a certain way, intermixing Spanish and English as if to obscure both my proficiency in one and my deficiency in the other. I wore a conspicuous Mexican serape of heavy cloth through Harvard Square. I sought rebellion. I wanted to be exotic. I grew a beard and long hair. I drank Mexican beer. I continued in vain to search Boston, and later New York, for *real* Mexican food. I constantly complained about the cold; I told nostalgic stories about the California sunshine that I was sure was keeping my friends and family warm and happy. I tried to forget that I wanted to be someplace else. Anyplace else.

Above all, I was preoccupied with what I considered the extraordinary significance of being Latino at an elite, predominantly white school. Maybe I sought peace with the past. Maybe I intended to distance myself from the traditional image of a Harvard student in the hope of also distancing myself from Harvard's tradition of excluding people like me. Resisting assimilation, I wanted to be noticed, seen as different. I wore my ethnicity as a badge. No, a shield. Like a Halloween costume, I slipped it on in October and left it on until June. I was desperately trying to be something that I was not. My father might call it, disdainfully, "playing the role." Even my name changed. I found myself with my father's name, as it was called out decades ago by his parents to the ten-year-old who hauled pails of water across long rows of grapevines. *Rrrubén!*

At once, I was reincarnated. I was *Rrrubén Nava-rrrre-te.* The name had a harder sound. It would not break under pressure. It was name of a stranger, a foreigner, someone to be respected. It would protect me. Perfect, I thought. Just perfect.

Eventually, I would understand that my gesture was hollow. I would realize that I could assume my father's name much easier than what really mattered—the life experience that gave it all meaning.

Harvard had, for me, lost most of the glamour of its recruitment brochures, which I suddenly realized, had made no mention of messy subject matter like race relations on campus. It was not the educational promised land that I had envisioned. It was instead, with its faculty of white males and its investments in South Africa, in the rhetoric of the ethnic left, the *oppressor*. Those were times of disappointment and disillusionment. The myth of Harvard had been shattered, but there was, for students in general but minority students in particular, still nothing to take its place. Even the symbols that had initially lured me to Cambridge now seemed superficial and irrelevant. The Kennedys, I realized, were not Mexican-American.

All of this had the dual effect of bringing me closer to some of my fellow undergraduates and further alienating me from others. There was a developing interracial bond between African-American, Asian-American, and Latino students on campus. Strangely, the connection was based not on what we were, but on what we were *not*. Ultimately, though we would not admit it at the time, our only common characteristic was that we were all nonwhite. We were linked not by a shared history, culture, language, or religion but by the lack of a particular pigmentation. There was nothing linking the Korean from New York City to the African-American from Atlanta to the Chicano from East Los Angeles except that they were all unlike the white, third-generation Harvard student from Greenwich.

Still the camaraderie seemed real enough at the time. I noticed, and still remember fondly, the occasional silent acknowledgment from black students whom I did not know. As I passed them on my way to class, we would make eye contact. They would smile and nod. The gesture reminded me that, although we were not completely alike, we were in the eyes of John Harvard both different. It is testament to the strange ability of a predominantly white school to unite nonwhite students that some of my closest friends and my first real girlfriend were not Latino, but black.

Near the end of my freshman year, I became president of a campus organization that intended to serve as an umbrella group for the various ethnic student groups on campus. It included African-American, Asian, Puerto Rican, Native-American, and Chicano students. We took an aggressive, at times even antagonistic, approach to the administration. We argued for ethnic study programs and campus forums on race-related issues. We demanded a Third World Students Center, similar to the structures that had appeared on other campuses, including Princeton and Yale. We protested the lack of minority faculty and advocated the hiring of more people of color.

That is what we called ourselves, "people of color." The term seemed inclusive enough to accommodate the glaring differences among the various kinds of minority students. Apart, in each of our respective organizations, we were few. Together, we tried to be many. I wonder now. Could our understanding of racial division be so incomplete that we believed an Asian-American professor or an African-American dean could somehow, vicariously, enrich the college experience of Chicano students from San Antonio?

And my ethnic awakening brought alienation. The very term, "people of color," was by its nature not only inclusive but also exclusive. Did our narrow application of the phrase mean that my white roommates were, by implication, "colorless"? I am embarrassed to admit that is precisely the way that I treated the two of them. No one suffered more from my racial role-playing. My ethnic zeal excluded them, lumped them together as part of an amorphous mass of people. White people. Without regard to them as individuals, I instinctively considered them, based on their race, to be privileged and detached. I assumed that they did not have, and could not have, an understanding of my experience before Harvard and that experience on campus could never be nearly as traumatic as mine.

I assumed them to be indifferent to institutional racism. Throughout American history, hadn't their ancestors been its biggest proponents? I treated them as ideological whipping boys. Had they offered their own personal perspective on suffering, I might have laughed out loud or argued. Always we argued. I dreaded those confrontations, some of which lasted until three in the morning. Coincidentally, the three of us were enrolled in a course whose subject matter lent itself to debate in and out of class. It was not long before political discussions became personal. It was not long before political attacks became personal ones. Always I fought to win, had to win. My honor seemed at stake. More than that, the honor of "my people" seemed at stake.

I accused them of being so consumed by the professed color-blindness of northeastern liberalism that they ignored the massive implications of racial differences between human beings; they accused me of being so consumed by those differences and by my own ethnic nationalism that I could see nothing else.

"Why is *everything* race with you? Why are you so angry?"

"Why is *nothing* race with you? What are you running away from?"

"I asked you first, goddammit!"

"Hey, fuck you!"

They angered me. Liberals. So eager to point the finger of racism south toward Montgomery or Jackson, and yet so reluctant to see it in the streets of Boston during the busing crisis or at a whites-only country club in Connecticut? I did not respect them. I did not consider my roommates to be racist, only racially insensitive. What's that they say about liberal politicians having passionate discussions about poverty, over lunch?

Still my roommates were right about me. Just like the young woman who I had met at the admissions office the year before, I had become consumed by race. My perspective was shallow; my temper was short. It was no small irony, or tragedy, that as someone whose predecessors had been brought to these hallowed halls to somehow make amends for the killing of Martin Luther King, I should desecrate his spirit by judging others solely by the color of their skin and not by the content of their character.

As the schoolyear drew mercifully to an end, there was a sense of emotional and intellectual exhaustion that shrouded our dormitory room. We had argued everything, settled nothing. The only thing that we knew was that we could not live together the following year. We left one another, as if to attempt friendship.

In our final weeks together, there was peace. The kind of tranquillity that follows the devastation of war. When one of them was sick with a spring cold, I went into the Square for medicine and orange juice. In May, on my birthday, one of them brought me a pint of Häagen-Dazs in what would become a private ritual. As we dug into the container with the same spoon, we agreed on at least one thing—the lack of intimacy in our relationship with Harvard.

"You know, Ruben, I realize friends of mine from high school might go home for the summer as cheerleaders for their colleges. They might love their schools. But I don't love Harvard . . . Harvard doesn't let you love it, doesn't expose itself to your love. But I'll tell you, I fuckin' respect Harvard. . . ."

I listened as his voice trailed off to more quiet reflection. I agreed with what he had said. I did not love Harvard either. And I knew Harvard, although it may have finally been willing to acknowledge my presence at the end of our first year together, did not love me either. Love is shared between intimates who leave themselves vulnerable to each other. Harvard, it seemed, was vulnerable to no one. As I took my last final exam and packed my belongings into storage for the fall, I knew that my school and I had a relationship. That's all.

My roommates and I were affectionate with one another in those final days, when it was almost too late. I may forever regret that, blinded by a boy's prejudice and paranoia, I had not done my part earlier to share more affection with what, I have since realized, were perhaps the two most caring, most loyal, and most supportive people whom I knew at Harvard.

I remember that during an argument, one roommate—the more outspoken one—challenged my platitudes about suffering and alienation. He said that I was wrong about him. He claimed that he did know about what it felt like to be under siege for being oneself, to be the outsider unsure of belonging. He said he knew alienation and loneliness and pain and prejudice.

"There's shit you don't know about me . . . ," he said under his breath.

I was sure that he was caught up in the heat of argument. He was a third generation Italian-American from the wealthy suburbs of Connecticut. Pictures of his hometown looked like a Norman Rockwell painting. Everyone was smiling. His neighborhood, as he had described it, was safe and warm. In high school, while I was fighting off the accusations of classmates, his biggest concern was likely coordinating the senior prom. I considered him to have a sheltered life that was oblivious to the kind of differences between people of which I was so aware. There was, he had explained, very little racism in his hometown or high school. Of course. How could there be racism, I remember thinking, in an environment in which only white people lived?

What did he know about oppression and intolerance? What could he tell me about prejudice, about being alienated?

"Okay," I poked him. "Tell me. What do *you* know about how I feel . . . ?"

"Not now," he said with a mouthful of ice cream. "Later . . ."

CHAPTER 5

STRADDLING SEPARATE WORLDS

"THE WOODS ARE LOVELY, DARK AND DEEP,
BUT I HAVE PROMISES TO KEEP,
AND MILES TO GO BEFORE I SLEEP.
AND MILES TO GO BEFORE I SLEEP."

ROBERT FROST

HARVARD COLLEGE, CLASS OF 1901

If my freshman year in college had been circumscribed by borders—between me and my roommates, my surroundings, my school—then, my trip home for a much-deserved summer vacation provided a unique opportunity to cross some of them.

I told my parents that I would be home two weeks later than expected because I had decided not to fly home but to take a train instead. They asked me if I knew just how far three thousand miles was on the ground. I told them no. That was precisely the point. I had no idea, and I intended to find out. I gutted my account at the bank in Harvard Square and repacked my father's army green duffel bag, as I had months before. My plan was to catch a series of automobile rides from Boston to Washington, D.C., then board a train from Washington to Fresno. In Connecticut, I hiked up mountains that overlooked countrysides that reminded me, fondly, of home. In New York, I ate hot dogs at Coney Island and stared out across the Atlantic. I remembered chasing waves on the beach of the Pacific as a child. I realized then that although some people live near one ocean or the other, very few of them have cooled themselves in both. In Washington, I took the subway to Arlington National Cemetery, where I knelt quietly beside the gravesites of John and Robert Kennedy. I realized that I was standing many miles away from the grape fields of Delano where, twenty years earlier, Robert Kennedy had knelt beside an ailing Cesar Chavez.

Harvard had come in too fast. The memories crowded in my head. I was unsure of what it all meant, unable to place the changes in me in their proper perspective. I knew a five-hour flight would not help me sort it all out. Once on board the train, I was afforded ample time for reflection as America's beauty passed by my window for hundreds of miles, accompanied by cold chicken salad sandwiches, newspapers, and Walkman rock and roll. I was allowed three stops. Like a presidential candidate looking for maximum effect, I chose them carefully. Consumed with the metaphor of travel, I thought about where I had been, where I was, and where I was going.

As the lush green countryside of Virginia and the Carolinas passed before my window, I prepared for my first stop in Atlanta. There, I stayed with a friend from Canaday. Months earlier, we had joked with each other in the Union about Harvard's ineptness at dealing with the race issue and bathed in the martyrdom of being nonwhite in a largely white setting. As an African-American and a Latino, we shared a kinship of difference and each, a reciprocal preference for the women of the other's ethnic group.

Suddenly, I realized that I was in the fabled American South. I remembered junior high school textbook pictures of attack dogs and segregated lunch counters. At stops in Georgia, and later in Mississippi and Alabama, I noticed the groups of people waiting on the platform at the various train stations. Always the same, two distinct groups, one white and one black. What had once been mandated by law was now accepted as preference. Strangely, even passengers on board the train conformed to the rule. At one point, I swaggered through three cars, each full, on my way to the cafe. One car contained all white passengers; the next, all black; the final one, all white. I was amazed at the resilience of custom. I was even more amazed at the confused stares that I received from both white people and black people who, apparently, had grown so accustomed to a world of two colors that they were distrustful of a third.

Also unsettling was my encounter on the train, somewhere in Mississippi, with two African-American men. They both seemed older than me, perhaps in their late twenties. One appeared well-educated, boasting to his companion of the college degree that he had recently secured. He leafed through a book that prepared people for the LSAT, the law school entrance exam. The steward asked him politely if he wanted coffee. He declined politely. I contrasted him with the young man who sat across the aisle from him. He was louder, more disruptive, and less refined than the would-be lawyer. He was unshaven, wore a baseball cap, and spoke with a slur. The steward asked him to remove his feet from the seat in front of him. I was mesmerized by the element of difference. Both men were the same color and perhaps the same age, but any similarity between them ended there. One seemed acceptable, the other threatening.

In the Mississippi of the 1960s, the two young black men would have been treated, mistreated, in the same fashion. But in a new age, education and refinement distinguished one from the other. As the steward interrupted my reading to ask me, politely, if I wanted coffee, I wondered. How would he have viewed, next to me, a second-cousin of mine—someone with darker skin, poor diction, and a more threatening mannerism? Had just one year of college provided me with a gift, something that went well with intellectual enlightenment? Was I now, by virtue of the behavioral assumptions surrounding those who attend schools such as Harvard, somehow less threatening and more acceptable to white America than other, less-educated

Mexican-Americans? And, if so, what would that mean to those, once so much like me, who were not similarly blessed? I was confused. I wanted to go home.

Later in New Orleans, I learned more about religion and ethnicity. I noticed the Catholic influence that defined the old French city. I saw the cathedrals, and thought it odd that black Creoles with French last names could share *my* religion—the faith of Mexican priests and Spanish missions. I watched parades of people in outrageous costume. I drank hurricanes at Pat O'Brien's along Bourbon Street. Though its children would not be represented in the rigidity of a Harvard application form asking for "race," the city was of course quite ethnic. As with my exposure to Little Italy or South Boston or Fresno's historic Armenian Town, I was beginning to fully appreciate the richness of America's ethnic tapestry and to become distrustful of the sort of narrow racial categories employed by bureaucrats such as those at Harvard. Maybe you didn't have to be black, brown, or yellow to be a "person of color."

In Houston, ten days after I had left Cambridge, I finally started to feel a bit at home. I met family members whom I had never known before, who had been telephoned by my grandmother to expect me. I savored the first authentic Mexican food that I had tasted in several months. A New England winter makes homemade flour tortillas taste even better in summer. But along with nostalgia, there was more confusion. I noticed that most of my newly introduced cousins did not speak Spanish, something that they did not seem to worry too much about. They brought to mind over two dozen first-cousins back home and the realization that, as poor as my own Spanish was, it was perhaps the best in the lot. My cousins in Texas drove pickup trucks and listened to country music. Still, their lives could not be termed inauthentic. Someone mentioned a recent divorce, someone else told me that she had dropped out of high school. Not simply Mexican-Americans, these were *tejanos,* my mother's people. Spanish or not, I saw realism in their lives; it was hard and precious.

As I reboarded the train and it labored across the vastness of Texas, I found myself questioning the ethnic assumptions of my first year in college. A real Mexican. That is what I accused other classmates of not being. That prejudice was nourished in

the sterile, pristine world of the Ivy League. But out here, in
the so-called real world, how could a spoiled kid from Harvard
begin to assess the ethnic authenticity of people who did not
flaunt Spanish in Mexican restaurants or wear serapes but who
nonetheless lived real lives of promise and pain? Did I even
have any idea of what a *real Mexican* looked like?

The flat Texas plains yielded to the rustic colors of New Mexico. As roadrunners scurried alongside the iron horse, I recognized the orange and red mountains as remnants of an
earlier world. A purer world, undisturbed by the corruption of
progress. An Indian world. Indians, like the ones whose turquoise adorned my father's wrist and hand and whose rugs
decorated the family den. Indians, the Mexican lovers of Span-
iards and the Mexican descendants of a forced union. My maternal ancestors. Dark skin, bronzed and reddened by the sun
like my grandfathers'. Yes, I was getting closer to home. The
San Joaquin Valley became a beacon. How many days left? I
want to go home.

New Mexico became Arizona. I noticed in the heat of the
desert, the cacti, a kind of hard serenity. There was an emptiness to the open space, but also a sense of freedom. There are
no second chances in the desert. No mercy. To step off the train
and wander in the sun was certain death. Life as a pioneer on
the way to the Pacific, not following a road map but creating
one for others to follow after you. Life without a net, pure and
unforgiving, like a young man's time at Harvard.

When the train stopped for a few hours in Los Angeles, I
wandered away from Union Station and found Olvera Street.
The mariachi music at the wooden bandstand, the old grandmothers grinding cornmeal into tortillas for tacos, the crepe
paper souvenirs and burnt milk candy, *leche quemada,* from
Tijuana all seemed to welcome me home. A tourist couple who
had boarded the train in the Midwest snapped a picture to
share with friends back home. These were the trappings of culture, familiar but foreign. Dated and hollow, even to me. They
were not its soul. That, I sensed, lay ahead, deeper in the heart
of California. As if transcending the layers of Dante's inferno,
I anxiously prepared for the final portion of my three-thousand-
mile journey, the four-hour trip north to Fresno. Passing the
grape fields around Bakersfield and Tulare, I admired the Si-

erra mountains to the east. As a boy, I had stared at those mountains from my grandparents' ranch in the country. I had wondered what lay behind them, so far away. Now I wondered no more. Just a few weeks after my nineteenth birthday, I knew exactly what lay to the east. And I was glad to be home.

As the train pulled into Fresno, I was comforted by the sight of my cousin waving to me from the platform of the old Santa Fe station. Like a structure on Olvera Street, the station boasted a Spanish-style architecture. It spoke of the old Southwest, of missions, and of Mexicans. Funny, I had never noticed that before.

My journey cross-country had been long and tedious. I vowed to never do it again. Still, there were lessons along the way and I had enjoyed the solitude of reflection. The geographic metaphor of travel whispered a challenge: What if the distance between Harvard and Sanger—between where I went to school and where I lived—could be converted somehow from a liability, as it had been in my own culture shock, to an asset? What if I could harness the intellectual energy and character of these two places, the one that I fled in the San Joaquin Valley and the one that I had entered so far away? Could a young man then meet Camus's definition of greatness, that of touching two extremes at once? I wondered how difficult it could be to straddle two opposing worlds.

Slowly, over the years, through a dozen plane trips between Boston and Fresno, I would struggle with formulating an answer. It came subtly in a thousand responses. For nine seemingly never-ending months, Cambridge had given me some insight into the question through culture shock and racial role-play. Now, for three months at home, Sanger would provide its own lessons—not all of them pleasant—through the familiar medium of family and friends.

The first lessons came early. As my cousin and I were leaving the train station, various aunts, uncles, cousins, and grandmothers were busy gathering at my house. My parents were hosting a graduation party for my younger brother, and they did not expect me home until the next day. My early arrival was a complete surprise to them and to the rest of the family. As I passed through the crowd of friendly faces, I had an awkward sense that I was being viewed differently than I would have been just months earlier. There were polite, quiet smiles and suspicious stares. I had just completed, survived, a year at Harvard. Had I changed? Should they expect a dose of the fabled Harvard arrogance to spew from my mouth? Was that confidence they smelled coming from my direction, or condescension? Did I think myself better than them? "*Se cree mucho . . .*" Those suspicions seem trivial now. Yet, I remember that at the time, for many people in my hometown, I was the only person they knew who could boast of having a year of Harvard under his belt. And so, as with any oddity, they wondered. Much as my white roommates had wondered in their first intimate encounter with a Mexican-American.

A cousin about my age ventured forward. We greeted one another with casual smiles, but all we could manage after months of growth apart from each other was superficial cocktail conversation about our respective lives.

"So, *primo*, how's it going?"

"Not bad, man, how's it going with you?"

"How's 'Hahvahd' . . . ?"

"It's good. It's there. What about that new job I heard you started?"

The secret, I realized early, was to deflect questions whose answers might reveal too much too soon. Answer the questions of others with questions of your own. Always change the subject, evade, hide.

What could I tell them anyway? Something told me to keep my experience hidden, to ration it out quietly, separately, to a trusted few. A voice in my head whispered for discretion. No, don't tell them about culture shock, roommates from Connecticut, homesickness, loneliness. Don't tell them about snow and slipping on ice and suicides and drinking binges that ended at the foot of a toilet. Don't tell them about wanting a statue of a dead white man to kiss your ass, or about your new name, your new dress, your new life. Surely they will break into hysterics at such revelations. You have thought more about race in one year than they have in their entire lives. Don't tell them. Why worry them? Why confuse them, don't they think that schools like Harvard are the gold at the end of the educational rainbow? Don't spoil their fantasy. Don't expose yourself. Don't.

"How's Harvard . . . ?" The question so often heard, simple and yet so difficult to answer.

"Fine . . ."

I remember here that although my parents and siblings were consistently supportive of my Harvard adventure, there were some in my extended family who had a mixed reaction to it all. When I first applied, an aunt with children my age openly voiced doubt that I would ever be accepted. Something about how I should know better than to think that I could go to Harvard. "A school for rich people. . ." When I was accepted, another relative wondered what I was trying to "prove" by going to such an elite university. She thought that I considered myself better than those I left behind; after all, hadn't the colleges in California been "good enough" for her children? Later, a cousin admitted to me that he had wondered why I would subject my parents to what he and others assumed to be the massive cost of sending a child to Harvard. There was skepticism and cynicism, and likely, more than a bit of jealousy as well. As the first Mexican-American graduate of the town's only high school to attend a school such as Harvard, what could I have expected? The first anything always generates its share of suspicion.

Among friends, too, the reaction to my return was mixed. Most of those who had endured since high school were supportive but, like some family members, suspicious. I suppose they expected me to have an air of superiority about me after my first year in Cambridge. Most of them considered me to be arrogant in high school, so what kind of monster might they expect after Harvard, of all places? Some were not as easily convinced that my experience had been "fine"; they pressed for the real story. Would I drop out? And what was it really like out there for people like us, anyway?

The most interesting perspective of all belonged to someone who still remains a close friend. In high school, he had taken my classes and, in many cases, matched my grades. After graduation, his closest friends fled, searching for new lives in new cities. Palo Alto. Berkeley. Davis. Los Angeles. Cambridge. He stayed in our hometown and attended Fresno State, where he excelled. Still, he was unhappy and equated much of his unhappiness with what he considered a chance to escape that he had passed up. He confessed to me much later that he felt that our circle of friends had disbanded around him, abandoning not only our hometown but also those in it, including him. I tried to comfort him, reassure him that he had not been forgotten. I empathized. After all, if Harvard had left me with just one thing, then it was an appreciation of loneliness and the sense of being left utterly alone.

Summer vacation gave me a chance to rest my head and get my hands dirty. I passed up offers of cushy employment in law firms and business offices to take a different kind of work. Simple, hard work. The kind that typified my parents' teenage years but had eluded those of my brother, sister, and me. Along with not speaking Spanish, my parents also resolved not to subject us to the kind of fieldwork that they had known so well in summers past. We did not pick grapes or peaches or cotton or strawberries, as they did. My hands were soft, and that simple fact filled me with a sense of guilt that called out for redress. Upon my return to the Valley, I felt that what I needed most was not soft hands but the sort of hard experiences that promised a solidarity with my parents' laborious past. I wanted credibility to distinguish me from Harvard's soft world of privilege. Most of all, I wanted legitimacy, clean work that leaves your clothes filthy.

I went to work at a local packing house, the kind that have for generations surrounded my hometown like a fortress of low expectation. It is hard to find someone, anyone, in that town who has not worked in one of the five or six houses that saturate the place. *El empaque*, both my grandmothers call it. Low-paying jobs passed like batons from mothers to daughters to granddaughters.

My job had come to me, at least in part, as a legacy from the past. A good story. Thirty years earlier, in the 1950s, a young Armenian boy who was working in the fields had been put under the supervision of my grandfather. African-Americans and Latinos do not have a historical monopoly on the kind of ethnic repression that has characterized the San Joaquin Valley for much of this century. Those Americans of Armenian descent who still populate the area have their own stories. A girl I knew in high school told me that her grandfather, seeking to protect his family from discrimination, had changed the family name when he first immigrated to the United States near the turn of the century. Armenian laborers who worked in the fields along-side Mexicans endured harassment in the form of vicious, big-oted comments from German-American foremen and owners. A friend of the family, an older Armenian man, developed a strong affection, and loyalty, to Mexicans in the heat of those summer days. He remembers being picked on by the Germans who owned the land. He remembers their suspicion and their bigoted remarks. He remembers feeling alone. And he remem-bers the nameless, faceless Mexican workers who shared their lunches with him. For years, he has nurtured a strange affinity for tacos. Likewise, owing to my grandfather's high character and low level of tolerance for bigotry, there was a high level of respect that permeated his work crew at a time when that was not to be taken lightly. The young Armenian boy appreciated that. Thirty years later, as the wealthy owner of his own pack-ing house, he noticed a familiar surname in a stack of appli-cations and returned the favor. For that, my grandfather's *nieto* will always be grateful.

I arrived at work on the first day, excited about the possibility of "rejoining the masses." Being a full-fledged member of the proletariat, as they say in the Harvard government department. Ironically, owing to my background, I was at first assigned tasks in paperwork. Then, on my request—one considered odd by the boss—I was moved on-line. I humbly took my place at the beginning of the human assembly line. A rumor circulated among the cute Mexican girls who graded fruit across the plant. Was it true that I went to Harvard? Then what was I doing here? I stacked forty-pound boxes packed full of tree fruit for ten or twelve hours a day. A few times, I fell behind. I was rescued by a Chicano co-worker with a full mustache and tat-toos; he was just a few years older than me, supporting a wife and two kids on the modest wage provided us by that back-breaking work. I deferred to older Mexican men as experts. I watched them admiringly, the fine-oiled machines. The days were unmercifully hot, loyal to July and August days in the Valley. Days off were scarce and never long enough. Often I would not come home from work until late at night. My back hurt, my arms hurt, my legs hurt. One night, I actually fell

asleep in a cool shower. I was thankful for two things: the summer would eventually end; and I had been spared the much
more excruciating ordeal of picking the fruit that we packed
and stacked.

At home, I first assumed the role of a visitor. For the first half
of the summer, I yielded. I was polite to my parents over morning coffee. I read quietly as my brother talked on the phone. I
deferred in the usual family arguments that typified our lives
together. I was uncomfortable, a foreign guest in a house in
which I once had lived but to which I had since relinquished
any claim. On board the train, in dozens of inanimate cities full
of strangers, I had wanted simply to go home.

Home meant family, security, warmth, and acceptance. Now,
having arrived home, I realized nothing as clearly as the
changes within me. I was impatient with my surroundings. Our
hometowns are so warm in memory, yet so cold in person. Norman Rockwell never painted the emptiness along Main Street.
I was bored easily. Nights lasted forever under the strain of
having nothing to do. Had it always been this hot in summer?
Had there never been anything to do, anything at all to keep
one from going mad?

I pitied those around me—especially young people my age
who had never left the state, boarded an airplane, or tasted
gumbo in New Orleans. I pitied them as might someone
whose life was changed by a rare and brilliant comet, but
who stirs in the quiet frustration of not being able to share
the experience with those around him who missed the fiery
spectacle. Walking through downtown Sanger late at night, I
wondered how anyone could endure the cultural and intellectual constraints of such a place. Even in the nearby city
of Fresno there was no symphony house, no string of art
museums, no coffee houses open until midnight, no abstract
arguments until dawn. Dare I admit it? I missed the East
coast. How was that possible? Boston had so much. New
York had much more. What did a farming town like Fresno
have to keep a restless, disloyal native son from straying
into the seduction of a city's bright lights? Yes, in the chaos
of the East coast, I craved silence, peacefulness. But not
emptiness, not death.

I pitied them. But it was I who deserved pity. Pity the poor bastard who longs for home, comes home, and cannot find home. Pity a man without a country. A pathetic character from a Bob Dylan song, lost with no direction home, like a rolling stone. As the summer drew to a close, I said good-bye again to family and old friends. Once on board the plane, I realized that I had not seen, or did not recognize if I had seen it, the image of home that had nursed me through cold nights in New England. The image that I had tried to hold like water in my cupped palm seeped through my fingers and washed away in a pool of nostalgia. I was confused. Again. And hadn't my parents been confused one night at dinner when I had inadvertently referred to Cambridge as simply, home?

Sophomore year would be different, I told myself. I no longer felt illegitimate, most memories of high school accusation had faded. Those that remained seemed childish and petty. I had proven my resilience by surviving the academic and emotional challenges of freshman year. I was more confident. I watched the new batch of freshmen wander cautiously through the Yard, climb out of taxicabs, and struggle with suitcases. I offered them help, directions to the post office. When asked for advice about which classes to take, I counseled new students as I had been counseled. Having conquered the demons of illegitimacy and culture shock, the only insecurities that lingered dealt with what I still considered to be the profound implications of my own ethnicity.

As an elected member of RAZA's steering committee, I was trying to be less critical of those Mexican-Americans on campus who had distanced themselves from the group. This was especially difficult because I still believed that strength came through numbers and because I recognized their refugee status as an embarrassment to the organization. After all, how effective could RAZA delegates be, sitting across a table from the dean of the college demanding minority faculty when the dean himself knew that the group spoke for only a tiny percentage of the tiny number of Chicano students on campus?

I focused my attention away from the dissidents, as if they no longer existed. Instead of dwelling inward on my own identity,

I directed my energy outward to form a campus agenda. It was simple: the acquisition of institutional power to enhance the student life of Mexican-Americans at Harvard.

It was in my sophomore year that I finally realized the development of a siege mentality among some minority students.

I witnessed, and to some degree facilitated, the subconscious dividing of the Harvard community in two camps. *Us* and *them.* We were advocates—progressive Chicano students who "knew who they were," embraced their culture, and were ready to uphold their sacred responsibility to *la comunidad* and sympathetic white liberal faculty who tried to ease our alienation. We were "down with brown." They were detractors—conservative politicians appealing for the votes of those who felt reversely discriminated against, professors frightened by classroom populations that were changing colors, newspaper columnists talking about merit who had forgotten that their first break in journalism had come from an influential uncle, and fellow Chicanos seeking acceptance by denouncing affirmative action benefits that they had already accepted. We considered Them to be all those who had never wanted Us to attend schools like Harvard in the first place and now wanted to limit our numbers or encumber our experience. We wanted to destroy a status quo that had systematically disenfranchised our parents and our parents' parents. They wanted to maintain that status quo and pined away for the good ol' days when one could go one's whole life and never encounter a Mexican as an equal. Mexican-Americans at Harvard . . . imagine!

If Us and Them were at war, then paranoia defined the battlefield. Those who were not friends were automatically enemies. Trust was a precious commodity, distributed sparingly. I was still convinced that there were inflexible standards for what constituted a Real Mexican. Instinctively, unscrupulously, I applied those standards to other Mexican-Americans on campus, including those in RAZA, in a kind of ethnic litmus test to assess authenticity. I remember that, in my mind, authenticity implied loyalty. A foolish assumption of youth: Those *most* like you will not betray you.

What eventually ensued on our campus and, I would learn, on other college campuses around the country, was a messy game of ethnic "Truth or Consequences."

The exercise was conceived in difference. There were differences among the one hundred twenty-five Mexican-American undergraduates at Harvard just as there are differences among the twenty million Mexican-Americans in the United States. Some students were from mixed marriages; some were not. Some were from upper middle-class families; some were not. Some had worked in the fields as children; some had not. Some spoke Spanish; some did not.

The exercise thrived in difference. The rules of the game were simple. The contestants might be two Harvard Chicanos, similar yet different. The difference is noted. It might be a difference in skin color, Spanish-speaking ability, religion, even political affiliation. At first glance, it appears unlikely that both people can be authentic. The difference dictates that one must be a real Mexican, the other a fraud. The objective of the game becomes for the contestants to each assert his or her own legitimacy by attacking the ethnic credibility of their opponent. *More ethnic than thou.* The weapons are whispers. A pointed finger. A giggle. A condescending remark from one to another.

"Oh, with your background, I don't think you'd understand my point. . ."

Owing to rigid, traditional—some might say stereotypical—conceptions of Mexican culture, *authentic* meant dark-skinned, Spanish-speaking, Catholic, lower-class, and loyal to family. So a young Mexican-American man with light skin and an Irish surname, or a young Chicana who votes Republican and whose mother is a college professor might both start off at a disadvantage. I remember a beautiful girl with a Mexican-American mother and a white father who, as a freshman, was told by a senior in RAZA that she might have difficulty being accepted, trusted by the group because of her mixed lineage. This, of course, after he slept with her. Sex, I learned early, is the oldest weapon of all.

Finally, the game ended in a cynical pool of hurt feelings and lost friendships. The winner, having savaged their opponent with slander, accusation, and innuendo stood victorious; reward took the form of that elusive Harvard carrot, acceptance and respect. A reward, if not from the institution itself, at least from fellow Mexican-Americans there.

As an overzealous proponent of ethnic "Truth or Conse-quences" at Harvard, I was blind to a glaring reality. That is, if RAZA intended to build a fortress of ethnic authenticity around itself to ward off detractors, then the Harvard admissions office had given the group very few bricks to work with.

At RAZA meetings, didn't I notice the rows of light-skinned, middle-class kids, many of whom between them could not put together a phrase in Spanish?

Given my preoccupation with ethnic loyalty, there is no log-ical explanation for the fact that the object of my first signifi-cant college romance was not a Latina, there being no logic to love. On a college campus that touted liberalism as openly as did Harvard, idealistic young people are tempted to make up their own rules of whom to date. As Johnston Gate slams shut behind you, the precious opportunity arises to reinvent oneself. What is acceptable outside the gate, in the so-called real world, is of no consequence whatsoever. The immigrant student from India is allowed to explore his fantasy of falling in love with a blond American princess from Indiana. The blond princess can climb into bed with a Puerto Rican classmate and revel in her friends' giggles in the cafeteria: "Is it true what they say about Latin lovers?"

Little do the idealists know at the time that as they so freely explore their own sexuality, they are exploring also the outer realms of prejudice. Sometimes the two worlds collide. Parents come to visit. Ask questions. Are introduced. Smile politely. Later, alone, have long discussions with their surprised chil-dren about how this is "fine" for their limited time in college but that graduation will have to mean good-bye. Young people realize, in their broken hearts, as images become smaller in the car's rear window, that the tolerant playground that they built for themselves over four years was made of paper, easily crumbled up and discarded by the prejudices of the real world.

Though she was stunning, I remember most clearly that it was her strength of mind and character that enticed me toward her. That face, perfect and soft. That smile, warm and inviting. That heart, vibrant and vulnerable. Her mind was sharp. She was beautiful, intelligent, ambitious, kind, and loving. She was perfect, it seemed. That is, except for one thing—something that is not supposed to matter.

Given the thin color line that separates the handfuls of Latinos and African-Americans at predominantly white schools
such as Harvard, my experience was not completely unfore-
seeable. A nod, a wink, a silent gesture in Harvard Yard quickly
evolved into a common campus agenda for *minority* students.
My closest friends were black; they were my allies in impromptu lunchroom arguments over race and, along with
RAZA, my most trusted confidants regarding the shared pressures of our distinct, yet similar experiences. In that context, it
was not unreasonable that my first heart-wrenching relationship in such a place should be with a black woman.

At that point, we had no real expertise in negotiating any
racial dilemma that might be posed by our affection for each
other. I came from a town that had no black people living in
it. Through high school I saw black teenagers at the mall in
Fresno or when our football team played one with black players
on it. I had no experience in falling in love with people who
appeared so different from me. Likewise, she was from a city
that had no Latinos, on a coast whose conception of Mexicans
was limited to the servers of margaritas in restaurants and
black and white films starring Marlon Brando as Emiliano
Zapata.

Our arguments, and there were many, had more to do with
the normal trials of love than with race. She was sympathetic
to my concerns; she understood the emotion in my voice when
I ranted and raved about the English-only movement. I was
sympathetic to hers; I may have helped build a shantytown in
Harvard Yard to protest our school's huge investment in companies that did business with South Africa, but she was naturally more deeply touched by the issue than I was. Still the race
issue was always there. I could never shake the thought that
she might be happier with a black man; she hinted that she felt
the same way about my Mexican girlfriends, platonic or otherwise, back home. At Harvard, we had taught ourselves to
stick close to those who were most similar to us; for her and
me, that meant a loyalty to two separate groups of people.

And, of course, there was home. The real world, so to speak.
One night, sitting in my dorm room, she playfully twisted my
high school ring on her finger and posed a most memorable
question. She asked, "What do you think your family would say

if you brought home a black girlfriend?" What would they say? I thought to myself. Whew! I answered her as diplomatically, and as dishonestly, as I could.

With my parents, it was never spoken, more understood, that some things were not, well . . . encouraged. Family members had never expressed reservations about miscegenation, per se. Though it would have been unthinkable for members of my parents' generation to cross a color barrier that was then set in concrete, my generation was changing that precedent. I knew numerous family friends about my age, Mexican-Americans, who were dating or had married white people. In fact, of the half-dozen great-grandchildren who now wander in and out of my grandmother's house, each one of them is half Mexican-American and half white. As I play with them, I marvel at the bizarre combination of their blond curls, family features, and Spanish surname.

Still, I sensed my own relationship would not be accepted as readily. My mother asked about my new girlfriend over the phone, what color was she anyway? I told her. She was silent, not shocked or disapproving but certainly not supportive either. The reason is simple and ugly, especially to a proud young Chicano desperate to make metaphorical love to his people and his culture. The unpleasant truth is that whether or not Mexican-Americans consider interracial relationships to be acceptable has everything to do with the specific race involved. The clearest analogy: a ladder. The *social* ladder, if you will. At the top of the ladder is the color white, owing to generational assumptions that the fair-skinned shall inherit the earth. At the bottom is the color black, the color of subjugation. Inferiority. In the middle, nesting precariously between the extremes, is the color brown.

For parents consumed with family progress, the practical objective of their children dating is for them to move up the ladder and never down it; movement being measured in terms of still-unborn grandchildren. A curious aunt might wonder to herself why a family member would introduce a darker pigmentation into the gene pool after it had graciously disappeared generations before. And I believe, much of that is called racism. And what does an idealistic young man who is feverishly spouting rhetoric about fighting racism in the world do when he finds its distasteful remnants among his own people, among his own family?

It was not always that way. In an episode similar to those recalled by Armenian laborers, I remember that my grandfather's strength of heart knew no color. One day, at the beginning of a lunch break in the fields, he noticed a black laborer sitting alone with no lunch of his own to eat. With limited English but with no hesitation, he invited the stranger home with him for a lunch of *frijoles, carne, y tortillas*. My grandfather, a man of Mexico, had no interest in American prejudices. In the nineteenth century, Mexico did not permit slavery in the territory that was to become Texas; since then, the Mexicans that have arrived in that territory from Michoacán or Nuevo León or Chihuahua have fortunately not understood the legacy of that American institution.

Unfortunately, the same cannot be said for the children of Mexico. In this country, the American offspring of Mexican parents attended segregated schools where they learned that while they were despised as inferior, their only comfort was that there were others who were more despised and more inferior. They knew that their mistreatment by white people in schools and in the workplace had been based, at least in part, on pigmentation. And the other group of people *were* darker, after all. Our parents' distorted lesson was that, no matter how lowly the social stature of Mexican-Americans, they were at least superior to blacks. I had heard words in my childhood, years before I could ever know what they meant. *Prieto. Negro.* Later, in high school, around friends who played against black athletes from other schools. *Mayate.* Though the tone of their voice was seldom mean, it was never respectful. How would they react to my college romance?

Time passed. The young woman left my life as discreetly as she had entered it. Our feelings for one another faded. There were lots of reasons for that, none of which had much to do with race. Years later, I still think of her on occasion. When I do, I cannot help but think also of the cultural unpleasantries that my affection for her brought to the surface. I remember her pretty face and the tears that welled up in her eyes whenever we fought and the way she made me feel. And I smile.

*   *   *

My memories of college roommates are not always as fond. In my sophomore year, I lived with two young men from California. Because we were from the same state, I expected that they would be somewhat sensitive to the cultural and geographic adjustments in going from California to Cambridge. They were. They knew what it meant to hate snow or miss sunshine. Unfortunately, when the issue of race came up, as of course it inevitably did, the fact that we were all from the same state seemed to matter very little. It was then that I realized that a little knowledge of ethnicity is more dangerous than none at all, especially when mixed with substantially more ignorance.

One roommate was from San Diego, a blond, blue-eyed surfer who considered himself quite familiar with Mexican-American people and their culture, both of which he professed to appreciate as if they were his own. He fashioned himself a fluent speaker of Spanish, a connoisseur of Mexican food, and an admirer of Mexican women. He had gone to a racially integrated high school, where he had been exposed to nonwhite classmates, including Latinos. Still, it was clear to me that among his neighbors, closest friends, family members, and old girlfriends, Mexican-Americans were a rare commodity. In his teenage years, Tijuana was his Disneyland. On adolescent Friday nights, he and his friends found liberation from California's drinking laws in Mexican bars. The more daring might have left their innocence in the darkness. In college, he extolled the virtues of tequila and consistently preferred Mexican beer to domestic brands. I took him to RAZA parties, where he satisfied his taste for Mexican women.

He tried to reassure me of his affinity to my culture and my people. Ironically, his Mexican performances only made me nervous and defensive. When he attempted a Spanish phrase at dinner, I squirmed uncomfortably in my seat. When he offered a perspective on Mexico in a discussion, I bristled. When he challenged my viewpoint, I was enraged. I was critical. I was short-tempered. I was defensive.

Was I being unfair? Hadn't I wished that my freshman year roommates had known more about people like me and our experiences with people like them? Should I not be relieved to live with a roommate who already knew something about my culture, one whom I did not have to educate in the nuances of eating tamales?

No. This was my culture, not his. I was unexpectedly territorial, even protective. Spanish was my dead grandfather's language, and while my roommate spoke it as badly as I did, what was far worse was that he spoke it carelessly.

"Hombray, key-eres una ser-vay-sa?"

The butchering of language was something that I had tried to avoid in my Italian class freshman year. Italian was not my language. I did not presume to own it. It belonged to someone else's dead grandfather. I had no stake in learning it correctly. It was "cute" that I would even try, someone had said.

They were wrong. There is nothing cute about someone carelessly picking at Spanish as if it were a taco bought on the streets of a border town, spilling out its contents for cautious examination. This was my culture, a part of my soul really— not something to be toyed with like a wooden puppet bought for a handful of quarters on a street corner in Tijuana.

The innocent ignorance of one roommate had been replaced by the precocious presumption of another. The Californian's conceptions of Mexican-Americans, favorable or not, had been cast in concrete long before we met. There was not much else that he felt others could tell him. He had his own memory. He had his own opinions.

All of his life, the young man had been near Mexico and Mexicans. San Diego is, after all, the city of the old Mission, the northern capital of Mexico, the city of a Spanish priest. He knew about the Mexicans. He had heard them mentioned at dinner, had played with them on playgrounds, had seen them selling fruit along the highway. He knew them, was sure he did. They were the gardeners, the quiet ones in elementary school, the parking attendants at the best restaurants in La Jolla. They were different. Always different. Not as good. Left behind. At high school graduations in San Diego, white students fleeing to the Ivy League can be confident that the next classroom they sit in will be filled with far fewer brown faces than the ones to which they have grown accustomed over the years. What a surprise it must have been for people like that to walk into places like Harvard Yard and find someone like me.

I remember visiting my roommate one summer in San Diego. I took a friend with me, another Mexican-American who spoke even less Spanish than I did. One afternoon, we left his upper middle-class neighborhood near the state university and took a trip to Tijuana. We converted money; the immense strength of the dollar versus the peso seemed oddly reassuring. Before entering I paused at the customs booth in momentary fear of the unknown. Then I stepped forward. We walked across the border. We walked across time. The pace of other tourists was faster than mine. But I was not a tourist, anyway. Was I? In any case, I had no idea where I was going so I was in no great hurry to get there. Besides, I wanted to keep the border crossing in sight. I was desperate to keep my bearing. And so, the blond surfer led the two Mexican-Americans through Mexico.

I had been to Tijuana once before. When we were very young my parents took the three of us through there in the old green pickup truck. I remember dusty roads and the incomprehensible Spanish and being awakened by the flashlight of a border guard upon our return. Since then, I had not been back. As a teenager, Tijuana—T.J.—did not mean legal beer and bartered goods and whorehouses. Some friends would drive down to San Diego for a baseball game, and then go into Tijuana at night. Mexico meant nothing to me. The word brought to mind images of *piñatas* made of bright crepe paper, overweight *policía*, and *dulce de leche*. Mexico was uncivilized, poor, hungry, criminal, corrupt. It was unsafe, unclean. It had bad water. An American joke. In the United States, I knew that, given the chance, I would never drink Mexican water, the water that my grandfather had bathed in as a young boy.

As we passed taco stands on street corners, I suggested stopping at one. Our guide warned against it.

"No way!" he said shaking his head. "You don't know what they put in those things."

I shrugged and heeded the advice. What did I know? But wasn't it strange for my roommate to discourage me from buying a taco on a street corner in Tijuana, when months earlier, I had seen him buy a hot dog of equally dubious quality on a street corner in Manhattan? Did he have any better idea of what he was eating then? The next day, back at home, my father asked if I had tasted the authentic *taquitos* that he remembered they sold from street carts down there. I felt as if I had missed something.

We were trapped in a CNN documentary on the Third World. Indians with bronzed, weathered faces begged for loose change. They were millions of miles away from the power brokers in Mexico City, those who spoke perfect English and were many shades lighter. Dark-skinned little boys sold Chiclets, descending in packs on unsuspecting tourists. My Mexican-American companion ignored our guide's advice to ignore them, cashing dollar bills into quarters and passing them out like lollipops at a day-care center. It caused us, him especially, physical pain to see children in poverty. He whispered to me that they reminded him of those baby pictures of him that his mother kept tucked in the closet back home.

Everything was for sale, it seemed. One got the sense that for the right dollar amount, one could haul the whole country back up the interstate. Still it was one thing for me to think that to myself; it was quite another for our tour guide to express that sentiment out loud. I had no doubt that if he were bidding on the country, he would not spare it the insult of chiseling it down to a bargain-basement price.

Cuanto? No, no menos. . .

I wondered, if we were on the other side of the border, would he whine and snarl with white merchants along Rodeo Drive?

At one point, I lost my temper. I had asked a man, in my best and least conspicuous Spanish, for the price of a shirt. *Cuanto?* He told me. Our guide urged me to bargain. I resisted. He persisted. *Cuanto? Menos . . .* The man refused and startled us by walking away. Embarrassed, my roommate tried to explain the merchant's impatience with American tourists. He chose entirely the wrong words.

"You know," he said with the look of someone who has just solved a riddle. "It's midafternoon. That's why they're cranky. They don't want to be here. This is the time for their *siesta.*"

My mouth dropped open. Did he just say what I thought he said? Siesta? Talk about stereotypes! We argued feverishly as we walked back toward the border before dark. Why was I so offended? he asked. Our companion cashed more dollar bills into quarters. The border guard let us pass without inquiry, our loud argument was spewing Harvard English so well.

My other roommate from California was linked even more closely to my past, a past with which I was not at all comfortable. While it was true that I was the first Mexican-American graduate of my predominantly Latino high school to attend Harvard, I was not the first overall. One year earlier, there had been another student—a white one—who had been accepted into the university.

During those spring days of innuendo, it would have been nice for me to have received the least bit of moral support from my Harvard predecessor who had learned via telephone lines that I had applied and had been accepted. Perhaps a phone call from Cambridge congratulating me on matching his feat. There was none. Only a loud silence. I concede that his ambivalence toward my accomplishment might have been due to his academic workload or the fact that, though we knew each other in high school, we were hardly friends. Still I am more inclined to believe that his personal resentment of me played a role. It is likely that he resented my conspicuous and arrogant intrusion into his private world of achievement. I remember that, when he was accepted into Harvard, there were, in contrast to my experience, no raised eyebrows among faculty and students. Quite the contrary, much of the response from teachers and administrators alike was congratulatory. They respected his talents. They thought him completely worthy of Harvard's accolades. "Did you hear about our Harvard student?" I overheard one teacher say to another. "We're all so proud of him. Oh, he's going to do such great things one day."

Now, only a year after his ascension to sacred ground, I had ruined his little monopoly on hometown newspaper headlines: "Local Boy Does Good!" And in time, I would completely steal those headlines from him. All of this may have only strengthened his contempt for the concept of affirmative action, which he considered my chief benefactor, my rich uncle who played golf with the dean. He may have considered Harvard's elite doors to have opened too wide, and wished they had remained closed after he had passed through them.

It was a bad practical joke by the Harvard housing office that found the two of us sharing space as roommates in a room that was much too small for two such massive egos. During the year, in discussions that digressed into disagreements, we were repeatedly confronted with our radically different viewpoints and the chief personal characteristic that accounted for much of the difference. In a dorm room along the Charles River, as it had been three thousand miles away in the small farming town that we both called home, the race issue simply would not go away.

One night, he walked into my bedroom holding a pamphlet distributed by Harvard's Office of Career Services and intended for undergraduates contemplating application to law school. Given its gloomy forecast of the stiff competition that Harvard graduates would encounter in the application process, the booklet might have been entitled: "Stop wasting our time! You can't go to law school!" My predecessor had read the material; he was devastated. He was convinced by a few words on paper that he had no life after Harvard, not in law school anyway. For some reason, he approached me. Uninvited. Unannounced. After he explained his worry, I tried to rebuild his shattered confidence. I belittled the booklet as "bureaucratic babble," and told him that I was sure that he and I would do "just fine" whatever the nature of our graduate school plans. Stunned by my optimism, he tactlessly implied a reason for it.

"Why are you so confident?" he asked with a dose of thinly veiled scorn in his voice. "You know that no matter what happens with undergraduate admissions, that the graduate school process is a whole new ballgame."

He must have noticed the confusion in my face, and so he continued the process of shoving his foot deeper down his throat.

"What I mean is that graduate schools [in admitting students] are going to pay a lot less attention to other factors, like . . . ah, well . . . ah, geography, where you've come from, your background. . ."

Geography? Where I come from? He had diplomatically avoided saying what he really meant. He lacked the unabashed directness of my high school classmates. Still, the message was the same. I recognized it. I knew it well. He was growing more nervous by the second, afraid that I would prod him into a full admission of what he really meant by all that double-talk. I did. He admitted. He said "geography," but he meant "race." *Hello, Mr. Bakke.*

Furthermore, in addition to being timidly presented, his theory was also profoundly incorrect. He thought it was unfortunate that affirmative action was practiced in admissions at the undergraduate level. Still he took some comfort in his assumption that the practice somehow miraculously disappeared in the graduate school process. At least he hoped it did. He considered himself to be quite liberal on most issues, and seemed to view race-consciousness and preferential treatment as a kind of historical atonement to be tolerated by superbly qualified white applicants like himself. But if atonement was what it was, then why extend it indefinitely? It should be a one-time payoff, I understood him to be saying, like government reparations for the wartime internment of Japanese-Americans. No, there should be no extension of affirmative action into graduate school or, worse yet, into the job market. I could just imagine him saying to African-American high school students: "Okay, slavery was bad, yeah . . . okay, so we'll let you into college and then we'll call it even, okay? Just don't come back for another helping for law school!"

He would be disappointed to know that, in the reality of graduate school admissions, the opposite is true. Given that the truest objective of affirmative action is not to atone, but to adjust—to alleviate what have continued to be the vast disparities between the numbers of whites and nonwhites enrolled in colleges and universities, it follows logically that such programs would be more, and not less, desirable in graduate school in which the number of minority students is even smaller than it is at the college level.

One night, my roommate and I argued relentlessly until four in the morning about the "morality" of affirmative action. *Morality*, a convenient term for Harvard liberals. To be used at whim and for their benefit. There was, after all, no morality in the segregation of my Mexican grandparents in the Texas classrooms of the early twentieth century, or in the subsequent mistreatment of my parents in public schools brimming with racial discrimination, or finally in the snide innuendo that tarnished, for many of my generation, the glory of a highly coveted letter bearing the Harvard crest and embodying the long-overdue destruction of an antiquated and immoral status quo. The discussion grew louder and more volatile as minutes passed into hours. As with those who debate this horribly divisive issue in the national arena, there was simply no convincing one another of the merit in opposing positions.

The one thing that I remember most clearly from the argument was that my opponent seemed completely unwilling to consider even for a moment the possibility that the beneficiaries of race-conscious admission programs might be conventionally qualified. Always, in his employment analogies, the moral dilemma was whether the fictitious employer should hire the Mexican or the most qualified person for the job. Had he forgotten that my academic record in our old high school had been better than his own?

In his limited perspective, the "Mexican" and the "most qualified" were never the same person.

CHAPTER 6

HARVARD HOMEBOY

"I'M A HOMEBOY NOW. AT HARVARD, I DIDN'T FIT . . .
I WAS CONFUSED. NO ONE UNDERSTOOD ME.
I WAS TORN BETWEEN HAVING TO BE OVER THERE AND
WANTING TO BE HERE. I DIDN'T WANT TO BE THERE."

JOSE LUIS RAZO

HARVARD COLLEGE, CLASS OF 1989
(AFTER HIS ARREST FOR ARMED ROBBERY
IN ORANGE COUNTY, JULY 1987)

"I WALKED A MILE WITH PLEASURE, SHE CHATTERED ALL THE WAY;
SHE LEFT ME NONE THE WISER, FOR ALL SHE HAD TO SAY.
I WALKED A MILE WITH SORROW, AND NOT A WORD SAID SHE;
BUT OH, THE THINGS I LEARNED FROM HER, WHEN SORROW WALKED WITH ME."

ROBERT BROWNING HAMILTON

I have not forgotten, will likely never forget, that phone call from my father on that especially warm July afternoon. I was in Sacramento, spending the long hot months between my sophomore and junior years in college serving as a special assistant to the state's Chief Assistant Attorney General. Content with the superficial appreciation of menial labor gained by a summer of stacking boxes in a packing house, I had finally allowed myself the softness of an office job. And anyway, if the previous summer job had been intended to bring me closer to my past, then working in a legal environment would prepare me for the future, specifically a career as an attorney.

Just twenty, I would greet the guard who sat behind the bullet-proof window each morning. I would walk the halls of the Department of Justice, attired in flashy ties and suspenders and occasionally sipping a carton of chocolate milk. I flirted with the pretty young girls in the secretary pool. I had lunch with attorneys twice my age. I took the elevator to the top floor where I handled bite-size administrative projects. I bathed in the attention of being so young and so privileged.

Harvard had brought me there. My stint at Justice was the first of several dream jobs that I was fortunate to have during college. Months earlier, in Cambridge, I had met a political operative who had come to deliver an address at the Kennedy School of Government. We had talked over late-night pizza. He had listened to my interest in law and offered a contact, someone he knew. That is the Harvard way. I took a name, made a call, sent a resume, was hired. My new friend's old friend happened to be California's Chief Assistant Attorney General. He had a framed picture of Robert Kennedy on his wall. We bonded instantly. I left for Sacramento a week after flying home from Boston. As I settled into the daily routine, I wondered how I had gotten there. Yes, I was the youngest person in the building and one of the few Latinos as well. But I was also the "Harvard guy." That single fact seemed to give me an air of legitimacy. Harvard Chicanos are rarely at a loss for exciting, well-paying offers of employment. A Congressional aide. An intern at *Newsweek*. A clerical assistant with Solomon Brothers. These were ripe, sweet plums never really earned, yet truly enjoyed.

That day, however, I would not enjoy. The ringing phone broke the sterility of my bureaucratic sanctuary. My father was calling from Fresno, from the cubicle that he occupies there as an investigator for the District Attorney's Office. He was asking if I had seen a curious, disturbing headline in the morning paper.

My father's voice was familiar, but it had a solemn tone. I sensed that he had something disturbing to say. Something terrible. Had there been an accident? Was someone hurt?

"A guy from Harvard was arrested in Orange County," he

said amid the shuffling of papers as he tried to recover the
article in question. "His name was Joe . . . Joe . . ."

"Joe *Razo*," I whispered into the phone, finishing his sentence for him. "It was Joe Razo, wasn't it?"

I listened intently to my father's recital of the article that he
now held firmly in hand. My heartrate quickened. My replies
were growing more breathless each second. I sat down.

Weeks earlier, in the most exciting of my summer assignments, I had prepared for statewide distribution to law enforcement agencies throughout California an official Spanish
translation of the infamous *Miranda* warning—a safeguard
against self-incrimination. It was a feather in my cap, a résumé
filler. My father, the proud cop, had a laminated version of the
new warning, my cryptic creation, mounted on a plaque en-
graved with a ceremonial inscription. Little did I know, as I
pored over case law and made notes on a yellow legal pad, that
soon, and less than five hundred miles to the south, Jose "Joe"
Razo, a classmate from Harvard, would himself be Mirandized.

You have the right to remain silent . . .

"It says that he was arrested for armed robbery," my father
continued.

*If you give up that right, anything you say can and will be
used against you in a court of law . . .*

"As many as fifteen counts [of armed robbery]."

*You have the right to speak with an attorney and to have an
attorney present during questioning . . .*

"He's being held in Orange County" he went on, no doubt
wondering, given the stunned silence on the other end of the
phone, whether I was still on the line.

*If you cannot afford an attorney, one will be provided for you
free of charge . . .*

"He's got a public defender," my father added.

With these rights in mind, do you wish to speak to us now?

Joe spoke.

According to the national news reports that I felt compelled
to pore over in the several weeks that followed, the twenty-
year-old honors student had gone to the La Habra police station
one afternoon, seeking the attention of an audience by claiming that he had information about the murder of a nine-year-

old girl; he had none. The police grew impatient. They would have dismissed him except for one thing. At one point, in a casual tone, he reportedly mentioned to detectives something like: "You know, I've done some robberies."

After waiving the protections of *Miranda*, he proceeded to confess to, in what investigators considered remarkable detail, a series of armed robberies that had been committed at a number of fast-food restaurants and convenience stores in Los Angeles and Orange counties during time periods that coincided with Razo's summer and Christmas vacations from Harvard over a two-year period, along with a hold-up in Miami that Razo claimed to have committed during spring break. His accounts of the robberies were so precise, complete with specific references of how much money was taken at each location, that police were convinced that they now had in their custody, put there not by great police work but by his own volition, the individual who had become known by the local press as simply "The Ski-Mask Bandit."

During Razo's "speedy trial," which took place almost exactly two years after he was arrested, his confession assumed prominence as the major component of the state's case against him. With witnesses being unable to identify under oath the individual in the ski mask, or to agree completely on the height, weight, or ethnicity of the bandit, prosecutors held on to Razo's confession as the only real piece of evidence in their hands.

Razo later recanted the confession in a flurry of confused and contradictory statements to the press. After pleading "not guilty" at his arraignment and eventually being released on bail, he was asked by a mutual friend of ours why he would confess to crimes that he later claimed he did not commit. He responded that, although it sounded stupid, he was "just bragging [to police]." At Razo's preliminary trial, his attorney argued unsuccessfully that the damaging confession be suppressed because, at the time he issued it, Razo was in a "confused, vulnerable, and volatile mental state." The court was not persuaded that that explanation could account for the accuracy of Razo's confession, complete with details about which the police claimed only the true culprit could know. The confession was upheld and a fellow Harvard Chicano was held over for trial.

I am back at the Attorney General's Office. I am surrounded by lawyers. I am surrounded by red and gold books promising to hold truth. I am surrounded by shock. My father has stopped reading and has begun to ask me the type of straightforward questions that characterizes our relationship.

"Did you know him?"

Yes, I did.

"Did you have any idea . . . ?"

No, of course not.

"Why do you think he would do something like that?"

Hmm, that is the question, isn't it? A question that I and my Chicano classmates at Harvard would be asked again and again and again in the months after my father's phone call. The case was a horrible riddle. Harvard people do not commit armed robbery, after all. Insider trading, perhaps, but not armed robbery. We would be asked for the riddle's solution by friends and family who assumed that, as Harvard Chicanos, we might have special insight into this bizarre tragedy that had claimed one of our own. Were we to somehow climb into our classmate's mind and bravely search its recesses for a true motivation?

Why?

Why would a bright and talented Latino on America's educational fast track throw it all away and choose instead to fade into the impersonal world of criminal statistics? Cynical mumblings over the morning toast, *Just another Mexican robber . . .* Why? The question with no answer. The question that Razo himself, now sitting in a Folsom jail cell, has consistently refused to answer. And yet the question to which tantalized spectators could not resist proposing an answer of their own.

Liberal theories absolved the young man of any guilt of his own and shifted the blame to larger, more sinister institutions. There was the respected professor of Chicano studies in California who, having never met Razo or visited our campus, nonetheless reasoned that Harvard was the most likely villain in the drama.

"He was miserable there," the angry professor speculated to an audience of young Latinos in California, with an extended index finger presumably pointing toward Cambridge. "He committed those crimes as a way of escaping."

Maybe. Weren't we all miserable there? Maybe he wanted an

escape route, like the rest of us. Maybe, unlike the rest of us, he had the courage to forge one. But what courage does it take to wave a gun in the face of a cashier working at a fast-food joint? In any case, what I found most curious about the professor's simplistic theory was that it provided both sympathy for Razo and venom for the blue bloods at Harvard. Evil, racist Harvard. I wondered which of his dual objectives he would consider more important.

There were those who supposed that Razo was simply a scared young man on a fast-moving treadmill on which he was placed by a well-meaning society, and now he wanted off. Perhaps. It is a kind of understood belief among Latino and other minority students at schools like Harvard that—no matter how lonely or alienated one feels—few things are worse than giving up, going home, and "letting Harvard beat you." One young Latina, herself a close friend of Razo's, confessed to me that no matter how much she hated her Harvard experience at times, she would "never let Harvard win" by transferring to another, more nurturing campus in California. My own suspicion is that, at the end of his sophomore year, Razo was not nearly as afraid of confronting the American penal system as he was of explaining to his proud parents that he was unhappy at Harvard and wanted to leave. I empathized. Had I not been unable to bring myself to tell my parents of the trials of my freshman year?

According to newspaper accounts, Razo had, as a high school honors student and athlete, been courted by some fifty colleges and universities. He chose Harvard in part, the papers suggested, because Razo's mother and grandmother were "Harvard-struck," impressed with a school that they thought represented the absolute pinnacle of American success.

For Mexican-American parents who come to value the rewards of proper education through the filter of their own struggle in school, there is simply no convincing them that minority student life at an elite school such as Harvard is not all that it promises to be. After all, my parents' generation was consumed by nothing as much as the pursuit of access. The restaurant, the classroom, the college all barred access. *No Mexicans allowed . . .* The goal became access, and access alone. Access promised reward. Access was power.

My generation was left to muddle through the murky waters of what came next: What of the quality of life for minority students once admitted? To even raise the question was to sin against progress, to seem ungrateful for experiences that had been denied our parents. I remember my own father's disbelief during one of many conversations about the place. "How can anyone be *unhappy* at a place like Harvard . . . ?" Very easily.

There were also those who suggested that Razo was pushed into a life of crime by financial need. The string of fifteen robberies to which he confessed had netted a sum of money estimated to be between $27,000 and $30,000. After his arrest, Razo told a reporter for *The Los Angeles Times* that he "needed money [at Harvard] and that was a way to get it." Even with a generous scholarship from Harvard, Razo had the usual expenses: airfare to and from California, money for food and entertainment, money for books and alcohol.

Like many students at Harvard, particularly like most Latino students there, money was no doubt a constant irritation. My parents sent an occasional card with money in it, sometimes as much as fifty dollars a month. Still, there were times, few but memorable, when I had nothing in my pocket but a wish for the future. I had to borrow quarters to do laundry. I could not afford to buy an expensive textbook for class. I could not afford to leave town for the weekend when keeping my sanity required it. I could not afford to go to movies or out to dinner with a girlfriend. Could not afford! Could not afford! Could not afford! In New York, I once ate cardboard pizza every night for a month, welcomed a stranger buying me a free beer at an Irish bar, and walked fifty sweaty blocks up Broadway in uncomfortable shoes in the middle of July rather than surrender the single subway token that jingled with a few nickels in my pocket.

These stories are universal. To be a college student, even at a wealthy college, is to be poor. And not everyone who has gone without for four years, hoping that, upon graduation, John Harvard will provide, turns to a life of crime to supplement their income. Besides, Razo's reported take of $30,000 would buy a lot of plane tickets, pizza, and beer. No matter what liberal apologists argued at the time, I sensed that there had to be more to the story than financial need.

Another popular explanation, the most colorful of the bunch, provided Joe Razo with an alias—that of Robin Hood. In a newsroom somewhere, Razo was transformed into a modern-day Joaquin Murrieta, the defiant angel of Mexican-American folklore. Romantic theories of the redistribution of wealth suggested that my classmate was stealing not from the Sheriff of Nottingham but the Evil Empire of Corporate America donating the profits to those less fortunate. Razo told reporters that he had given much of the money away to family and friends in need. "Whatever my family wanted, it got—food, bills paid, furniture," he said. Though Razo admitted that he kept his criminal escapades secret from his family, he claimed that it was because of the crimes that he was able to help out his family with household expenses. His claims were not supported by a story in *The Boston Herald*, in which two of his sisters seemed to contradict that contention. One sister called her brother's claim "ridiculous," and said that family members had not seen any robbery money. Another sister went further, recalling that her mother "always sent [Razo] money," and even went without paying bills at times so that she could send money to Cambridge. Clearly, notwithstanding a working-class sympathy for Robin Hood–type bandits, there again seemed to be more to the story than that provided by such a theory.

Though the liberal theories of why a Harvard Chicano would commit over a dozen armed robberies seemed flawed, more conservative ones were not much better. A few weeks after Razo's arrest, an irate, white alumnus from California reportedly called the undergraduate admissions office to complain about the negative publicity dealt our alma mater and to assert that, in his day, things like this simply did not happen. His pre-Chicano days, that is. Thus, he assumed that affirmative action was not only opening Harvard's doors to incompetents, but also to criminals. I imagined his stuffed-shirt arrogance aboard a yacht. "Now you see what happens when. . ." Later I joked with the office worker who relayed the story to me that, if the caller was at a loss for other Harvard alumni who had run afoul of the law, he should consider Ivan Boesky and many of President Nixon's Watergate bunch. That was different, I imagined him saying. Joe Razo had not committed his crime by using a computer or a black bag of dirty tricks; he had used a gun. At a place like Harvard, that sort of thing is considered, well . . . vulgar.

My own father at first suggested, with a shake of his head and the notable bias of a career cop, that it all seemed to add up to a case of being able to "take the kid out of the barrio, but not the barrio out of the kid." If that was true, liberal educators around the country were likely to be heartbroken by the futility of their efforts to "rescue" minority children by recruiting them to more enriching, if foreign, educational environments. I was not persuaded by my father's pessimism. And yet given the other explanations that were circulating at the time, it seemed as plausible as anything else that I'd heard.

If one seeks tragedy, dishonor if you will, the Razo drama will not disappoint. But though disturbing, the tale was strangely not all that original. It had all happened before, a variation of it anyway, two summers earlier and three thousand miles away on a block of warm concrete in upper Manhattan.

It was a reporter for *The New York Times* who, in the initial seventy-two hours of Razo's confession, first drew a comparison between the story of the Harvard Hold-up Man and that of the late Edmund Perry. I learned the details from friends in New York. Perry was a seventeen-year-old African-American youth who, on June 12, 1985, was shot and killed by an undercover police officer near Columbia University. Like the Razo story, the tale of Edmund Perry had evolved slowly. At first, there was little concern in the press over what seemed to be simply another young black male casualty of inner-city violence. Soon, however, there appeared, from a stack of notes on a copy editor's desk, a hook.

The press learned that Edmund Perry had, just weeks before he was killed, graduated from Phillips Exeter Academy, perhaps the most prestigious prep school in the country, and had accepted a full scholarship to Stanford University. Like Razo, a dazzler, Perry shone in Harlem's public schools—impressing his teachers and testing past the twelfth grade level when he was in the eighth. He was offered rescue from his environment. Through the outreach efforts of the Boston-based educational organization "A Better Chance," he had been placed at Exeter, where he likewise excelled academically.

There was another, more shocking detail, that made the story of Edmund Perry not only disturbing and sad, but also—like that of Joe Razo—confusing and messy. At the instant that he was shot, he and his alleged accomplice, his older brother Jonah, were supposedly mugging the undercover cop. Again, disturbing headlines for the morning papers. Again, the why?

The truth may never be known about what actually occurred on the corner of 114th Street and Morningside Drive, just after dark on that warm night in June. The version of events told by the young, white plainclothes policeman who was on "mugger duty" that night has, over time, remained unchanged. He testified that two black men came up behind him, that one got him in a chokehold while the other went through his pockets, and that then they punched and kicked him until he fell to the ground. Bleeding and about to lose consciousness, with thoughts of his young wife and unborn baby, the officer reached for his ankle holster and fired into the night. One of his assailants fled the scene, the other fell to the ground.

Whether one believes that the police officer acted in justifiable self-defense, as a police review board and Manhattan grand jury concluded, or that the incident is simply part of a pattern of the sort of police violence against inner-city black males so aptly depicted in the videotaped beating of Rodney King, the mind-boggling end result is the same: the unconscious, unmoving body of seventeen-year-old Edmund Perry on a street corner in New York City, many miles away from the pristine New England academy that, it was intended, would spare him such a fate.

Eventually, it was revealed that a panicked Jonah Perry—himself then a sophomore at Cornell—had, on the night that his brother was shot, blurted out to neighbors that he and Edmund had gone to "the Hill [Morningside Park] to rob somebody," but that they had "picked the wrong guy—a DT [detective]." After the revelation, Edmund Perry was no longer, in the minds of those who read the morning papers, a "good victim." The roar from the African-American community in New York tapered off to a whimper. Confronted with mounting evidence that their martyred honors-student-victim-of-police-violence was actually simply a mugger, and not a very good one at that, an embarrassed set of local African-American leaders dropped the case, and along with it, the important issues that I believe it presented for those nonwhite students educated at traditionally and predominantly white schools.

Before long, the tale of Edmund Perry faded into obscurity. Life in New York went on as before. The subway trains ran. Vendors gathered in the Village. Couples on blankets listened to Shakespeare in Central Park. Other people died. And newspaper writers moved on to other stories of human despair. But urgent socioeducational issues ignored do not go away. They only reappear in time. And ironically, when Jonah Perry was later brought to trial on charges of assault and attempted robbery, the witnesses to his supposed panicked confession were not found credible and a jury acquitted him on all counts.

That confusing summer finally came to an end. It ushered in, what would be for Harvard Chicanos, an even more confusing autumn. After his arrest, a friend visited Joe Razo in jail. Razo told him of his only consolation, that at least he "did not have to return to Harvard" in the fall. The rest of us were not so lucky. We did return. And we dreaded the discussions to come. We knew that it was likely that many students, instructors, and administrators had by then heard of the Razo affair via a flurry of negative publicity heaped upon an institution that dealt with success much, much better than it did failure. Certainly, *we* all knew. Through the discomfort of July days spent at home in places like San Antonio, Phoenix, Los Angeles, and Fresno, Harvard Chicanos had kept vigil through television reports and had scoured local newspapers for any mention of their fallen classmate. Now, our return to Harvard forced us to sort out, if we dared, what the Razo tragedy meant for those of us who remained.

There was above all, I remember, a clear defensiveness that September. During my first ten days in Cambridge, I walked through Harvard Square, a bit on edge. Perhaps I was afraid that someone would approach. They would mention seeing Joe in a hometown newspaper or maybe on television. Inevitably, mercilessly, they would, I feared, lure me into a discussion that I was unable and unwilling to have. *Why?*

Then someone said it, the single admission that none of us

had been willing to make. A RAZA member confessed to how "embarrassing" it all was for the rest of us; she implied that her roommate was looking at her a little differently these days, perhaps even afraid to leave anything of value lying around the room. Suddenly, we were all placed under a microscope of sorts, and for minority students delicately trying to fit into foreign surroundings, that is an especially uncomfortable place to be.

On October 9, 1987, a special RAZA meeting was called to discuss what the organization felt compelled to issue as its "formal response" to the Razo affair. Someone actually suggested ignoring the whole thing and hoping the scandal would subside. My journal entry from that night suggests that some of those in attendance felt a renewed pressure to defend their presence on campus, reminiscent of the sort of affirmative action accusations that they had encountered years earlier in high school. I suspected that, whatever we had been through up to this point, our reaction in the months to come to the tragic demise of one of our own was going to be a test that would represent "our toughest and most important challenge yet." It was. For Harvard Chicanos, the measure of our reaction was no less than a measure of our true character.

Harvard's institutional response was predictably unimaginative. For reporters calling before deadlines, Razo's story was reduced to that of an "isolated incident." Ah. Some high-level bureaucrat in some office somewhere had decided that the best strategy was for the institution to drop its former student like a hot rock. Reprehensible statements circulated from the Undergraduate Minority Recruitment Program to campus press suggesting that Joe Razo, as a football player, had been recruited from high school not through their efforts but through those of the Harvard athletic department. That same office later circulated among all its minority recruiters, whom it feared might be asked difficult questions during their upcoming high school visits, a prewritten response saying something about how the Razo case was an "isolated incident" and that there were also, among Harvard's Latino students, many more success stories than otherwise.

Success, Harvard could handle. I remember Harvard administrators fawning over San Antonio Mayor Henry Cisneros during his visit to campus in my freshman year. Cisneros had done a graduate stint at the Kennedy School of Government before becoming the first Mexican-American mayor of a major U.S. city. He had assumed a national prominence. He was interviewed on the *Today* show and on *60 Minutes*. In 1984, he was considered by Democratic presidential candidate Walter Mondale as a prospective vice-presidential running mate.

By the time Cisneros was noticed by the media, he was already known and revered in much of the Mexican-American community in the Southwest. His reputation transcended the borders of Texas. The first, the only, Cisneros was a role model, a symbol of excellence. He was intelligent, articulate, and handsome. He spoke Spanish as smoothly as English. Among the Latino patrons of a coffee shop in Tucson or in the lunchroom in Los Angeles, he was, simply, "Henry"; the informality of a shared culture prompted us to claim him as our own.

Cisneros was what a proud parent wanted his child to become. I remember an evening when, as a fifteen-year-old boy, I was approached by my father as I studied in my bedroom. He was holding a magazine article, which he offered to me. The article was about the mayor, who I at first viewed as an obscure public official in a faraway city in Texas. So what? Achievement was familiar to me. Arrogantly, foolishly, I took it for granted.

Because I still had not begun to think of myself as a Mexican-American, because I had not yet realized that discrimination was more than just a dusty word in a history book, I did not know what my father knew: "These things are rare, *mijo*." The boy who had not lived his father's life, a life whose dreams were circumscribed by racism, could not understand the pride in his father's expression as he stared at a magazine story about a complete stranger whom he would likely never meet. Not unlike strangers excited by my entrance into Harvard, my father and millions of Mexican-Americans from a generation of deprivation could somehow gain vicarious nourishment from the distant success of a man like Henry Cisneros. My father read that Cisneros was a Harvard graduate and that carried its own significance. Harvard was a star-maker. Harvard promised reincarnation. Harvard could empower Mexican-Americans, could legitimize them somehow.

With my initial exposure to the persona of Henry Cisneros, Harvard, this mythical place that I had heard referenced only in connection with the Kennedys, came to represent, in the mind of a fifteen-year-old boy, an ethnic beacon of sorts. If educational achievement was indeed the best road to success for Mexican-Americans in the United States, then Harvard could pave the way. It was fitting, ultimately, for my association with Harvard to propel me much closer to Cisneros than my father could ever have hoped to be.

The Harvard Foundation for Race Relations had been created long before I arrived on campus; it intended to improve minority student life at Harvard. Its ambitious mandate notwithstanding, it did nothing more revolutionary than sponsor cultural events on holidays and arrange for ethnic superstars to speak on campus. Henry Cisneros was a superstar, and better yet, a Harvard son. Our roommates asked: "What's his name again?" But for the handful of Mexican-Americans from the Southwest who had been transplanted by ambition to this scary place, Henry was no less than our spiritual father.

The director of the foundation had taken a distinct liking to my outspoken nature; he asked me to deliver the closing address at a campus luncheon honoring the mayor. Without a moment's hesitation, I cut class and nervously prepared the speech of my life. As I walked into the room, I was escorted to a seat marked by a small strip of cardboard. I realized then the rewards of the chosen. I was sitting next to Papa.

The old saying suggests that victory has a thousand fathers, but defeat is an orphan. The phrase was likely coined by a Harvard man. Success was something for which Harvard had no trouble claiming credit. Good publicity meant large checks from wealthy alumni. On the other hand, failure was someone else's responsibility.

There was a rumor among students, particularly minority students, that Harvard had in its disciplinary arsenal a weapon far worse than expulsion. When Harvard wanted to dump you like a high school crush, when Harvard wanted absolution for the error of ever making your acquaintance, when Harvard wanted to forget that you ever existed, Harvard could make you disappear. A student could be expunged. The idea, incredible anywhere else but very credible at Harvard, was that school officials would go through your records, through all your administrative paperwork, and destroy them all. Someone said that one unfortunate soul, having met such a fate after assassinating a head of state or some such thing, had carved his initials on a desk in Widener Library; the desk, it was said, simply disappeared. Legends endure, truth blurs together with fiction. The importance of stories that Harvard could actually expunge someone, rob them of their existence was important for only one reason: true or not, the Harvard students I knew believed it. I believed it.

Joe Razo with his ski mask and pistol and embarrassing headlines was, after all, no Henry Cisneros. If the public success of one had proven Harvard to be gracious and proud, the public failure of the other would show it to be fickle and disloyal. When the pretension and the tradition and the exclusivity wilted away, the truth was inescapable. Harvard was a whore.

Another group that was responding to the Razo tragedy in a predictable way was our fellow Chicano students at other Ivy League schools, a competitive group skilled in rubbing salt in an open wound. These were, in many cases, talented and well-intentioned young people who would spend hours and days recruiting bright Latino high school seniors to their schools like Yale and Princeton and Columbia, only to see them end up at Harvard instead. They complained about the alluring power of the Harvard name and reserved in their hearts a dark place for those of us who had turned down admission to their colleges in favor of one we simply considered to be better. I remember, for instance, the venom from the Princeton recruiter when I told him that I had chosen Harvard. It was with a distinct joy, then, that our counterparts would in subsequent years point out perceived flaws with our chosen campus as often as opportunity afforded them the chance to do so. And the sad, confusing tale of Joe Razo provided them with such a wonderful opportunity.

During an inter-campus conference, I asked a classmate if she had a response to what I anticipated would be a flurry of accusatory questions about Razo; she winced and said that she doubted the issue would come up at all. In disbelief, I responded that she must be joking. I guessed it would be one of the first three questions that we were asked. "How was your trip?" "Would you like a drink?" "What the hell did you *do* to that kid from LA?" I was right. Later that spring, during the ever-competitive recruitment season, I could almost hear the phone lines from New Haven to high schools in the Southwest: "You know, Razo was obviously not happy there and Harvard and those white-washed Mexicans up there just let him fall right through the cracks. . ." Tsk. Tsk.

Finally, looking for answers among the rubble of lost futures, psychologists studying the cases of Joe Razo and Edmund Perry offered up casual theories, labeling them self-destructive "sun children."

Sun children are poster children for the American Dream. Psychologists designate them a rare breed. They are bright minority students who, despite economically or educationally disadvantaged backgrounds, excel academically. Through excellence, they earn separation. They are rescued from their surroundings, their families, their friends, and themselves. They earn the reward of admission to elite, predominantly white schools where it is assumed all will go well. They are spared the torments of destiny.

But unforgivingly, the parade turns to a funeral march. Inexplicably, the psychologists warned, these sun children sometimes turn away from the guiding light of success and instead burn out like an abrupt comet. For sun children, the experts guessed, something as harmless as summer vacation might be traumatic. I sensed that they were closer to solving the riddle than they realized.

Perhaps it is shame that fuels destruction; the recognition, as described by one author, that you hear your parents speak in a way that your teachers discourage as improper. Perhaps guilt; an old friend from kindergarten, a fellow Chicano, whom you run into at the 7-Eleven—you in your Harvard sweatshirt and him carrying his two-year-old daughter. Perhaps it is simply loneliness, the overwhelming fear that Thomas Wolfe was right and that you will never be able to go home again.

Whatever the reason, the result was the same: vulnerable youth enduring an undeniable loss of intimacy with a community left behind; no longer part of the oppressed, now in league with the oppressor.

The development of a theory, regardless of its validity, meant that Harvard might be wrong. The Razo tragedy might not be "isolated," at all. These random acts of human destruction might not be random at all. For those sun children who re-

mained at places like Harvard, there was an odd sense of uncertainty that called out for resolution. It had to be confronted
and conquered. And, if Harvard would not face it, then we
would have to. If not, any one of us might be the next casualty.

My junior year was helplessly entangled with the tragedy of
Joe Razo. Every dimension of every event, every day of every
month was filtered through the episode. Had anyone heard
anything from California? No. Piles of news clippings grew
taller, but I was no nearer to an understanding of the truth now
than I had been when my father had first told me of the events.
Still the why remained. Insufficient theories floated through my
head. *Sun children . . . You can take the kid out of the barrio
. . . At least, I don't have to go back to Harvard . . .* I was drinking again. Now the tinkle of ice against glass epitomized not
rebellion, not reincarnation, but respite. Our classmate was
three thousand miles away, awaiting trial in a jail cell in California. Yet he was with us. He walked to class with us. He had
mesa with us. He mourned the loss of California with us. His
spirit roamed freely through Harvard Yard, haunting those of
us who had not been able to escape so easily.

It was March. In New England, March is nature's cruelest
tease. After a long, cold, and wet winter March promised compassion. A milder climate. Passing months assured that spring
was coming, but when? In Los Angeles, March meant spring
break and bikinis. In Boston, it meant keeping your winter
clothes on a while longer as it granted no reprieve from an icy
wind chill. I hated March. In the vulnerability of my first year,
March had nurtured leftover doubt from autumn about
whether I belonged at Harvard in the first place. In the defiance
of the next year, March had permitted me to consider a transfer
to Berkeley to arrogantly refute the air of legitimacy that Harvard bestowed on a commoner. And now, in the confusion of
my third year—had time gone by so quickly?—March had left
me obsessed with loss. I knew the month. If March had a soul,
then it was black and cold. If March had a will, then, I was
convinced, it was focused on my destruction.

Again, I was alone. Again, I sought comfort in familiarity.

Each year, during Thanksgiving weekend, one hundred
or so Mexican-American students from throughout the Ivy
League gather at a designated campus for Pachanga, a cultural

celebration organized for the benefit of those who cannot afford to fly home for the holiday. It provides a chance to catch up with the experiences of old friends from places like Yale, Columbia, and Brown. It allows for the drinking of large amounts of tequila and perhaps a one-night stand with a familiar stranger.

In addition to Pachanga, there were also, during the school year, two other organized gatherings of Mexican-American students in the Ivy League. The one in October was traditionally set aside for the discussion of issues involving the more effective recruitment of Chicano students; the one in April usually concentrated on the more difficult question of the retention of those students once they arrived on our campuses. Appropriately, just months after Joe Razo's arrest, along with its implication that John Harvard had shown his ineptness in retaining at least one of his students, it was our turn to host the spring conference.

A RAZA committee selected as the conference's theme something that was a unique and disturbing subject matter—ourselves. The Sun Child Conference was intended as an introspection into the uniqueness of our experience as Chicano students at predominantly white, Ivy League colleges. The stage was set for an emotional, and eventually disturbing, two-day session of soul-searching about the significance of that odd distinction. We wanted to test the psychologists' hypothesis. Were there in fact certain universal pressures beholden to Chicano students on elite, white campuses? If so, could they be conquered before they conquered us?

We gathered to answer those questions and to explore the significance of our presence on sacred soil for our families, our communities, our people, and most importantly, ourselves. Always in the past, we had discussed, in abstract workshops, political topics such as affirmative action or language rights—issues of importance to us. This time, the topic *was* us.

I remember an articulate and passionate address by the conference's keynote speaker, himself a Latino graduate of Harvard and a professor of sociology somewhere in the Midwest. For over an hour, he allowed us to struggle with the complexity of our college experience. When he unexpectedly, and unforgivingly, made a reference to Joe Razo, he did so to remind us of our implied responsibility to one another. He retold a story, one that I will likely never forget, about standing in his kitchen and feeling helpless as his wife accidentally cut herself. He was paralyzed, unable to help her. Later, he tried to explain his failure to act, to comfort. *What could I do?* She responded that he could have held her, told her that he loved her, and reassured her that she would be all right.

As I listened to the story, I looked over at the old friend who sat next to me; he seemed to read my mind and to know instantly that I was thinking of Joe Razo and of what may have been, for Harvard Chicanos, our greatest collective failure. *What could we do?* We could have held him. We could have told him that he would be all right.

Later that night, at a party that served as the conference's main event, we drank and danced and tried to forget. After too much drink, I watched helplessly as a close friend, someone who I cared for as a brother and who seemed to identify with the pressures that had conquered Razo, appeared close to losing his mind. Surrounded by three people who watched him closely, he lay on the floor in a curled-up ball of confused, muffled whimpers. He mumbled about being "just like Joe." He confessed loneliness. He confessed alienation. He cried uncontrollably in drunken slurs about being unhappy and having to succeed to please too many people who were too far away. And the music played on.

The following night, a small group of us gathered in someone's room for a private "head-session" to hash out our impressions of the events of the conference and finally reveal our feelings about the Razo tragedy, by then nearly a year old. No press statements, and no punches pulled. For six hours, we talked and listened. Joe's spirit entered and took its seat near the stereo.

Arguments and tears and admissions filled the room. Someone said that he felt guilty for succeeding in a school system in which others like him had failed. *There, but for the grace of God, go I . . .* Someone else joked about not having anything in common with her parents anymore; she recalled silence at the dinner table during summer vacation. No one laughed. Suddenly, one of the strongest, brightest, and most talented people that I have ever known broke down and cried, as she admitted guilt over the fact that her parents had had to mortgage their house to pay for airfare to attend her graduation. We were consumed with simply finding a precarious place to perch between two opposing worlds—one which we had been allowed to visit for four years and one to which we knew we must somehow eventually return. The sun came up over the Charles. We wiped away tears, hugged one another, and, with nothing resolved, finally went off to bed.

These were people poised to conquer the future, but who had not yet reconciled themselves with their past. We were torn, divided, conflicted. I loved and respected my parents and yet I wanted nothing as much as to live a life that was different, better, than theirs. I had avoided being part of a sorrowful statistic—"50 percent of Hispanics drop out of high school," the commentator on the evening news said—and yet instead of feeling lucky, I felt guilty, illegitimate, embarrassed. I felt like part of the educational system's dog-and-pony show, paraded in public to convince the audience that people like me could attend places like this. People like me. John Harvard was the ringmaster.

The day after the head-session and for many days after that, as many as a dozen of us wore the RAZA sweatshirts that we had designed and ordered. We wore them with a distinct, new-found pride. We wore them to the gym. We wore them to the dining hall. We wore them to bed, and again the next day. Perhaps we were afraid to take them off because of the security they afforded us. These were our colors. We were eager to display them to others on campus. Like a letterman jacket in high school or a gang insignia, the sweatshirt was our reminder to those around us that our experience was unique and worthy of respect. A prominent historian once said of slavery that it is best understood by he who has endured; the same may be said of sun children. We understood. We had endured. We had lost one of our own. And still we persisted.

Later that week, walking alone along the river, I finally allowed myself to think of my own experience with Joe Razo. Months earlier, my father had asked through a phone line, "Did you know him?" Yes, I had said. But there was more that I had not said, had not told to anyone.

For two years at Harvard, Joe and I were friends. Though that would itself become a point of contention among other Chicanos, I still feel that is fair to say. We felt comfortable with one another, I think. It was our school that Joe never felt comfortable

with. Well beyond being merely preoccupied with racial difference, he seemed to pass through a ritual that some scared and
alienated minority students in elite schools go through. He wore
his ethnicity like a badge. Or was it a shield . . . ?

I remember Joe in the costume of an East LA homeboy—the
khaki pants, the Pendleton shirt, the bandanna around his
head. I remembered his tattoos and his homesickness for
Southern California. I remembered his broad shoulders and
tough exterior. I remembered seeing him with a black eye one
afternoon and hearing him tell me that he had been in a fist-
fight with a couple of white, local townies because of an alleged
racist remark that they made. Town-gown relations are somewhat tender because young working-class whites in Cambridge
sometimes resent the presence of Chicano and African-
American students on an elite hometown campus that remains
largely closed to them. It is ironic that Joe felt shut out from
our campus as well.

I imagine the sort of penal institution that will likely house
someone I once knew for the rest of his twenties, years never
replaced. The dismal monotony, the stench of urine, the separate ethnic gangs stalking the exercise yard. A horrid institution in a horrid correctional system that scars and beats and
sodomizes, but seldom corrects. Against that hard reality, I
played with a much softer array of memories.

I remember a bright young man with a good, kind heart. As
part of an offensive line during a not-so-friendly intercampus
football game at Pachanga, he repeatedly allowed our dimin-
utive quarterback to get smeared in the grass rather than risk
using his two-hundred-pound frame to accidentally hurt someone. "C'mon, guys, it's only a game. . ." I remember him saying
with boyish innocence. He seemed more like a teddy bear than
a gangster.

I remember him coming by my room one night to show me
a letter that he intended to send to the *Harvard Crimson*. As a
freshman, I was quoted in the *Crimson* as being critical of Harvard's failure to provide support systems for its minority students. Joe came to my defense by commending my efforts and
attacking my critics. I did my best to discourage his involve-
ment, but he persisted. Loyalty was important to him. He felt
that as Mexican-Americans on unfamiliar ground, we had to

look out for one another because no one else would. At least someone understood that.

I remember running into him each day during one semester of our sophomore year, as we hurried to separate classes at the same time in the same building. He told me how excited he was to be returning home to California for vacation. I, too, was homesick. But given his profound unhappiness at Harvard, home represented something more for Joe. It was salvation, an escape from Harvard and Boston and snow and New England liberals and bad Mexican food and arrogant, competitive classmates.

Still, of course, our experience was not all bad. The idea of attending Harvard was saturated with prestige. It was prestige that had lured generations of young people to Cambridge. And in a sense, it was prestige that kept them from leaving. No matter how miserable they were. Once when one of our discussions turned to graduate school plans, Joe confessed an intention to go to law school. The only question that remained was, where? I told him that I intended to return to California and pursue graduate study there. Not him. I was shocked to learn that he was seriously considering attending Harvard Law School. Why? Why on earth, I asked, would anyone who hated our school as much as he seemed to hate it want to spend three more years in it?

"Well," he said with an innocent shrug. "I figure that when you graduate from a place like Harvard Law, well . . . no one can give you shit."

I nodded, conceding the point. We shook hands and said goodbye. He walked away. We would not see each other as free men again. The next time that I would hear his name it would be from my father on the telephone. As his image faded into the scenery of Harvard Square, I realized from his blunt answer to my inquiry that my friend was, in his lingering insecurities, still afraid of people "giving him shit." I interpreted that to mean the denial of something that we all expected as a reward for hard work. Something that should, but does not always follow the act of attending Harvard. Something called respect.

Harvard Homeboy. What an idea! What one bright young man caught up in a lonely game of charades seemed not to understand until it was too late is that between the separate worlds that those two words represent is a barrier that perhaps should not be crossed.

CHAPTER 7

CHEATING THE DEVIL

"ULTIMATELY A HERO IS A MAN WHO
WOULD ARGUE WITH THE GODS
AND AWAKEN DEVILS
TO CONTEST HIS VISION."

NORMAN MAILER

HARVARD COLLEGE, CLASS OF 1954

Buried somewhere in my morbid collection of newspaper articles about the arrest and pending trial of Joe Razo, there was a single editorial of extraordinary significance. It detailed with insight the emotional pushes and pulls of being an ethnic pioneer, an overachiever, a "sun child," or whatever one wanted to call students like us. It invoked the profound metaphor of two worlds, separate and conflicting, and professed a difficulty in simultaneously maintaining a foothold in each. It confessed the author's own intellectual estrangement from his less-educated parents through his own education in elite schools and argued that, though painful, such distance was a necessary concession to success in America.

The editorial cited the Razo case as an example of the dire consequences that face those who resist such concessions. In the author's opinion, the Harvard Homeboy had met his tragic fate in large part because he had tried to have his culture cake and eat it, too. It was like some bizarre late-night movie, the kind that gives you nightmares. The commoner wants success and acceptance badly enough to strike a deal with the devil. *Fame and fortune; your soul in return . . .*

Razo wanted success in one world—a Harvard diploma, even admission to its law school. Still, he was reluctant to pay the inevitable price. The author defined the price of success in the new world that we had entered as the surrendering of the cultural restraints of the old world that we had left behind. Razo struck his deal, along with the rest of us. He was rewarded, placed among the sons and daughters of the world's elite. But then, he flaunted his ethnicity. He flirted with separatism. He tried to cheat the devil. And was punished.

The enigma of being a Mexican-American at Harvard was not enough of an oddity to satisfy my colleague; he felt compelled to take an already profound statement and place an exclamation point after it. Not merely a Harvard Chicano, but a Harvard *Homeboy.* Twice separated. A bandanna worn as a crucifix, perhaps to ward off Lucifer. A homeboy was someone to be feared, respected. A romantic symbol. A thug. Someone who refused to be broken. Someone who would not, as Razo had said to me, be "given shit."

In that sense, Razo's provocative costume was not only a badge and a shield, but also a billboard. It boasted boldly of ethnic defiance. It was sewn together delicately with cultural trinkets smuggled aboard an airplane from Los Angeles; bandannas, khakis, tattoos, and a *pachuco* strut were the colorful threads that comprised the tapestry. Yet if the author's cryptic speculation about the inevitable concessions of success were correct, then the charade was being performed in vain. Concession to Harvard was inevitable. Razo would eventually have to remove his radical garb, if only to replace it one day with the more traditional trappings of a cap and gown. He had re-fused to change his wardrobe, and so the devil had left him standing naked in Harvard Yard.

But even a friend's peril was not enough to convince me. I was not resigned to accepting the author's theory. I was too idealistic to concede inevitability so easily. How could I? I had my own ethnic pride. I had my own costume. A serape had been my bandanna, my billboard. I, too, was trying to avoid cultural concession. I, too, was trying to cheat the devil.

Thus, I wanted, no *needed*, to believe that academic success required no real sacrifice in culture, that it had no price in family intimacy. I needed to believe that one could have his cake and eat it, too. After all, I had already accepted the role of provider. My cake was promised to others back home. The evidence was everywhere. The proud smile of parents who lived vicariously through me. The handshake of Mexican strangers who watched my progress. The hope. The expecta-tion. The shared nourishment of a feast put out by a cruel entity that played favorites—the American educational system. A sys-tem that invited me to gorge and let other Mexican-Americans starve.

One had been educated to somehow empower thousands of others. At Harvard, one hundred twenty-five carefully chosen Chicanos represented millions of Mexican-Americans. We were expected to act as role models for youngsters back home. A separation from them would have been a betrayal. A broken promise. Pocketing the educational loot, refusing to share.

Vete, pero no me olvides . . .

In Tijuana, I saw graffiti on a wall near the border. It was a directive for those who left behind family, friends, and famil-iarity in search of something better. It was a pathetic plea from Mother. *Go, but do not forget me . . .* Please. On the border, Mother was Mexico. In the Ivy League, Mother was memory. And in my culture, one does not disappoint *mamá*. "Don't for-get where you come from," an uncle admonished me when I left for Harvard. I *had* to remember, I told myself. To forget was to sin against culture.

But I was forgetting. I could not remember the warmth of the San Joaquin Valley sun. I referred casually, ungratefully, to

Cambridge as home. Even the birthdays of family members got lost in my daily planner, buried underneath scribbles about the due dates of papers and RAZA meetings.

Especially disturbing was that though time was suspended for me at Harvard, back home, time moved on. Friends got engaged, got married, got divorced. I was helplessly vulnerable to change. During my junior year, my father, I later learned, had suffered a minor stroke. His face was a chilling contortion. My parents graciously hid the news from me. "We didn't want you to worry. . ." They were afraid that the news would interfere with my studies. But of what importance is a final exam under such circumstances? My eighty-year-old grandmother slowed her daily routine, ran fewer errands to town, stayed home more often. For a time, she confessed to me a morbid resignation to dying. She confessed this to me, of course, through the sterility of a telephone wire.

I could not condone Joe Razo's criminal actions, but I did not repudiate what seemed to me to be his admirable intention of staying connected somehow with the familiarity of home, of straddling two opposing worlds. I was beginning to see his robberies as a cynical way of disproving the old adage, of trying to go home again. *Harvard Homeboy.* The concept was ludicrous and liberating all at once. I rationalized that the failure of Razo's endeavor lay with the individual. He was weak. The mission could have been accomplished by someone stronger.

It could be done, I sensed, this simultaneous touching of two extremes. It seemed a sociological experiment. It dared to be tried again. Razo had walked a tightrope between two worlds; he had fallen. But the tightrope could be walked, I sensed. It just required someone with a better sense of balance. It required not negative energy selfishly directed inward for personal profit, but positive energy selflessly directed outward for the benefit of others. The effort was bold, perhaps even dangerous. Joe Razo had it backwards, I was sure. It had to begin not with the transplanting of culture from California to Harvard, let alone in the form of trivial trinkets, but with the introduction of Harvard's culture into California. There, not here. Airfare, yes, one would need airfare. Above all, the effort needed sincerity, needed to be rooted not in robbery but in reconciliation. Yes, I resolved. Arrogantly. Foolishly. Yes, I could do it.

As my junior year came to an end, the surest motivation for me to actually carry out my ambitious plan was for someone, anyone, to tell me that it could not be done. After all, my ego devoured challenges. *There has never been a Mexican-American graduate of this high school who attended Harvard . . .*

Then, one day that spring, I stumbled upon the challenge. Its herald was a book on a shelf at the Harvard Coop. Two hundred pages whose very premise was concession. It represented a sustained assertion that Mexican-American students at elite, predominantly white academic institutions could not expect to maintain what might loosely be termed "culture." They should not expect to keep their intimate ties to their families or to the world that they had left behind. The inference was that to try was sheer folly. This was the cost of going to school with Kennedys, the melting-pot price of the American Dream. The book's argument was familiar. Its author was the same person who had penned the provocative editorial on Joe Razo.

His name was Richard Rodriguez. He pronounces it without accent. *Rich-heard Road-ree-guess*. The book was *Hunger of Memory*, what the author himself described in its introduction as an assortment of "essays impersonating an autobiography."

There are those occurrences, seemingly unremarkable at first, that simply change the course of your life. There are people you meet, jobs you take, friends you make, love you find and lose and find again. There are even instances when a single piece of literature might affect your life's course so profoundly that it ceases to be merely rows of words on paper but becomes a beacon of sorts. A living, breathing entity that whispers to you from your bookshelf. You dare not put it down, anticipating each sentence before you read it. A classic, not to be read too quickly but to be savored in a gradual digestion. And so it is that two hundred pages of print—lone among the multitude of bound paper that I read and recited and forgot in four years at Harvard—changed the course of my life. Changed it, unforgivingly, at the precise moment when it seemed most structured and surely destined for great things.

Richard Rodriguez knows firsthand the solitary experience of straddling opposing worlds and feeling at ease in neither. A product of parochial school and elite universities, he describes his childhood as one of "intense family closeness." At the beginning of his education, he was close to his family and particularly loyal to his parents. Family members addressed each other warmly in Spanish. They laughed at dinner. With his parochial teachers' insistence that he stop speaking Spanish at home (the nuns believed that juggling two languages was hampering the boy's progress) he unwittingly underwent what he considered a gradual, yet definite emotional and intellectual separation from his less-educated parents. The family no longer laughed at dinner. Rodriguez submitted that familial intimacy had been sacrificed to an elite education. Further, in the part of his argument that I was most unwilling to accept, Rodriguez concluded that such intimacy was *necessarily* sacrificed. Education was not really the culprit in the drama, but the savior in it.

I was not content to merely repudiate the author's theory; I felt somehow compelled to go further, to repudiate the individual as well. I held trial in my own conscience. The charge: an unspeakable sin. A public sin. Rodriguez had exploited his God-given gift as a writer of beautiful words by being publicly contemptuous of his parents, his past, his culture, and his people. The evidence: He had, in *Hunger of Memory,* not only professed intellectual alienation from his parents which I considered disrespectful and ungrateful, he had also openly questioned the legitimacy of government practices such as bilingual education and affirmative action, each of which was considered sacred to Mexican-Americans concerned with educational progress. It took me only minutes to pass judgment: Guilty. He had not shared cake. He had turned against his own.

And for what? A spot on a bestseller list? I considered Rodriguez an opportunist who was willing to barter "memory" for money and success. In my mind, he was nothing less than a sellout. And Latinos know well the concept of selling out, reserving a special place for it in our collective hearts. A dark, foul, ugly place.

My friends in RAZA would have considered a sellout to be someone who sacrifices his own cultural identity for some degree of success. In Spanish, the word for such a person is considered an insult, one of particular bite. Even among the angriest of Chicano activists, it is used sparingly and rarely in mixed company. It is a private accusation to which there is no real response. We say it with scorn: *vendido*.

There are other, more colorful euphemisms used to express much the same sentiment. *Un Tío Taco*, a Mexican variation of the character of Uncle Tom in Harriett Beecher Stowe's classic. *Una mosca en leche* (a fly in milk), referring to a dark object trying to blend into lighter, foreign surroundings. And a time-honored favorite, coconut; you know, brown on the outside...

I knew those words. In fact, I knew everything—such a fortune to be bestowed on a young man of twenty. I hated Rodriguez. I hated him without knowing him. In my own ignorance and defensiveness, I had mentally tried and convicted a complete stranger of serious cultural sins. One other thing: I had done so before reading a single word of his book.

After reading the book, finally, I felt conflicted. I riddled its margins with schizophrenic scribbles. *Great! S.O.B.! Great!* I reluctantly recognized in Rodriguez's brilliant prose the uneasy solitude that I myself had experienced during my brief visits home from Harvard. There *had* been silence. There was apprehension. What could I tell my parents of my college experience? Would they understand the significance of my travels, of the exciting new thoughts that crowded my head like cars in a parking lot? Would they be overly concerned with my encounters with sex, love, alcohol, hope, fear, loneliness? What would they make of the rapid changes that I had undergone? They seemed eager for me to share with them news of my schoolwork as if to check the return on their financial and emotional investment. But what would they really understand of my lessons? What had they been taught in state and community college of Plato or Locke or the historical complexities of the Civil War?

Rodriguez wrote that, as a college student, he noticed upon returning home a loud quiet at the family dinner table accentuated by the "tinkle of iced tea." For me, the tinkle was grimly familiar. During vacations, Silence sat at our family's dinner table like an unwelcomed guest. He sat next to the Harvard guy, threatening to intercede in the discourse. In truth, I felt that I was being educated so much, so fast, that other family members would never catch up. What a disrespectful thought!

I felt guilty for my modest enlightenment, which only seemed to worsen my alienation from home. In that sense, I was heartened by the emergence from lines of print of an indication that my feelings, though ungrateful, were not unique.

Also, although I was angered by what I perceived to be Rodriguez's disrespect for his parents, his distaste for his heritage, his abandonment of culture, and his shirking of responsibility for his people, I was nonetheless inspired by the author's courage in saying such things out loud. In Mexican culture, as in others, disturbing childhood or adolescent memories are usually kept to oneself, seldom shared. You will not find the Latina incest survivor describing her ordeal on "Oprah." Never written about. Rodriguez's own mother had said as much in a letter to her son after he published his first autobiographical essay. In the book's final chapter, he shamelessly recalls her concern over the telling of family secrets. "Why do you have to tell the *gringos* about our lives . . . ?" she had written. The dutiful son, I savored the tempting impulse of another son's irreverence. It seemed liberating, somehow. It was a sure way to throw off the weight of a parent's proud expectations. But I was embarrassed to admit the allure. I was embarrassed to admit that the book's last chapter was fast becoming my favorite.

Rodriguez was a teller of secrets but his betrayal, if it might be termed that, was not limited to his parents. Several of the book's chapters, including those dealing with the long-standing cultural insecurity of many Mexican-Americans about lighter and darker skin color, seemed to publicly air the dirty laundry of an entire race of people.

After the highly successful publication of *Hunger of Memory* and with the subsequent publication, during the 1980s, of several dozen articles and numerous public appearances, Richard Rodriguez assumed a more pronounced "public self"—his words. I would hear his name come up over dinner in a New York restaurant, in a bar in Houston, or from friends in Los Angeles.

Rodriguez has been called by some, "the greatest Hispanic thinker of our time." It is, I would learn, a distinction that the author resists and, at times, even resents. He is a writer, he would say. Someone who makes his living in quiet through the seductive power of words. Not a great *Hispanic* thinker or a great *Latino* thinker. But simply a great thinker. The way that Supreme Court Justice Sandra Day O'Connor need not be distinguished from her colleagues as a great *female* legal scholar.

I remember a piece that he did for *Time*, in which Rodriguez devoted a thousand cumbersome words to the idea that as Latinos grow in number, we will become so diverse that conventional notions of culture will no longer do. He urged a wider consciousness and the discarding of labels that restrict the complexity of the human experience. It must have been with a mixture of amusement and frustration then, that he noticed the editor's subscript on the article: "Richard Rodriguez is an expert on Hispanic affairs."

Such distinctions did not befall the writer by accident. They were, in fact, courted by him. His early work was exclusively about Hispanic themes or Latino issues or Mexican-American culture. He wrote about affirmative action, bilingual education, immigration, farm workers, and Mexico. One article was about Catholicism in Latin America, another about the Mexican bandit Joaquin Murrieta, and still another about the Mexican-American middle class in the United States. If he was not simply "a Hispanic thinker," he was, at least, a thinker of Hispanic issues.

And yet even then, he was also much more than that. Reluctantly, in my dismissal of his thesis, I recognized Rodriguez as a brilliant and prolific writer. His words were chosen carefully. They were at once graceful and powerful. They dripped from the pages of national magazines and newspapers like honey.

Still, some think the honey sour. Rodriguez has critics of all races, to be sure. Yet with regard to Latinos and particularly Mexican-Americans, the venom of censure for the writer has always seemed especially bitter. He assumed a distinct infamy within various quadrants of the Latino community. Often, in the 1980s, the reaction to the author's work, among Latinos, was one of distaste, disappointment, even disgust.

Without exception, the harshest comments about Rodriguez came from what might be termed the Latino elite. These critics were his contemporaries, his former classmates in the pristine academies of the late 1960s and early 1970s. Some of them had received their doctorates by virtue of the same programs that the author had criticized in his book. They had become college professors; many taught Chicano studies on campuses in the Southwest. They were a close-knit group of Latino educators. When they somehow crossed my path, perhaps as speakers at a Harvard forum, they were not pleased by my growing interest in someone whom they considered a blasphemous demagogue.

One professor from Berkeley, a friend there told me, had cited Rodriguez to his students as a prime example of what they should not become. A professor from Texas concerned with the advancement of Latino students was particularly scornful of Rodriguez's work; when I told him that I thought that Rodriguez was not completely wrong, he responded to my comment by telling me that if I considered Rodriguez to be any sort of expert on education, then I had "fucked up already." Another professor claimed that Rodriguez "hated himself." Another professor said in a condescending tone that she felt "sorry" for the author. In a speech to a roomful of Latino college faculty and administrators, a Chicano president of a university reversed that sentiment, claiming sympathy for Rodriguez's parents, who, he presumed, had been scarred by their son's reprehensible admissions. Still another professor had refused to bring Rodriguez to her campus because, she told me, her Chicano students were "screwed up enough [about identity]." This odd assortment of Latino professors was not used to agreeing on matters of controversy. Yet in their shared contempt for a certain Latino writer, there was an amazing consensus.

These critics represented the first generation of what Professor Stephen L. Carter of Yale Law School termed, "affirmative action babies." Their mother was a foster mother really, assigned to them reluctantly by a social agency named the Johnson Administration. Her name was affirmative action. I was, of course, also an affirmative action baby. The difference, one defined by generation, was that, if I was conceived in controversy, my older brothers had been conceived, fifteen years earlier, in complaint and concession. Their experience had been more traumatic. And because trauma breeds intimacy, my older brothers were closer to our mother than I was. They worshipped her. They ignored her imperfections. They did not notice the blemishes on her face or the thinning of hair. They forgave her wrinkles and scars. All because they felt that they owed a debt to her that they could never repay. Oh, how they loved her! She was

Mother. She was to be nurtured and to be protected from criticism.

One day, a horrible son, a disrespectful bastard of a son, showed contempt for Mother. He accused her of playing favorites in the children that she adopted and took under her care. He accused her of skimming the cream, helping only those who did not need help, of passing over the handicapped and the ill-educated, and of nourishing only the well-fed. Worse, he accused her in public. Worse still, in print. Mother's other sons were more behaved, more loyal, more trustworthy with family secrets. They had grown up and made Mother proud. They had become lawyers, doctors, politicians, and college professors of Chicano studies. They heard their mother scream from the bastard's assault and came to her defense. They attacked her attacker; they savaged their renegade brother and tried to destroy him. They denied his charges. They spoke out against him and labeled him disloyal. They tried to get him committed to an insane asylum. They tried desperately to validate their own existence by discrediting his. Most of all, they instructed younger brothers to ignore his tantrum and the embarrassment that it had caused the family.

A baby in my crib, I heard the warning and heeded it. I would not listen to my crazy, bastard brother. One day, though, I heard his whimper as he sat crying—alone, an exile from our home. I approached, lured by his defiance. I was much too curious, much too intrigued to pass up a conversation with this exile of my blood.

Richard Rodriguez and I first met in San Francisco in May 1988. It was a week after my last final of junior year and my abrupt departure from Cambridge. It was a month after Harvard had granted me a leave of absence for the coming school year. Rodriguez had received a letter from me, inviting him to Harvard to speak at the Sun Children Conference the month before. He had declined, citing a trip out of the country. A lie.

His real reason for refusing the offer, he told me later, was a suspicion that he would be subjected to a tirade of personal, perhaps insulting accusations at the hands of an elite bunch of arrogant Ivy League Chicanos who, in the presumption of youth, had settled all questions of their own ethnic identity and were now eager to help a middle-aged man with his.

So, Mr. Row-drrree-guess, why do you hate your parents?

The author's suspicion was, I think, a good one. Arrogant and presumptuous, I had intended to strike the first blow myself. In any case, even in his refusal, he had been good enough to invite me to lunch and conversation in my favorite city. I had accepted. I left the Valley at around eight-thirty; three hours later, I was in San Francisco. I arrived at the address on his letterhead, a Victorian-style apartment building. I pushed a doorbell, marked humbly with masking tape. *R. Rodriguez.*

A few seconds later, the door opened and a Mexican man stood before me. He had dark skin and a handsome face. He was a stranger. No, an old friend. I recognized the face, a younger version of it anyway, from the cover of a paperback book that I had worn out with bent pages and scribbles of red ink. He smiled. A broad, kind smile. He put out his hand and introduced himself to me. Introduced? I needed no introduction. His autobiography had, for months, been my bible. I knew about his childhood, his adolescence, his college years as if they were my own. I probably knew what he had eaten for breakfast. He seemed smaller in person, though. He invited me inside.

I recall that there was something odd, perhaps even unsettling, about my first few minutes with this man who I then revered and despised all at once. As excited as I was to be meeting him, he seemed just as interested in hearing about me, about my life, about my family, and the pressures of identity that he assumed had brought me to the doorstep of that Victorian building. Before long the journalist in him interrupted the innocence of our meeting with questions. With questions of my own, I reluctantly found the roles of interviewer and interviewed reversed.

"There's so much that I want to ask you," he said as he reached for his London Fog. He motioned to lead the way back outside. "But first, what should we eat?"

I explained to him that after nine months of a culturally sterile New England environment in which one was expected to stomach the culinary atrocities of *arroz con pollo* served separately and tortillas in a can, that I was looking forward to "real Mexican food." I suggested the Mission District.

"Are you kidding?" he said. "What I mean is . . . well, the Mission's fine, but we can have anything you want."

I understand Rodriguez's surprise at my request much better now than I did then. There must be a hundred nationalities represented on various menus across San Francisco. Two well-educated Mexican-American men should have felt comfortable eating Thai or Russian. One did, seeing it as an entitlement of his sophistication. The other did not want to spark a complicated debate about entitlement; he only wanted real Mexican food. Finally, the author relented. We soon found ourselves at a quaint, Mexican restaurant where the Mexican customers already seated seemed not to care in the least about the odd discussion that led us there.

After less substantive pleasantries, I explained to Rodriguez that, though I agreed with many of his observations in *Hunger of Memory* and applauded his courage for writing such things, I felt that the book's central premise was incorrect. I told him that I was not willing to concede that a well-educated Mexican-American necessarily had to endure an emotional and intellectual separation from his or her parents, family, culture, and heritage. I submitted that, the tragedy of Joe Razo notwithstanding, the metaphor of two separate, opposing worlds was not a liability, but an attribute. The worlds could be straddled effectively, I argued, if the bridges were built under the right circumstances. Finally I concluded that for my generation of highly educated Latinos to concede a paralyzing detachment from the lives we once lived was to undermine the educational and social progress of all Latinos.

After all, had we not been taken like babies stolen in the night from the warmth and security of our cribs in the neighborhoods of the Southwest and placed at the doorstep of remote places like Harvard, Yale, and Princeton all for the benefit of not only ourselves, but of others as well? Were we not role models for an entire race of people? Were we not expected to share our success with strangers? And how might we do that, I asked, if we all made the Richard Rodriguez concession of separation?

I went on to describe my plan. This bizarre experiment that I had been slowly mapping out in my head for weeks. I would use my leave of absence from Harvard to return to the San Joaquin Valley, to Sanger, for one school year. I would live at home with my parents and my two teenage siblings; that was essential. Anyway, how difficult could that be? I would enroll in the fall as a visiting student at California State University, Fresno, where I would take a full load of courses in Chicano-Latino Studies. I would study the history, culture, and character of the Mexican-American people, all of which I knew almost nothing about. I would reintroduce myself to the San Joaquin Valley, in all its complexities. I would study the scars on its face, drink its water, eat its food, date its young women. All to capture and hold in the palm of my hand, if only for a moment, the soul of this place called home. I was not entirely sure what I would find, and that was, after all, precisely why I felt compelled to return.

The author listened intently. He took a sip of his coffee, put down the cup, and smiled again. "So," he said with a hint of skepticism. "You are, in essence, trying to show me up . . . to prove me wrong."

I smiled back and nodded.

He said nothing. He paid the bill and we left the restaurant. Outside, as we walked along the street, he spoke suddenly as if to answer a question posed hours before.

"Good luck," he said. "I hope you succeed. Be warned, though. It may not be as easy as you think to 'go home again.' There may be moments, lonely, horrible moments, when you do not recognize your surroundings as being the same ones that you left behind. You may not like what you find . . ."

I stopped and looked at him. Our meeting over, we shook hands and promised to stay in touch. Even with our differences, informality took hold.

Good-bye, Richard.

Good-bye, Ruben.

Later, on the drive home, I realized with some amazement that I had not met the monster that I had expected. Not a bastard or a devil. Not a sellout or a traitor. Simply a man, defying the expectations of others and boldly putting forth his own definition of self. And couldn't the same be said of me?

In addition to disputing Rodriguez's thesis of concession through separation, there was another more practical reason for me to carry out my journey home. It revolved, oddly enough, around the excitement of something as simple as taking Chicano studies courses at the state college. How I looked forward to sampling a curriculum based on the history and culture of my own people. A rare delicacy. Sadly, although I was rapidly approaching the threshold of my graduation from perhaps the finest institution in the country, I had, at the time, only a remedial knowledge of anything derived from Mexican-American studies. These were the sorts of courses that a $20,000 annual tuition at Harvard had not been able to provide me. Had not provided because Harvard did not want to provide it. There was no Chicano studies at Harvard; the incongruity of the mere phrase was enough to make Chicano students there laugh irreverently. *Chicano studies at Harvard?*

Twenty years of complaint, petition, and protest for a college curriculum that reflected the ethnic diversity of the United States had largely fallen on deaf ears. Only modest concessions had been made and those for more vocal groups. After a band of students seized University Hall in the 1970s, administrators conceded a handful of courses in African-American studies. Still, the Afro-American Studies Department, several of my black friends were quick to point out, was like a sick child wheezing in the night. It was poorly funded, housed in an old wooden building away from campus, and staffed by only a sprinkling of professors, each of whom had to fulfill the odd requirement of holding an appointment in other, more credible departments like English or Government. Such a grand concession for the dramatic seizing of a building.

Meanwhile, women students were celebrating the end of a long struggle to get the University to create a Women's studies department. It had come in spite of defiant letters to the *Crimson* by tenured white male professors who opposed the action. Opposed it perhaps because they opposed the sharing of prestige with their female colleagues. Opposed it perhaps because they were opposed to change in any form. Or because, in the spirit of Harvard pretension, they believed that their curriculum had been bestowed on the institution from God and that it was above passing fads like progress.

I was glad for my African-American and women friends. Their battles for diverse curriculum had been hard-fought;

their victories were well-deserved. They had been given a degree of academic respect. It was a historical acknowledgment, for instance, that the lives of Harriet Tubman, A. Phillip Randolph, and Malcolm X mattered somehow. It was a concession that the achievements of Susan B. Anthony and Margaret Sanger mattered somehow. Magically, academic respect filtered down to students as *individual* respect. Harvard was saying that these historical figures were worthy of respect, so students could assume that they, too, were worthy. It may have validated, for African-Americans and women, their presence on campus to see themselves in the curriculum or on the faculty. Harvard became somewhat less foreign and somewhat less frightening.

But for Mexican-Americans on campus, the curricular neglect was constant and unchanging. There was no academic or individual respect. Harvard was still foreign, still frightening. We did not matter.

Usually when our issues were brought to the forefront of class discussion, the initiative had been our own. For instance, we routinely did term papers on Latino subject matter. This was, of course, no small effort given the scarcity of primary material related to such things in Widener library. A library system comprising ten million books could manage only thirty or forty titles related to the experiences of Mexican-Americans. We did our class papers on farm workers, welfare reform, Latino politics, and other related topics.

So I recognized that if I wanted to drag Harvard kicking and screaming into the twentieth century, then my options were few. I could not organize enough Chicano students to seize a building and I did not have ten years to wait for some Harvard concession that might never come or mean very little when it did. There was urgency. It burned in my gut. I honestly believed that, in three years of study, Harvard had possibly done more harm than good to my sense of history with its idiotic philosophy that it was better to learn less than more.

One example. In my sophomore year, a liberal white professor had been gracious in his analysis of a paper that I had written on Mexican-American social bandits in the nineteenth century. "Superbly written and researched. Well done," read the comment written in blue ink. The grade brought relief: *A*. "Just one thing," the professor had written. "The paper may have been even stronger had you omitted your reference to the legendary California bandit, Joaquin Murrieta. You know, of course, that legend is all that he is, that Murrieta never really existed . . ." I knew no such thing. I had read in books and learned from numerous accounts that Joaquin Murrieta, who won fame among Mexicans for opposing the nineteenth century Anglo occupation of California, did in fact exist. Always among Western historians like Leonard Pitt the question was only of the character of Murrieta: Was he a mere bandit or a righteous avenger of the injustices inflicted upon his people in the 1860s? Throughout the Southwest, Murrieta's existence was never in question. At Harvard, it was.

Furthermore, there was no real progress anticipated in bringing Chicano studies to campus. In a meeting with the chairman of the history department, I voiced my concern. There were, I explained to the ancient man before me, incidents in American history that had occurred in the Southwest since the Mexican War that I had, in his department, been taught nothing about.

In listening to my friends from schools like Berkeley describe taking courses in Chicano studies departments with full listings and with full faculties, I was quite jealous. More ironic was that I had myself, years earlier, turned down admission to Berkeley. I was searching for something better. What I had found was only something whiter.

I had half a mind, I told the chairman, to storm down to the term bill office and demand a refund. The old man listened quietly, maybe formulating a grocery list in his head. When I had finished, he urged patience. He explained that he planned to study the question further. Study it with no real urgency, I expected. Perhaps, he said, they could offer something uniting many groups. Hispanic History. Yes, how did that sound? It would take time to put it together, of course. Say, four or five years. I let out a sigh. I forced an insincere smile. I thanked him for his valuable time, this despite the fact that I considered my time to be just as valuable as his. I left his office.

Harvard was, at least, consistent in its approach to race.

Whether the issue of the day was Chicano faculty or African-American studies or an Asian-American cultural center, one could almost hear the ghost of John Harvard whisper in the ears of timid administrators:

Ignore it. Ignore it and it will go away . . .

I would have been willing to attribute such suspicion to my own cynicism had it not been for an illuminating discussion that I had initiated in my sophomore year with the chairman of the sociology department. I frankly explained to him my belief that Harvard was consciously shirking what I considered to be its responsibility to provide support systems for minority students, including studies programs and faculty role models. I submitted that administrators were intent on ignoring racial differences in the student body rather than dealing with their consequences. Finally, I wondered why those administrators had resisted the racial reforms of sister schools like Princeton, Brown, and Yale, and why they seemed determined to treat minority students no differently than white students.

The chairman, himself a white male, listened politely to my ramblings. He smiled occasionally, nodding his head. When I finished, he responded. His words told me that he was satisfied with my observations. It was as if I had just deciphered some great three hundred and fifty-year-old riddle. I expected bells to go off and confetti to fall from the ceiling in his office. A beautiful woman would storm in, smiling, and tell me that I had just won the grand prize: transfer to a college with an environment that was culture friendly.

Instead, the chairman agreed with my assessment of Harvard's reluctance to address the challenges of racial difference. Among the reasons that he cited for such timidity was a recent history of having dealt with the issue rather ineptly. In the 1970s, Harvard had experienced its share of campus chaos involving race. There were demonstrations and protests and disruption. Poetically, the powers of Harvard—the president, the various deans, and tenured faculty—found themselves in the embarrassing position of being engulfed by a concept, the complexities of which they knew very little about. Think of it. The American intellectual elite, boasting a multitude of degrees from Harvard, Oxford, and other premier academic institutions, were shamed by their complete lack of knowledge about what Jefferson called "the American dilemma."

Students were demanding to be taught about not just the Mayflower but also Malcolm X. They wanted instruction not just in the significance of Julius Caesar but also in that of Cesar Chavez. As an institution ruled almost exclusively by white males, Harvard found itself embarrassingly ill-equipped to provide the kind of education that was suddenly being asked of it. Ironically, it was likely that, from personal experience, an elderly black grandfather in Birmingham knew more about Martin Luther King, Jr., or the rift between the Southern Christian Leadership Conference and the Student Non-Violent Coordinating Committee, than did a high-priced, well-educated white professor in Cambridge. Likewise, there were Mexican-American children in the Southwest who had been taught more in elementary school about the Treaty of Guadalupe Hidalgo which ended the Mexican War than I had been taught about the subject in three years of studying American history at Harvard. Futhermore, as members of a racial minority group, it could be argued, persuasively I think, that the black grandfather and the Mexican children were more emotionally involved in discussions of race and racial oppression than those who belonged to the dominant racial group.

As such, with the beginning of the clamor for racial adjustments at Harvard, a largely white ruling body was pressed to admit its own intellectual deficiencies. That would have required humility, the loud acknowledgment in academic circles that "the best and the brightest" did not know everything. Humility being in short supply at a place like Harvard, it was easier to ignore the clamor for adjustment, ignore race altogether in fact, and treat nonwhite students and faculty as if they were white. Some might have considered this approach to be admirable. Not me. Given the fact that minority faculty had been hired and minority students recruited in full recognition of racial difference, I viewed Harvard's racial change of heart once we arrived on campus not as admirable, but rather as irresponsible, dishonest, and hypocritical.

And so, at the end of my junior year with graduation clearly in sight, I left.

I fled to California like an old prospector searching for shiny trinkets in a tin pan. On the day that I left Cambridge for Logan, the May air was still cold. Against my skin, it felt unyielding and uncaring. As I departed, as it had been when I had arrived years earlier, Harvard hardly noticed.

CHAPTER 8

BRIDGES

I was not frightened by Richard Rodriguez's warning about "not liking what I find." Nor was I especially concerned about the possibility that I might somehow follow in Joe Razo's troubled footsteps. Yet, there *was* some degree of fear surrounding my mission. The idea of going home for a year, like the idea of first leaving home for Harvard years earlier, was at once exhilarating and frightening. I had heeded Emerson's sadistic advice, to continually seek growth by doing exactly what you were most afraid to do. At that point in time, just eight courses away from a Harvard diploma, what I was most afraid of was going home, not for a few days but for several months. The idea was to live with my family again, as if to flirt with the life I once led. I was afraid of not being able to bridge the chasm. I was afraid of feeling out of place among loved ones and old friends. I was afraid of being alone in a sea of familiarity.

The experiment had been baptized in fear. Months earlier, what I had been most afraid of was telling my parents my plan. I knew at least two things. First, they would likely not understand abstract platitudes about disproving the theory of a Mexican-American writer who had been, until recently, a complete stranger to me. They would only appreciate a more practical motivation for my endeavor; there had to be something that a year in Sanger could provide me that a year at Harvard could not. Second, regardless of the stated pretense for my return, I sensed that the gesture would cause my parents immeasurable worry. They would worry that my brief leave of absence was really an excuse for me to then leave Harvard altogether and never return. They would worry that there was something about my three years in college, something terrible, that they knew nothing about. There was, of course.

Most of all, I sensed that they would worry that I was being reckless with a precious opportunity. *Our* opportunity. In many ways, my Harvard education meant more to my parents than it did to me. For one thing, they had more invested in it, including not only money but a personal history of denial, discrimination, and deferred dreams. As *la escuela de los Kennedys,* Harvard represented a whole world to which they had been denied access years earlier.

Through hard work, perseverence, and sacrifice, my parents were able to overcome the obstacles of poverty, racism, and low expectation of Mexican-Americans in the public schools of Texas and California. Eventually, they would assume the sort of jobs that were, in the years before the civil rights movement, considered unattainable to many of their race.

My father's twenty-five-year career as a law enforcement officer is without doubt his life's proudest achievement. He savors it all the more because it is an accomplishment rescued from the ashes of discouragement. As boy in the 1940s, he startled my grandfather one day by announcing that he wanted to be a policeman. He had stumbled upon a book with a picture in it of a kind policeman helping a boy and girl remove their cat from a tree. The image captivated him. He was intrigued by a profession based on helping people. After his son had explained his career goal, the old man shook his head, perhaps in deference to the fatalistic traditions of Mexico. He told the boy, in solemn Spanish, that he would never be afforded such an opportunity. Given what he knew of American society in the 1940s. After leaving Chihuahua for the American Southwest, my grandfather had learned firsthand about discrimination and economic exploitation. He had been taught most clearly the American ethic of limited possibility. He had learned that there were certain professions, usually those of prestige and good wages, that were simply off-limits to *mexicanos*. Had my father told him that he wanted to be a picker of cotton, a warehouse supervisor, or a truck driver, he might have given his blessing, thinking such opportunities possible. But a policeman?

My grandfather considered such a prestigious profession nothing less than a beautiful girl, elusive to the touch. People of darker complexion never dared court this blond-haired, blue-eyed angel. Pursuing her would only bring eventual disappointment and a broken heart.

Although he valued nothing as much as my grandfather's opinion, my father was not completely discouraged. After a tortuous time in the public schools of Sanger Unified in which teachers ruthlessly reinforced the idea of limited expectation, fate intervened. A two-year stint in the army gave my father the discipline and focus that had eluded him for so long. The young man who, throughout his life, had been taught by authority figures that for Mexican-Americans and other racial minorities, life's choices were limited, learned a new democracy. Suddenly, there was no color, only rank. White, black, brown, and yellow soldiers were lumped together in collective contempt without preference for any particular group. After his discharge, my father went back to college, taking night courses while working during the day. Later, a flurry of written and oral exams and a blur of faces. *Thank you, Mr. Navarrette. It was very nice chatting with you. We'll be in touch* . . . Diligently he progressed from the position of a police officer in our hometown to that of a police sergeant. The old scrapbook of newspaper clippings filled up. The den wall became crowded with citations. Old men waved hello to my father in restaurants, respectfully deferring to him as if he were mayor.

Finally, he accepted a hard-earned position with the local district attorney's office, where even in a county that was almost 40 percent Latino, he was one of only a handful of Mexican-American investigators. A maverick at the DA's office, he would leave home for work in the early morning. He would utilize instincts born of years of experience to complete huge volumes of cases. He would do so, however, in a brash and outspoken manner. He would walk into labor camps or economically depressed neighborhoods dressed in blue jeans, boots, and a cowboy hat. Invariably, he would find what he was searching for. Still, back at the office, he was an embarrassment to some. Those consumed with public image in a highly political position would have preferred him with a shorter haircut, dressed in a coat and tie, and with less chutzpah.

Some of the criticism was race-related. In one instance, the Mexican suspect in a high-profile case had fled home to Mexico. The DA's office needed the assistance of Mexican law enforcement agencies to locate and transport the fugitive. Anyone who knows anything about Mexico and its ugly history with the United States knows that such a request for assistance should resonate with respect and humility. A white supervisor with limited experience in dealing respectfully with Mexicans suggested that the request be more of a command. My father was somewhat skeptical that such an approach would work.

You give them an order and try to throw weight around down there, and they'll tell you to go fuck yourself. . .

Eventually, my father was able to use his own contacts in Mexico and an appreciation of his own Mexican culture to find the suspect. *"Gracias por la ayuda, Comandante. . ."* The supervisor who had suggested a firmer response, an approach not likely to have been considered had the country involved been Canada, stood rebuffed. On another occasion, the same supervisor went so far as to tell my father that he doubted that there was any hope for future advancement. He did so in a disrespectful and racially insensitive way, criticizing my father's ability to speak "good English." Lacking the acceptance of the "suits" in the office, he would progress no further. There would be no promotions. Younger people whom he trained would surpass him. Slowly, his energy and experience were stifled by a glass ceiling under which his supervisors kept those who did not fit their image of law enforcement officers in a new age. Before long, he seemed as tired leaving for work as returning from it.

No matter. Up until his death, my grandfather was noticeably proud of his youngest son's career achievements. The old man seemed especially to relish the sight of his son in uniform. He would leave our games of gin rummy to sit by the window and wait for my father to visit while out on patrol. He kept my father's picture on the shelf. He would brag to his old cronies at the public park about his son, *la policía.*

Still, several years after my grandfather's death, as my father contemplated retirement from an esteemed career that was never supposed to happen, he could privately concede the disappointment of limitation. The once-beautiful girl that he had courted for so long was no longer so beautiful. Furthermore, she was disloyal. She played favorites among her suitors. She would never be his completely.

A headline in the newspaper. An African-American police officer in southern California found in his locker, presumably left there by fellow officers, an unmistakable token of disrespect: a watermelon. A recruitment ad for the LAPD boasts: *Our cops only come in one color—Blue.* Near the end of his career, my father privately reflected on a quarter century of conflict, criticism, and commendation. Only then could he admit to his own son, and to himself, that while his profession may have claimed to notice only the color blue, it was in reality conscious of other colors as well. The boy once so intent on proving his father wrong might have done well to realize that in the old children's-book picture that first had set him on his life's mission, the kind policeman rescuing the cat from the tree was, of course, white. And so it was that, ultimately, the shake of my grandfather's head decades earlier had boasted prescience.

When my mother was a little girl living with her family in the poverty of South Texas, progress need not have meant a bigger house or nicer clothes. Instead, she would have been content with merely escaping the menial labor of agricultural fields and packing houses. Under such circumstances, office work of any kind was viewed as being as prestigious, and as elusive, as ascension to the presidency. After graduation from the local high school and two years of community college, my mother began a stint in state and county offices, and although her efforts were not likely to result in promotion, she had already, in avoiding a life of hard labor that ensnared so many of her contemporaries, accomplished a major goal for herself.

Despite the fact that she has worked through her adolescence and adult life, my mother has had no career, per se. Her lifetime of jobs was primarily a means of helping support her family and not a sustained effort to refine a craft or build a dossier. Although she entered the adult work force at the threshold of the women's liberation movement, she did not taste the fruit of social progress. She might even laugh at her son's use of the phrase, *women's lib*.

Like many Mexican-American women of her generation, my mother, in large part, lived her mother's life. She never lived alone or on her own, moving obediently from my grandfather's authority to that of my father's. She married under the impending fear of becoming an old maid at twenty-three. She understood early on that life meant labor and, with the boom of two-income families in the 1970s, never expected that her husband would be able to support the family without her help. Even so, she spent her marriage economically dependent on my father, who was always considered the household's chief breadwinner. Divorce would have meant economic devastation.

Through the years, nothing has been more important to her than her responsibilities to her three children. Without a doubt, my mother would consider her greatest domestic achievement the exhaustive balancing of efforts to care for her husband, raise three children, and maintain a household. In that last effort, she received little help from my father. As women her age went back to college and onto law school, she packed our lunches and drove us to school before leaving for work herself. As others organized political rallies and ran for office, she drove us to Cub Scout meetings, music lessons, and Little League games. As other women began a feverish effort to be considered just as good as men, her most pressing personal objective remained being a good wife and mother.

These days, she seems content with her choice. Although she would applaud the efforts of Mary, Queen of the Boardroom, she tells me that she does not feel left out of the women's revolution that defined her generation. Her satisfaction comes in the appreciative faces of her three greatest accomplishments.

On Easter Sunday of my junior year, after brunch, I finally braved the inevitable. I explained to my parents that I planned to take a leave from Harvard and return to the Valley. The reason? Several, I told them. I needed a break from a college education that was passing before me much too quickly. I wanted to rekindle what I considered to be a lost intimacy toward family and friends.

Finally there was, I told them, an academic motivation. I pathetically offered it up to my parents' concerned faces as an appeasement to practicality. I professed an interest in exploring a topic with a special significance to the San Joaquin Valley. I told them that I wanted to study the recent history of the United Farm Workers Union (UFW), the labor union that was founded twenty-five years earlier in the small town of Delano, just an hour's drive from my hometown. Upon returning to Harvard the following year, I could then incorporate my observations into a senior thesis in American history. My parents listened closely to all of this. They heard the part about my leaving school, but not much else. As expected, they expressed concern.

"What can you possibly learn in the Valley that you couldn't learn at a school like Harvard? Aren't you happy back there . . . ? Are you burned out? So, does this mean you're through with Harvard altogether? What will you do?"

I was smug in the reassurance that, at least, I knew my parents. I told them that no, I was not "burned out." I explained that "happy" had nothing to do with it. And I stressed that coming home, my private experiment, was just something I felt compelled to do. Finally I told them that I was prepared to do it with or without their approval.

Still, consistent with five hundred years of tradition, there I was, asking my Mexican parents for their ceremonial blessing for me to come home. Cautiously, they gave it. It was my choice, they said. They trusted my judgment, they said.

Later, I would learn that my mother was actually pleased by my news. With my being so far away, she had missed me incredibly in three years. As her firstborn, I shared a special bond with her. Once, when a neighbor asked about my progress at Harvard, she had suddenly broken down and started to cry.

My father had missed me also. But he had made a concession to prestige. He bragged relentlessly about my accomplishments to family, friends, and, on occasion, complete strangers. My mother would smile as my father launched into his prepared discourse of my accomplishments. "Oh yes, he loves Harvard. He's doing well there. He will be done soon. Then he'll probably go off to law school." With my announcement that I would be leaving the school—for good, he was certain—in which he had wrapped so much family pride, my father knew that he would have a good amount of explaining to do to co-workers and family members. There were those who, anxiously expecting my graduation from Harvard, would be concerned. *Is he going back?*

There were, I knew, others, perhaps parents with children my age, who resented my father's incessant boasting. They would speculate, privately, that the answer to my parents' frantic question was obvious. *No, he won't go back.* In their minds, I would not be returning to Harvard. I had failed. I was coming home whimpering, with my tail between my legs. Beaten. I should have known better. *La escuela de los Kennedys . . .* Who did I think I was anyway?

My father knew all this. A slave to public opinion, he had always been extremely concerned about what people thought or said. After brunch, he was mysteriously quiet for the rest of the afternoon and evening. At one point, without comment, he walked outside alone for a breath of fresh air. And for the reassurance of a familiar small town in which he had lived all his life.

The alarm clock sounds. I peek out from underneath the covers. My mind needs orientation. *Where am I?* It is late August. According to tradition, I should be packing my bags for the flight to Cambridge. I should be saying good-bye to friends, telling them that I will see them at Christmas. I should be picking up a dozen burritos at a local restaurant, wrapped for the trip and ready for distribution among culture-starved Chicano classmates at Cambridge.

But no. I am in my room, in my bed. In the bathroom, I hear the sound of my father shaving. I hear my mother in the kitchen, the crackle of something frying on the stove. I hear my brother's alarm clock blare. Then my sister's. They will be leaving for high school classes in an hour. It has been three years since I have experienced such things. It is exciting. It is frightening. There is still doubt. Have I done the right thing?

Breakfast cannot keep pace with us. We are scampering through different parts of the house, tending to morning repair. *Has anyone seen the hair dryer?* My father finishes his cup of coffee, wishes me luck with a pat on my head, and leaves for work. My brother does not have time for breakfast. He'll get something later, he says. My sister sits with me at the table nibbling toast and glancing occasionally at her watch.

"So," she asks. "What time is your first class?"

"Early," I respond. "About eight forty-five, I think. I'll be leaving soon."

At the time, eight forty-five is early for me. For three years at Harvard, I was careful to choose classes that began no earlier than eleven. Now as a visiting student at Fresno State, I find myself enrolled in four courses in Chicano studies, two of which begin, on separate days, before nine. This was not such a good idea, I tell myself.

There are other adjustments that I must make before assuming my role as a student at a state college. As one of only six thousand undergraduates at Harvard, I was fawned over by administrators and financial aid officers. Problems with course schedules or scholarship money could usually be settled by phone. At a state college brimming with over twenty thousand students, I would no longer have such luxury. I would stand in lines with hundreds of other students to pay fees, buy books, and, God forbid, reschedule courses. I would helplessly surrender my individuality to an onslaught of administrative red tape, assuming a registration number in place of my name.

In fact, just getting to class had suddenly become much more difficult. At Harvard, I flirted each morning with the ceremonial chimes of Memorial Church. I could, under the worst circumstances, wake up ten minutes before class, splash cold water on my face, put on a baseball cap, walk across the Yard balancing a cup of coffee, and still find myself in a hard wooden chair seconds before the professor stopped shuffling papers and began to speak. At my new school, I would not have as much latitude. I would have to drive thirty minutes from Sanger to Fresno, fight for parking, find the building cited on my class list, and assume an inconspicuous seat in the back of the room. The drive would be especially troublesome, even dangerous, in the winter months to come when the usual blanket of fog rolls into the country roads of the San Joaquin Valley. I knew that, by Christmas eve, I would be lucky to see twenty feet in front of my car's headlights.

On this autumn day, however, the images of rural life that seeped through my car window were much more generous. Images that basked in serenity. Images from the Steinbeck novels that I had been forced to read in high school. New, old images once so familiar that I had come to take them for granted and was only now appreciating. The thirty-minute drive to campus was along a series of country roads. Along the roadside, long rows of grapevines dangled peacefully and crews of farmworkers scurried up and down the rows like armies of ants. Somewhere along the way, an old woman sold peaches and nectarines from a wooden fruit stand that exuded humility. Cows grazed in an open field and orange trees swayed in the autumn wind. My new surroundings were so unlike those of the cities to which I had recently been accustomed. All of it so vast and so pure.

When I arrived on campus, I was struck immediately by familiarity. I had been here before, coming on field trips when I was in junior high school. In early adolescence, I assumed that when I was older I would go to Fresno State. I would do so, primarily because, for decades, that is what people who grew up in the San Joaquin Valley did. There was no other four-year college in the immediate area, and so, for those not confident enough to venture off to schools in bigger cities like Los Angeles or San Francisco, the state university in Fresno had a natural allure.

There is another, more personal reason why the campus was familiar to me. And it is another reason why, growing up, I had always imagined myself attending school there. It all comes back to me in a comforting wave of sentimentality. I was here, in these halls, as a child. There were those nights, fifteen years earlier, when I tagged along with my father to night school courses. Maybe my mother was working. Maybe, late for criminology class, he could not find a babysitter and decided to take me with him instead. Or maybe he simply wanted, even then, to expose a boy to the world of university cafeterias, bookstores, and professors in the hope that I would eventually assume my rightful place in such an environment. I sat in the back of dusty classrooms, surrounded by men and women old enough to be my parents. I colored and sketched drawings and mumbled quietly to myself. My father's plan worked. Many years later, as I entered high school, the only question left in my mind was not whether I would go to college, but which one I would eventually attend.

In an odd coincidence, I discovered in my first class a living remnant of my father's college experience, a Mexican-American professor who taught him when the department was called "La Raza Studies." Now the same professor stood before me, dressed humbly in slacks and an open-collar shirt. He wore no coat and no tie.

Remembering the professors that I had learned from in Cambridge, I savored the contrast. At Harvard, most of the professors seemed older than this one. As students there, we had instinctively deferred to what we assumed to be their superb qualifications. Arrogantly, we trusted Harvard's selectivity. After all, Harvard had chosen them, as it had us, from among the best in the country. Yet in their excellence, they seemed somehow unapproachable. As a freshman, I once stood outside the office door of one professor for twenty minutes trying to decide whether or not I should disturb his study with a knock. The round-faced man before me looked more like a *tío* from Texas who might drop by grandma's house on holidays than an academic with a Ph.D. Partly because of our shared ethnicity, the line between teacher and student—always distinct in the Harvard environment—discreetly faded away in warmth and informality.

I noticed even more glaring differences in the student bodies of the two schools. At Fresno State, the students appeared to be more at ease with one another, and with their surroundings, than I expected them to be. Like their counterparts at Harvard, they dressed in blue jeans and listened to rock music and drank and most likely experimented with sex. But unlike them, this group seemed not to take themselves, or their problems, too seriously. They joked about missing class and complained only mildly about the "B" that should have been an "A." Most did not live in dormitories, only parked their cars in the parking lot and visited there for a few hours each day. They viewed school as merely a job, and a part-time one at that. Perhaps that is why they were not *consumed* with the experience of going to college which, after all, is supposed to be fun. I had almost forgotten.

They were enjoying their youth. They were putting themselves through school. They were taking six and seven years to complete a four-year degree. They assumed, foolishly, that there were jobs waiting for them after graduation. They were avoiding growing up and the responsibility that comes with it. There was very little pressure to excel. There were no suicides.

The Mexican-American students, of which there were fifty times as many as there were at Harvard, embodied the most striking differences. They were unlike any that I have ever seen. Certainly, they were different than their counterparts in the Ivy League. Yet in many ways, their lives might be considered more normal than ours. They were all near my age, and yet the experiences of those years had been so much different than mine. I studied them.

In my first class, I met a young man in a baseball cap. He had driven from another small town, an hour and a half away, along solitary country roads. Although he lived at home with his parents, he financially supported his own education. He worked at two jobs, including one as a janitor. He struggled to find time to study during breaks. One day, when my father came to campus for lunch, the fellow joined us. In the ensuing conversation, it seemed to me that my father was looking in a mirror, conversing with a younger version of himself. Strangely, the young man's experience was more like that of my father's than had been mine, that of his own son. I considered that experience to be rough, jagged. Later, after meeting and talking with a few more people (Did they realize that I was more interested in studying them than the books in front of us?), I realized that I did not know the true meaning of words like rough and jagged.

I met a young woman who was six months pregnant. It was her second child. She was unmarried, had never been married. She was alone. A statistic. She went to school in the morning, so as to work a double-shift in the afternoon and evening. The week of our final, our professor told us the joyous news. She was not in class. She was sleeping in a hospital room after giving birth. A boy. But, she was still alone. She would make up the class next semester, he said.

I met a young man who told me that he did time in juvenile hall as a teenager. *No big deal . . .* He looked matured. Weathered. He had tattoos and a full mustache. His muscular arms bore a few scars. I thought I knew what they were; I did not ask. I recognized him as the caricature that Joe Razo sought to emulate. He was married. He had a daughter who had melted his heart. It was thoughts of her that brought him there each day. He was looking for something better, trusting that a college degree would mean a bigger paycheck and better Christmas presents for *mija*. Still, he struggled. He did not speak with my confidence. School had never been his thing, he said. His young eyes were sad, worried that *mija* would be disappointed at Christmas. So he tried harder.

I met a young woman who said that she dropped out of high school years earlier to have her son. Her husband worked construction. After class, she was supposed to pick up the boy at school and take him to her mother's house on her way to work. Near the end of the semester, she asked our professor for an extension on the paper that he had assigned. Her son was very sick. She was worried; neither she nor her husband had health insurance.

I met a young man who was thinking about graduate school. Was it true that I went to Harvard? *Yes.* I asked him if he was thinking of going there one day. He smiled nervously. He said nothing. I made a case for Harvard. *A nice place . . .* Still nothing. Finally, he sighed. He could never go to a place like Harvard, he said. He could never get in, he said. He could never afford it anyway, he said.

I sensed the presence of a familiar third party in our conversation. The cold spirit of *limited possibility.* An old adversary, I had not encountered it since high school in a small town that should have been named "Cannot, USA." The spirit laughed at me. *Fool! You wish to recruit into Harvard those who have barely graduated from high school? Why? To ease your conscience, perhaps?*

I turned away from the cold. But the young man had left, off to his next class and his next responsibility.

I was alone, left only with irony. I had been taught that I was worthy of respect. For twelve years, an educational system had labeled me "special." Harvard considered me special and, for three years, gave me the chance to walk in the footsteps of old heroes and speak at luncheons in honor of new ones. I had been allowed access to boardrooms in which I was the youngest person and banquet rooms where the only other Mexican in the room was placing slices of roast turkey onto my plate. All because I was *special*. A Latino honors student. A bright star in an educational black hole. Special, different, better.

I am free of the responsibilities that strangle my new classmates. I have no wife, no children. I am too arrogant to be constrained by racist limitation. I stare down the familiar spirit. And yet, I recognize the lives of my new classmates as being more "real" than mine. And suddenly, I do not feel so worthy of respect. Suddenly, I do not feel so special.

My professor congratulates me on the perfect score that I have managed on his most recent examination. *"Good work . . ."* Work? I studied for ten minutes before class. The woman with the construction worker husband and the sick child and no health insurance could only manage a high "C" on the same exam. She will have to try harder, the professor tells her. But just how hard should one be expected to try? I hide my blue book in my binder. This is all a joke, I tell myself. A sick, twisted, unfunny joke. Maybe I will stop at the mall on the way home. Maybe, I will buy a CD. Maybe not. What difference does it make, anyway?

There are others in the room, living lives filled with a bit less drama. They have come to this class in Chicano studies, not as my Chicano classmates in Cambridge might have, not for cultural nourishment or academic self-esteem. They have not come because they have protested and demanded it from the university. They have come only because the university now requires the completion of such a course for graduation. They were given a choice between a class in Chicano studies, African-American studies, or women's studies. A bold few have ventured into one of the two other fields. Those sitting next to me have chosen what they hope will be familiar subject matter.

Still, they are more concerned with their economics test this afternoon than with the origin of the word *mestizo*. They do not care about *El Grito de Dolores* or Joaquin Murietta or the GI

Forum. They look at me as if I am crazy when I mention *Aztlán*, the mythical homeland of Mexican-Americans. Going to college in the San Joaquin Valley and not in Boston, they have been allowed to take racial difference for granted. In fact, it is likely that, in three years in the Ivy League, I have thought more about ethnicity and race than they have in all the years of their lives. Two friends from elementary school who visited me in Cambridge in my sophomore year liked my friends in RAZA. Just one thing, they said. Such an intelligent group of Mexican-American young people; why do they seem so obsessed with race? At Fresno State, during a lecture about the Brown Berets, a Chicano student reads discreetly from an economics textbook in the back of the room.

Some have come to the classroom lured by curiosity to learn about the past of their parents and grandparents. It has not occurred to them to ask their elders directly. They are in a generational war with their parents, sure that those who worshipped Elvis have no wisdom to offer a more complicated generation. They respect their grandparents, but cannot communicate with them. Their bilingual parents are the family translators. My broken Spanish reminds me that I am part of a generation that hears our grandmother's questions in Spanish but answers them in English. *Our* language.

Near the end of my semester at Fresno State, I found myself suddenly restless. I ran away temporarily. I took spontaneous, irrational, plane trips back east to New York, to Washington, to Boston. My parents were more confused than ever. Had I lost my mind? Had I not come home for a reason? I went to an inaugural ball, to surround myself if only for a night with the familiar electricity of elitism, power, and prestige. I went to the Yale game, willing to suffer through frigid weather for a dose of collegiate nostalgia. I went to Pachanga, surrounding myself with Ivy League Chicanos and enduring annoying questions about how my thesis research was going.

My "research" was going nowhere, of course. I was too distracted with my new, old surroundings and too consumed with trying to find my proper place in them. Besides, if studying the recent history of the United Farm Workers Union was merely a pretense for my own more compelling personal mission, then it was one that was wearing thin. I had been in the Valley for four months. I had attended campus lectures on the UFW. I had discovered new books on the subject. I had spoken with farmworkers. I had tried to contact union headquarters several times to arrange interviews with union officials. I had told the person on the phone about my coming from Harvard and about my intention of doing a thesis on the contemporary work of the UFW. I had asked to interview its president, Cesar Chavez. I had been told, sternly, that Harvard thesis or not, Chavez did not give interviews, something I knew to be untrue. I had also been told that if Chavez would grant me an interview at all it would cost me a tidy sum. Five thousand dollars was the normal rate for his speaking engagements, she said. Of course, she added, if I wanted to donate my time to the UFW grape boycott, in terms of office work or the like, they would welcome my services. I politely declined, thanked the woman, and hung up. I had not traveled three thousand miles and endured the skepticism of family and friends in order to stuff envelopes, even for a legend.

I will admit that I was somewhat shocked by the reference to cold cash by an official of a union that had always successfully portrayed itself to white liberals as a symbol of impoverishment and humility. After all, farmworkers are, according to Department of Labor statistics, consistently among the poorest laborers in the country. One would naturally expect the leader of an organization founded to serve them to be poor also. There is a popular story, sometimes recited in history books about Cesar Chavez going to Robert Kennedy's funeral mass at St. Patrick's Cathedral. Chavez supposedly stood in the back of the hall, dressed simply in his characteristic blue jeans and plaid shirt. White liberals love imagining that scene. There is something immediately charming to many about a successful and influential Mexican-American who seems, at first glance, unchanged by his accomplishments and accolades. Those who have, for three decades, successfully marketed to white liberal supporters the image of a little, dark-skinned Mexican man in blue jeans with an outstretched hand have always known that humility is ultimately rewarded.

There is no faulting the historical accomplishments of the

United Farm Workers Union. Its efforts to bring dignity into the
agricultural fields of the United States are worthy of praise and
admiration. Collective bargaining protection, clean drinking
water and toilets in the fields, and the ban of the infamous
"short hoe" were all necessary reforms. Before leaving Harvard, I considered the stature of both the union and Chavez to
be above reproach. Somehow, I instinctively equated the union
symbol—a black eagle on a red backdrop—with social justice
for all Mexican-Americans.

On one occasion, something called the "Hispanic Hall of Fame"
was dedicated at a *tortillería* in Old Fresno. Curiosity took me
there. A number of esteemed Hispanic figures were enshrined,
including Cesar Chavez. Invited to the ceremonial banquet
marking the event, Chavez sent his apologies and his chair at the
head table stood alone in a crowded room. A woman at the front
door collected a hefty admission price. Prominent Hispanic businessmen sipped cocktails from crystal glasses at tables covered
in lace. Pledging loyal support for *La Causa*, Chicano studies professors from the university argued politics over prime rib. A
woman walked in buried in a fur coat. Outside, in the parking lot,
a pair of Mexican farmworkers peered through the dirty windows
of an old Chevy at the spectacle inside the building. Maybe they
had heard of the event on Spanish radio. Maybe they were curious, too. Their clothes were torn and filthy; one wore a baseball
cap. Fresh from the fields, I thought. They saw the ties, the nice
dresses, the burly security guard acting as gatekeeper. They did
not stop their car, even to get a closer look. Instead, they drove out
of the parking lot and onto more welcoming city streets. In the
building, there was a toast of champagne: "to the *campesino* [the
Mexican farmworker]."

Meanwhile, it seemed that the UFW grape boycott, a weapon
to assert power in the union's perpetual battle with the agricultural industry, was having an adverse effect on a variety of
people. A farmer told me that he would likely never recover
his crop losses. Uncertain that he would be able to sell his
grapes, he was forced to convert them into raisins; in turn, the
raisins contributed to an existing glut of dried fruit. He grew
up in my hometown, but he was considering giving up farming
altogether ("not worth the trouble . . .") and moving away

("maybe down south . . ."). An American farmer. UFW literature never uses the word *farmer*, opting instead for a more ominous term: *grower*. Hence the image conveyed was not of a family business born of early hours, hard work, and faithful devotion to the earth but instead of a selfish, expanding entity, devouring all in its path—growing. One more thing. The farmer who was considering leaving his life's work was himself Mexican. He had been born in Mexico and had worked as a field laborer since adolescence. He had saved money and borrowed money. He eventually bought ten acres of grapevines. Then, with two children in college, the UFW boycott threatened his livelihood by lowering the market value of his crop, particularly in eastern markets.

Ironically, the Mexican farmer was being squeezed out of his profession by an organization headed by a man who was recognized as a hero to Mexicans. There was no shortage of irony in the drama of *La Causa*. Union rhetoric suggested racial repression of Mexican workers by presumably white "growers." Yet the San Joaquin Valley farmers adversely affected by UFW tactics include a large number of individuals who are Armenian and Japanese-American, each group being quite familiar with ethnic and racial discrimination.

Furthermore, the workers themselves seemed to suffer most from efforts intended to hurt those who normally employed them. In my hometown, I saw Mexican men who had given their life savings to ruthless smugglers, *coyotes*, and put their lives at risk to cross an arbitrary line in the desert, a line called the Mexican border. The oldest son or the man of the house, they had come looking for an elusive American Dream. They were prepared to work long, hard hours in the grape fields, albeit for low wages. I met them. I asked them questions in horribly broken Spanish. I could tell from the surprised looks on their faces and the cautious tone in which they answered me that they were not accustomed to being asked their opinion about such things. Most had not joined the union. There were many reasons, they said. Some did not want to relinquish the regular dues. Some did not have faith that the union could deliver on its promises. Some, coming from Mexico, suspected corruption. Nonetheless, most of them seemed to respect the aura of the UFW and its leaders.

In our conversations, I learned most, not from what they said, but from the words that they chose to say it. I noticed that they answered all my questions about the union in the third person. They consistently used the Spanish word *ellos* (they, them) and not *nosotros* (we, us), as UFW officials would have had me believe they would. Their response was a subtle, but clear indicator that they did not consider themselves to be even a figurative part of the labor union created in their name.

At harvest time, they were told by foremen that there was not enough work to go around. Smaller grape farmers, hurt by the beginning of what would be long drought in California and afraid that they would be unable to recover the cost of harvesting at market given the boycott, had chosen to let their crops rot on the vine rather than pay work crews to pick them. This year, there would be no money sent home to Mexico. In Sanger, some of the men, desperate for opportunity, went door to door in search of families to offer them a few hours of yardwork. One, a young man, sold flavored ice. He pushed a white cart with gold bells through town. On the street along which I had once walked to junior high school, I heard a chant reminiscent of Tijuana. *"Paletas . . . paletas frías . . . paletas . . ."*

One spring night, I received a phone call from a friend in New Haven. Had I heard? Cesar Chavez was speaking at Yale. He had reassured a roomful of supporters that, three thousand miles away in California, the grape boycott was flowing as smoothly as sweet wine.

The more that I learned about the contemporary state of the UFW, a quarter century after its founding, the more disenchanted I became with what I perceived to be the union's elitism, materialism, and overall irrelevance to the practical, everyday concerns of farmworkers. Gradually, a sour disillusionment permeated my sense of idealism like a cool breeze in a warm room.

I learned, finally, that the complex human experience that is carved out yearly in the San Joaquin Valley, in the grape fields of Fresno, melon fields of Firebaugh, and lettuce fields of Salinas, does not lend itself to simple analysis. Especially to those whose hands, like mine, are soft. It is pain in retirement, the smell of ointment in my grandfather's medicine cabinet. It is long hours and burning heat and dignified poverty. It is cold beer and shopping carts full of groceries and dances at the

Rainbow Ballroom and Western Union to Mexico. It is the private hope, above all, that one's children will never live this life.

It is an honorable ordeal. Not because some policy maker in Washington or some student from Harvard says so but because it is worthy of respect in and of itself. It is an ordeal that is best observed quickly before it is lost down the last row of grapes. My greatest lesson from the thesis that I never wrote was that only detached academics have the luxury of dwelling in the fields of the San Joaquin Valley. Farmworkers simply survive in them.

My observations, like much of the history of the United Farm Workers Union, are reduced harmlessly to the sort of abstract discussions employed by Latino professionals over happy hour. It is little more than intellectual chewing gum for those whose everyday lives go on completely unaffected and untouched by the drama that they so casually support or so callously ignore. Intellectual chewing gum also for a Harvard student trying feebly to understand how far the lives of his family and friends have progressed from the sweat-filled fields of summers past.

For the first few months of my experiment, I wallowed in the romance of my intellectual rebellion. I took neighborhood walks with my mother, listening to her renditions of family gossip. I visited my aged grandmother, marveling at the renewed sense of youthfulness in her eyes. I spent quiet evenings at home, sprawled out on the den floor in front of the television. I drank with old friends from high school, enjoying an intimacy that had been lost along a telephone wire. I dissected the provincial scribblings in *The Fresno Bee*, where just months earlier, I had started each day with the editorial pages of *The New York Times*. I ate *huevos con chorizo* and *tortillas de harina* in a tiny restaurant that exuded authenticity. I ate *pan dulce* from the old Mexican bakery in town, the one that I had never thought to enter in high school. I drank farm-fresh chocolate milk from a dairy. I exploited the mildness of the California climate, wearing shorts in December. I lifted weights with an old friend whom I had known since kindergarten.

At least initially, I peeled away each layer of the nourishing experience of being at home as if it were a sun-ripened orange picked from a tree and sold for a dollar a bag along a country road where months before, in a Boston supermarket, it would have cost much more. I savored the juice. I was comfortable and content at home. That splendid feeling would not last long.

As winter passed, I noticed a new skepticism developing slowly in me. The days were harder to face. I was more tempted to simply stay in bed. Family conversation seemed less interesting. Alone in the family car with my parents, I reached for the radio dial. At home, the family television blared down the hallway and toward my room, making study difficult. I was spending much more time on the phone, talking long distance with friends back in Cambridge, New Haven, or New York. Gossiping for hours. I was seeking intellectual nourishment— something, I had resolved, I could not find in Sanger. On the telephone, my friends, my dear friends, fed me. We talked about politics and education and love as if we were separated by inches and not by thousands of miles. We laughed as if we were seated together in a warm common room on a cold night. In New England, I could chart my unhappiness through a long parade of calls to California. Now, at home, my monthly phone bills were inexplicably larger than they had been in the East.

I was restless, again. I was unhappy, again. I resented my surroundings. I thought fondly of Cambridge. I reminisced about bookstores and restaurants and bars open until one in the morning. I remembered stimulating conversations with my old roommate from Connecticut. I remembered the lights across the Boston skyline and concerts and museums and plays in New York. I wore my Harvard sweatshirt again and again. I remembered the exhilarating feeling of being at what seemed like the center of the universe, near the very pulse of power and knowledge. I thought myself far removed from such things, exiled to a dark, far-away corner of that universe. I was sure that I was missing things. Important things. CNN showed Governor Mario Cuomo speaking at the Kennedy School of Government. I felt left out, and therefore left behind. During weather forecasts on the evening news, I found myself searching the northeast corner of the map for news about snowstorms that I would not have to walk through in the morning. I thought of touch football games with friends on the banks of the Charles. I was afraid to admit the obvious, the illogical. Incredibly, I actually began to miss Harvard.

But how was that possible? Hadn't I been miserably homesick there? Hadn't I hated the snow, the negative degree windchill? Hadn't I wanted, more than anything, to come home to California? Strangely, now that I was in California, I felt misplaced somehow. I felt suffocated. I took long walks alone. I took deep breaths of fresh air. I tried to rein in thoughts that flooded my mind, for fear of using it. I worked out my frustrations at the local gym. Three years had taken their toll on memory. I knew more about new restaurants in Boston than I did those in Fresno. I struggled with the names of once familiar streets. I had forgotten the names of once familiar people. I stewed. Time passed. Spring approached and with it, what was for me the menacing month of March.

By the time the calendar shed February, I was completely at war with my surroundings. I was more unhappy and more depressed. My daily jogs took on a therapeutic dimension. I talked even more on the phone. I admit that I was, in those months, more bored than I had ever been in my life. I felt trapped in the monotony of life in a small town. The days seemed never-ending. Each day looked unforgivingly like the one before it. I held a special contempt for the life experiences of others, especially those high school classmates of mine who had never dared leave the safety and comfort of our hometown. These young old men living their fathers' lives.

One night, a group of us gathered around a small bonfire in an open field. We drank bottled beer and ate tacos. They viewed their existence as a prison. They talked of simply "getting out." Their tone was desperate. My reaction was largely empathetic, but also somewhat harsh. I thought them emasculated by their own timidity and a constricting fear of the unknown. They had not seen a baseball game at Fenway Park, partied in Greenwich Village, walked the steps of the Lincoln Memorial, tasted New Orleans gumbo, danced in a Houston nightclub, or chased waves in the Atlantic. I diagnosed the source of the differences between us quickly, if condescendingly: I had grown; they had not.

While I could admit to unhappiness in high school, the college student boasted reincarnation. My old friends, however, seemed to be living the same lives that they had lived back then. And they were still unhappy. Most frightening of all to me was the possibility, however remote, that my brief return to the Valley might become indefinite and that their lives might once again become my own.

I was also bombarded by print, television, and radio commentary that I considered extremely conservative on a variety of social issues. And notwithstanding a population in the San Joaquin Valley that was nearly 40 percent Latino, I saw the popular opinion voiced on such mediums as being especially conservative on issues involving race. It was not likely that *The Fresno Bee*, beholden of a historically friendly relationship with Valley agribusiness, would editorialize the virtues of the UFW. A white television commentator called for stronger immigration laws and the universal speaking of English by the citizenry. And the popular host of a radio talk show, a white male, voiced his opposition to affirmative action in any form. Local politicians did not appear to be much more sensitive to racial issues in their opposition to bilingual education and affirmative action. They may have been afraid of seeming to pander to Latino voters, many of whom were not eligible to vote, at the expense of alienating white constituents, who voted in large percentages.

Certainly, I did not believe, even in the fire of youth, that the people of the rural San Joaquin Valley were somehow more predisposed to racism or ethnic prejudice than other Americans. I did not think that God had somehow populated the area from Stockton to Bakersfield with a disproportionate number of bigots. I was well aware that the east coast had its own racial scars, notwithstanding liberal efforts to hide them. Cities like Boston and New York, while stirring in my mind fond memories of bright lights and fast times, had infamous legacies of racially motivated violence and institutional bigotry. After all, wasn't it Boston—actually nearby Charlestown—that had witnessed angry mobs of white parents shaking their fists at little black boys and girls on a school bus? *Nigger, go home!* And wasn't it New York that had just recently endured the brutal attack of a group of black men by a white mob at Howard Beach?

Still, in the small farm towns of central California, racist assumptions were fueled by recent history. I had heard the stories firsthand, what my Harvard professors would have called oral histories. In conversations with my parents, with aunts and uncles, and with strangers about rural life in the 1950s and 1960s, I had learned that, in those years and for many years before that, the institutions of power, prestige, and influence had been controlled exclusively by white Americans. Naturally, even in the wake of the *Brown* decision desegregating public schools and other social reforms of the contemporary civil rights movement, power would not be relinquished willingly. The old man from Mexico who had discouraged his son from becoming a policeman was, at least, right about that.

Exclusion breeds prejudice. At the United States Naval Academy, that means that male midshipmen who attend daily classes with a percentage of female classmates that is significantly lower than the percentage that one might encounter in American society as a whole are afforded the luxury of prejudiced assumptions about the capability and readiness of female officers. They are allowed, and in some sense encouraged, to think of women as mere sex objects and not as equals. At Harvard, where I was taught by women professors, supervised by women deans, and accompanied in class by significant numbers of intelligent and capable female classmates, I was, thankfully, not allowed such luxury.

What "exclusion breeds prejudice" meant in the San Joaquin Valley was that a whole generation of baby boomers began to believe, perhaps unconsciously, in the innate inferiority of Mexican-Americans and other minorities. The rationale suggested that Mexicans and African-Americans and Armenians and Asians could not be teachers or policemen or doctors for a reason: simply, they were not naturally disposed to such professions. They lacked the skills necessary to succeed in the white-collar world. They were not intelligent. They were not motivated. And (a popular stereotype for Mexicans) they were lazy. Their attributes lay, as my mother had been told by a guidance counselor, in quick hands and strong backs. When Mexican-Americans did strive for betterment, they encountered resistance and outright discrimination.

Times changed. Racial discrimination, although not disappearing altogether, became more subtle. After the reforms of the 1960s, reforms that more easily controlled behavior than attitudes, discrimination became more like mercury, harder to pinpoint and corral. I have never been called "greaser." In the

American vocabulary, popular phrases like "Whites Only" and "No Mexicans Need Apply" were gradually replaced with ones like "token minority" and "glass ceiling."

My parents' generation, born of the original sin of racial discrimination, was determined to raise their own children to strive for the highest of goals, while making them aware of familiar attitudes that tended to resurface like an unpleasant virus.

Resurface like the day that I went to a mall in Fresno with my mother. I returned to a phone call from a friend and fellow Harvard Chicano, who was also from Fresno and who had that day been at the same mall with his mother. Coincidentally, he and I had both worn our Harvard sweatshirts. He told me that the father of a white young woman, a Harvard classmate of ours, had been at the mall as well. The father had commented to his daughter that he had seen a young man wearing a Harvard sweatshirt, presumably either my friend or me. The father, who was understandably proud of and horribly territorial about his daughter's association with Harvard, was outraged; he told his daughter that he felt like going up to the young man and "tearing that sweatshirt right off of him." This, because although he did not know the identity of the young man, the girl's father was "sure that he did not go to Harvard." Our classmate had relayed the story to my friend, who shared it word for word with me.

What my friend and I were both intrigued by was how the girl's father could be sure that a young man whom he did not know did not go to Harvard with his daughter. My grandfather would know the answer to that question. So would my father and mother. The answer, I would agree, lies in the fact that the older man recognized immediately that the young man, whether it was my friend or me, was Mexican-American. Maybe he saw the dark skin or the Mexican-looking woman walking alongside her son. In any case, once he had registered in his mind the image of a Mexican wearing a Harvard sweatshirt, his brain was as confused as if it had just seen a purple cow. He had responded cynically. There are no purple cows, he was *sure*. There are no Chicanos at Harvard, he was *sure*. Are there?

No, no one has ever called me "greaser." Instead, insult comes in a thousand muffled utterances.

I was, in my senior year in high school, intelligent, confident, and highly motivated. There was, I was sure, nothing that I could not do. I had rejected my grandfather's fatalism and my father's pessimism. I had disregarded my principal's low expectation and had applied to Harvard. Against heavy odds, I had been accepted as one of only thirty-five Mexican-Americans in an entering class of over 1,600 of the most talented young people in the country. Still, I had encountered the resistance of white classmates, born of jealousy and nurtured by narrow-mindedness at their parents' dinner table. They had been told by their elders, and they were eager to believe, that the only way that a member of a presumably less intelligent racial group could have outdone them in a competition for a coveted place at Harvard was if the competition was unfair in the first place. The fix, their parents had reasoned, had to be in. If not, then their generation's initial perceptions of the intellectual inferiority of people like my parents was incorrect, a lie. And that was not a concession that they were willing to make. In trying to comfort their children, as understandably any parent would, they anointed the disappointed young people before them as the new victims of something called "reverse discrimination." Their sons and daughters took comfort in that. They carried the phrase back to school, to the calculus class in which I had earned a better grade than them, and "graciously" shared it with me.

"If you hadn't been Mexican . . ."

Embarrassed and suddenly a bit insecure, I might have been tempted, had it not been for my ego, to follow the lead of other minority students and forget about Harvard altogether. And so it is that, for Mexican-Americans in the San Joaquin Valley, the only thing that stands in the way of future progress is a legacy of past prejudice. It is said that in the American South, all is forgiven, except race. Before long, I felt that the same could be said of the place that I called home.

In such an environment, I felt as if my idealism was under attack. Worse, it seemed to be retreating. I felt an encroaching sense of complacency. I questioned the viability of the social reform that had lured me to the Kennedys and to Harvard and to the grape fields of the San Joaquin Valley. I heard the familiar fatalism in my father's voice: *"You can't change the world . . ."* But I believed that my father was wrong. I was sure that each of us can change the world, with each effort of each day. Along with two dozen classmates of ours, my roommate and I had, one night during freshman year, built a shantytown in Harvard Yard to protest what was then our school's $500 million investment in companies dealing with South Africa. My father had instinctively disapproved, characteristically fearing the worst; in his mind, that meant that Harvard might throw me out. *"You can't change the world . . ."* Yet from the first moments of our infancy, Harvard taught its children that the exact opposite was true.

I especially despised the loss of anonymity in going from a relatively large city to a small town. The fact that I cashed my checks at the bank that had opened my infant account, mailed packages at the one post office in town, and shopped at grocery stores filled with old friends meant that it was impossible for me to find the occasional place to hide. Cambridge and Boston offered one the chance to be anonymous. On those days that I wanted the freedom of isolation, I could walk along Beacon Street or run along the Charles and still be reasonably assured that I would run into no one that I knew. In Sanger, I was rarely afforded such luxury. The simplest of errands through town was likely to send me into the path of an aunt or an old grammar school teacher or the woman who used to work with my mother two decades earlier. All with the same intrusive, bothersome question.

"So, is it true that you aren't going back to Harvard?"

Publicly, romantically, I began to fashion myself a twenty-one-year-old man without a country. Privately, I began to worry that I would never fit in anywhere ever again. I felt trapped. To be lonely and displaced at Harvard was one thing. But to be lonely and displaced at home? What sense did that make? And what refuge did that leave me, as I searched, simply, for a place to belong?

But notwithstanding the boredom and the conservatism with which I struggled upon returning to the San Joaquin Valley, nowhere was the task of going home again more difficult than within my own home. And at no time did I feel more alone than when surrounded by my own family members. The first and most obvious lesson was that my parents had, in the three years of my absence, not changed as much as I had. At dinner time, in the Mexican tradition, a generous one for men, my mother still did all the cooking, serving, and cleaning. My sister helped her in the

kitchen, while my father and younger brother watched television. It had always been this way; somehow I had never noticed
the inequity before. All of the family members must have thought
it strange then that I would volunteer to wash dishes as my father
and brother, instinctively, walked back into the den. I was also
more prone to jump to my mother's defense at those moments
when my father, who had learned such behavior from watching
his father, appeared to belittle my mother, as if to reassert his domestic control over her.

One night, when CNN brought images into our living room
of gay marches in San Francisco, I watched my parents'
stunned reaction. As my father disapprovingly spouted terms
like "queer" and "not normal," I engaged him in discussion.
No, rather, debate. Taking what I had learned from going to
college with openly gay students, I argued that bigotry was
wrong in all its forms and that, as Mexican-Americans, we
should be especially sensitive to discrimination, abuse, and societal prejudice.

My father was not so easily persuaded. Whether the issue
was gay rights or the professional capabilities of women or a
variety of other topics (thankfully, we did not discuss black girlfriends), I could never convince him that notions that had
rested in his head and heart for decades were now suddenly
backward and archaic. Still, I argued. Still, I persisted. I was
convinced that, as Robert Kennedy said, the harshest criticism
goes hand in hand with the greatest love. In my own arrogance,
I wanted nothing more than to make my parents better and
wiser and more tolerant people. In rejecting some of my parents' views and values, I found it difficult not to think of myself
as not only intellectually superior, but morally superior as well.
As it had been during summer vacations, the guilt surrounding
such judgments was overwhelming. The difference was that
with such an extended leave of absence, there was no threshold of September to offer eventual rescue. There was only another month, and then another, each filled with irritating
reminders of the life that I had once left behind, the life that I
had sworn to never assume as my own.

During my year at home, my arguments with my father were
the most contentious that I have ever experienced with anyone.
It was very likely that the older Ruben Navarrette had always

assumed that as his oldest son and namesake eventually passed through childhood and into manhood, I would be more like him than not. A behavioral inheritance was expected. My childhood had been spent in shadow. At family gatherings, I had been Little Ruben. *Rubencito* to my grandmother.

In junior high school, when I first developed a public image through local newspaper clippings, I resisted attaching the "Jr." to my name. I introduced myself to the presenters of academic awards as simply Ruben Navarrette, as my parents watched proudly from the audience. My father disapproved of my choice, in a sense laying rightful claim to a name that was his first. He worried that people might confuse the two of us, and indeed they might have. In high school, the behaviorial inheritance that my father expected may still have been possible. But later, with Harvard's immeasurable influence and my new skepticism of old ways of thinking, the possibility dimmed. In fact, through all my accomplishments, I was becoming most intent on succeeding in just one thing: I wanted desperately to not become my father. Finally, as I completed my tenure at Harvard, my father would no longer have to worry about people confusing us. The name in the newspaper or on the lips of the local attorney or on the desk of the council member was, more often than not, mine.

Although I respected what I considered my parents' incredible accomplishments, I was not blind to defects in our family fabric. My own family, I told myself, would one day be different. I meant, better. I would break what I considered to be a sexist cultural tradition of treating wives as children. I would respect and support my spouse. Perhaps my wife would ultimately make more money than me, as incomprehensible as such an idea seemed to many men in my father's generation. I remember, years later, the smirks from the conservative radio talk show host about Hillary Clinton making more money than her husband; I recognized his own insecurity immediately. If that were the case in my own marriage, I vowed, I would not feel threatened or any less manly. Rather, confident in my own worth and ability, I would be as proud of her accomplishments as I was of my own.

Above all, I was convinced, I would raise my children differently. I should say that I respected and admired my parents' selfless commitment to their children and their wish for our continued happiness. Still, there were moments, many of them, when suggestions sounded like commands. I told myself that I would have enough faith in my children's ability and judgment to allow them to live their own lives and even, if need be, make their own mistakes. I would not presume to know more than them about experiences that I had not lived. That was one area that seemed to give my father, in particular, special difficulty.

My father and mother had both taken a more active role in the education of their three children than their own parents had with them. Before I was old enough to attend elementary school, my mother was reading to me and teaching me to count in English and Spanish. My father remembers that once, when I was three, I insisted on reading to him. Of course, I could not actually read, but I managed to astonish him by precisely reciting the storyline of a children's book. At some point, he tested the feat by covering the words to the text. When I kept reading, he laughed and called my mother. I had memorized the entire story as it had been told to me and was merely parroting the words. By the time I entered school, I already considered learning to be fun and rewarding. My parents' full-time jobs notwithstanding, their support for our schoolwork was constant and unyielding. We were consistently praised for good grades, as if they sought to instill in us the kind of confidence in our ability and talent that had eluded each of them.

In a Kennedy tradition, self-doubt and self-deprecation were, in our immediate family, simply unacceptable. If we decided not to try out for the school play or not to run for class president, it was okay for us to explain at the dinner table that we did not want to compete. It was *not* okay for us to back away from competition of any sort because we were afraid to compete. The result, twenty years later, was three incredibly confident and motivated young people who were not content to simply meet standards but felt compelled to set them.

In kindergarten, on my birthday, my mother took cupcakes to school for the entire class. My father built the backdrops of science projects and occasionally chaperoned school field trips. Without fail, both attended back-to-school nights and PTA meetings and Christmas pageants starring their children. They bought books, and later computers, that they could not afford. They took us on trips outside the Valley. They spoke English

to us. The message to the three of us as children was unequivocal: Nothing is as important as education. Nothing.

It was perhaps because my parents had helped facilitate the
educational success of their three children that they extracted
from that an inferred personal investment in our educational
pursuits. My award was *our* award. My Harvard education was,
in a sense, theirs as well. My father, who was as an adolescent
denied the chance of even dreaming of attending such a school,
told me once that he felt that through my acceptance, he had
been vicariously allowed access to a world that had been pre-
viously closed to him. He was not alone. I heard the same sentiment from Harvard friends of all different colors regarding
their parents. In fact, in our freshman year, Joe Razo had mentioned that his mother, a clerk at a state office, was suddenly
being deluged with compliments and attention by fellow co-
workers impressed with her son's accomplishment. Women
who had never even said hello to her went out of their way to
invite her to lunch. My father told similar stories. Lawyers and
judges, entities that in my father's profession represent the pinnacle of prestige, stopped him in the elevator to excitedly ask
about the progress of Little Ruben.

I admit that the strange idea of one generation empowering
another is, at first look, somewhat charming. All is well that
ends well, they say. It is the way that America lives with itself,
this deferring of dreams. After crippling the productivity of
some of its citizenry, it rewards children for not becoming their
parents. Thus Harvard, in offering the child reincarnation, also
offers the parent redemption. But the exercise is primed for
failure, even disaster. After all, consider what happened at the
fateful moment when Joe Razo irreverently used tragedy to re-
claim his life from his mother's trophy cabinet.

Of course, my father, like my mother, lovingly wanted the
best for me. Still, my instinct is that my father was also tempted
to somehow use the glory surrounding my experience to live
his educational life over again. And so, my experiment and,
with it, the possibility that I might not ever return to Harvard,
was more than a threat to my own future wealth and happiness.
It was, in a wider sense, a threat also to my father's second
chance to succeed in the American educational system. When
he had been told of my scheme—the precise moment at which

the viability of that chance was first threatened—he had been silent. The quiet did not last long. In the months that followed, we argued incessantly. He seized any opportunity to remind me that I was playing with fire. Playing with redemption, really. All at once, the boy who could do no wrong was transformed into the young man who could do nothing right. It was March. And I was under siege in what was once my home.

The argument was always the same. At issue: the nature of my life's decisions. Whether the issue was time off from Harvard or the expectation that I would eventually go to law school or even the types of women that I was likely to date and eventually marry, I could expect my father to provide an unsolicited opinion. Worse than the opinion itself was its condescending tone, the fact that it was based on my father's presumption that older meant wiser, that young men were by their nature foolish, and, in the television culture of an older man's generation, that Father Knows Best. So had it been with my grandfather, the one person on earth whom my father respected most, even in death. And so, it was expected, that it would be between my father and me.

However, I was not willing to concede that older meant wiser. Opinionated and, as my father observed, "cocky," I would not budge. While my father had spent his own life with head bowed in deference to my grandfather, I was not prepared to follow in that tradition. I did not trust in some innate perfection in elders. As part of a generation of cynics, I had grown up a witness to the frailties and failures of adults. Watergate and Vietnam interrupted the cartoon hour. As a child, I watched my parents argue violently and heard them constantly threaten each other with divorce. In high school, Reaganomics taught me about inherited deficit and Beirut taught me about young men dying before their faces had cleared up. It was my profound opinion that my parents' generation, the Baby Boomers, for all their arrogance in the 1960s, had since then—in the political arena and at home—done a splendid job of screwing up American society.

At the threshold of my twenties, I had my own ideas of where my own life was going and why. And above all, I was not willing to concede complete wisdom to someone who, while presuming to have lived life, had not lived my life. I recognized that, given the limitation that permeated his own life experience, my father was no more capable of navigating my life's complicated and ambitious course than he was of piloting a spaceship. Besides, the support of my parents notwithstanding, I recognized that in the solitude of my Harvard experience, at those unforgivable moments in Cambridge when I was consumed by stress and loneliness and alienation, I was on my own. As such, I selfishly considered most of my success to be of my own doing.

My tone was horribly disrespectful. At times, instinct took over. Harvard had taught me to wound with words. When my father argued, I argued back. When he yelled, I yelled back. I approached him not as a subservient but as an equal, which seemed to unnerve him. He responded in sarcasm. *Well, I never went to Harvard, but . . .* He was a drill sergeant, bellowing commands in my face and perhaps worrying my mother that he would lose control. I was not afraid of him, which only seemed to make him more angry. In the Mexican way, respect, *respeto,* was everything. I did not care. I had been afraid once, a child cowering in my room when every misdeed warranted the discipline of a leather belt—another unflattering lesson that my father took from his father. I would be afraid no longer. The muscular six-foot frame of a young man stood where once kneeled a boy. If he hits me, I thought, then I will hit him back.

Clean your room! Something. *You should go to law school!* Anything. A time-honored favorite: *This is my house, so you live by my rules!* I was having the arguments that sixteen- and seventeen-year-old boys have with their fathers. Yet I was having them at twenty-two. I was breaking my father's heart rather than allowing him to break my spirit.

I was arguing not about borrowing the family car for the prom but about what my father believed was my irresponsible squandering of a precious gift. But, if it was a gift, then it had been given to me. Hadn't it?

"You had your life," I once screamed in the heat of battle. "This one is mine and I want it back!"

I stormed outside. The warm climate of an evening in May meant that my ordeal was almost over. I had already decided to spend the summer away, working in another state. In the beginning, sipping coffee in San Francisco, I had been so arrogant, so politically correct. I had been so intent on proving

Richard Rodriguez wrong that I had romanticized the idea of going home. Through the disillusionment, loneliness, and intellectual alienation of life in the San Joaquin Valley, I not only learned to appreciate how difficult it was to go home again but I remembered why I left in the first place.

Moreover there was a futility to the charade. I had to concede that a detachment from lives once lived was inevitable. In denying it, I had only sustained its existence. It was the uniqueness of my own experience, and the distance that it brought with it, that afforded me the luxury of reexamining the life that I once lived as callously as if it were a frog in a laboratory. The very fact that I felt compelled to reestablish intimacy with my family and hometown should have told me that it was already gone. My Chicano classmates at Fresno State—the tattooed drug user, the single mother, the person working two jobs— were not in a position to study the perils of their lives; they were too busy trying to avoid being devoured by them. A clinical observation was ultimately left to Harvard students who were free to extol the virtue of intimacy but only from a distance.

As cars passed in front of my parents' house, I cried hysterically on the front lawn. I cried desperately in choking gasps of air. Not whimpers but tiny fits of rage. *Please God, take me from here!* As my temper cooled, I felt terrible for the way that I had spoken to my father. I, of course, loved and in my own way respected a man who loved me more than life itself and who had always supported my every effort, however ridiculous. Still, I remember that I did not feel terrible enough to apologize. After all, it *was* my life.

I made a private concession to the night, a concession to Rodriguez. I had learned something that I should have realized earlier. If you take a fish from a small fishbowl and place him in an ocean, then it will swim freely and enjoy the space that you have afforded it. But if you then take that fish away from the ocean and put him back into the fishbowl that he once occupied, it will not swim at all. In fact, if you watch the fish closely, you will realize that it is slowly dying.

In the dark, I wept. Alone.

CHAPTER 9

PALACES ON THE SAND

"LOVE IS THE VOICE UNDER ALL SILENCES,
THE HOPE WHICH HAS NO OPPOSITE FEAR;
THE STRENGTH SO STRONG MERE FORCE IS FEEBLENESS,
THE TRUTH MORE FIRST THAN SUN MORE LAST THAN STAR."

E. E. CUMMINGS

HARVARD COLLEGE, CLASS OF 1915

"SAFE UPON THE SOLID ROCK THE UGLY HOUSES STAND;
COME AND SEE MY SHINING PALACE BUILT UPON THE SAND."

EDNA ST. VINCENT MILLAY

VASSAR COLLEGE, CLASS OF 1917

After stopping to play a few solitary games of blackjack in a Las Vegas casino, I had crossed the state line. The highway signs offered a greeting: *Arizona welcomes you!* After a period of penance at home, I had decided to spend the summer in a sprawling city built in the desert. Different people would have suggested different reasons for why I had come to Phoenix in its hottest and most unforgiving season. Family members thought that I had grown tired of Sanger and needed a vacation. My employer, an educational project sponsored by Arizona State University, assumed in me a burning desire to motivate young people to go to college. A few close friends suspected the truth; they smiled as they told me to be careful in my journey. Although I did need an escape and did care about motivating young people, I had gone to Phoenix mainly because I was in love.

I had for over a year been captivated by a young woman who, in my mind, embodied the best human qualities imaginable. She was beautiful and intelligent and caring and generous and strong. She felt equally comfortable hiking a mountain trail and studying the rhythm of an opera. She knew foreign languages. She spoke with humor and affection.

Though her stunning beauty was undeniable, I had long since begun to consider intelligence as the most important quality in the women with whom I chose to become involved. In that regard, she was no less remarkable. She was my intellectual equal, a characteristic she displayed in countless discussions with me. She was perhaps, in truth, even smarter than me—notwithstanding the unfortunate fact that she attended the second best college in the country. For the two years in which we wore the conventional titles of boyfriend and girlfriend, our respective classmates teased us mercilessly about this freak romance, this Harvard-Yale love affair. We had cultivated the teasing by constantly wearing each other's college sweatshirts on our respective campuses.

And, as a bonus of sorts, she was Mexican-American. Although it shouldn't have mattered, it did. A friend, a fellow Chicano who I consider to be progressive and enlightened, confessed to me once his inability to envision a sustained future with his white girlfriend. The reason—the kind of mother that he wanted for his children. He had always loved the fact that his own mother had raised him with such a profound sense of *cariño*. The word conveys a unique sort of selfless affection, arguably characteristic of Mexican-American women. Right or wrong, my friend assumed that his white girlfriend would not be able to love his children in the same way as would a Latina who was more like his own mother.

Despite the fact that, up to that point, I had lost my virginity to someone who was white, passed through a series of flings with women of all colors, and had fully explored the delicate realm of black girlfriends, I had come to consider a shared ethnicity to be a wonderful blessing. We understood each other's experience without having to ask about it; we had many of the same values, being raised by parents who conquered similar obstacles; and we bathed together in the affection of a shared culture, mixing into our conversations affectionate words in Spanish: *"Te quiero . . . " "Te quiero mas . . ."*

As I drove past cacti and through mountain ranges along the ten-hour journey to Phoenix, I had time enough to reflect on the metaphorical road that had brought me to that space in time. A lovely, yet perilous road.

Our courtship had been drama pulled from the pages of an Erich Segal novel. We met, appropriately, two years earlier in New Haven during a frigid rendition of the annual Harvard-Yale football game. I had taken a precarious seat with friends from Yale, discreetly cheering for Harvard from the opposing bleachers. A tight-skirted cheerleader on the field held my attention through four quarters of mediocre football. Harvard won the game, thus earning the visitors a round of gratuitous gloating during a series of drunken after-parties. The cheerleader was going home for a week-long Thanksgiving break. When she missed a midnight shuttle to the airport in New York, I somehow convinced a mutual friend to leave his warm bed and join me in driving her to the city ourselves. Along the way, our appreciative passenger cuddled in my arms and the two-hour drive seemed just minutes long.

In the months that followed, we called each other once a week, then twice a week, tying up phone lines from Cambridge to New Haven. At first, the tone was friendly, the relationship platonic. But as we shared intimate discussions about our respective experiences with romance, I began to slowly trust the warmth in the soothing voice on the phone. I began to wonder if, in recovering from the wound of an old girlfriend, I was emotionally ready for a new one. I resolved that, ultimately, the answer would depend on the girl.

The defining moment had come later that spring at Harvard

during an intercampus conference of Ivy League Chicanos. As usual with such gatherings, sleeping arrangements were somewhat disorganized. On the first night of the conference, I returned to my bedroom to find my new friend already comfortably buried in my covers. After accepting a coy invitation to join her there, I held her for several hours. Somewhere in our phone conversations, I had sensed a hardness, perhaps born of a fear of exposing herself to men. This was a woman who had been hurt before and, I sensed, would not easily trust again. Once in my arms, in my bed, I waited for something more. She told me how special she thought I was, how unlike other men whom she had known. Then, unexpectedly, I found the sign of vulnerability for which I was searching. Flowing down her cheek was a single tear. Consumed by vulnerability, we kissed each other until morning.

A few weeks later, I was in New Haven, surprising her with flowers. A week after that, she was back in Cambridge, escorting me to a Harvard formal. And, then suddenly in May there were finals to take and papers to make and we were restricted to phone calls again. Finally, through the familiar medium of a telephone, we confessed our love for each other just days before her plane left for Arizona. I was spending the summer in New York—something that I felt I had to do just once before graduation—working for the College Board to improve their methods for recruitment of Latino students. And so, our budding love affair would have to endure three more months of mere telephone calls and love letters.

At the end of the summer, she visited me in Manhattan for a week before going up to New Haven to resume her studies. It was in New York that we finally consummated our relationship. After a Broadway play and a late supper in Greenwich Village, we made love. It was as pure an expression of love and mutual respect as I have ever known. In the morning, she was gone, back to Connecticut for a cold winter without me. Our romantic interlude in Manhattan was at the threshold of my year's leave of absence from Harvard. In a few days, I cleared out of the New York apartment and returned to California.

The following months were difficult. Our "long-distance relationship" forced each of us to confront complicated questions about fidelity and implied commitment. The old cliche suggests that absence makes the heart grow fonder. Separated by three thousand miles, two young lovers trusted in the truth of that sentiment.

At first, with each passing day, we only seemed to miss each other more than we had the day before. We regularly sent each other flowers and love letters and balloon bouquets. I mailed her edible reminders of the Southwest in the form of home-made tortillas and *pan dulce*. We talked on the phone for hours and told each other how much we wished that we were to-gether. We left our song on each other's answering machines. Our love assumed a childish, playful dimension.

Still, we would eventually learn that while absence might make the heart grow fonder with people who share a distinct and well-defined commitment like engagement or marriage, the sentiment does not always hold true for those whose rela-tionship is more fluid. Sometimes in absence, hearts do not necessarily grow fonder, but merely grow apart.

Before long, my girlfriend began to resent what some might consider to be the necessary sacrifices and concessions of a mature, loving relationship. She complained that she felt smothered. She complained that I expected her to put her life "on hold" while I tried to rekindle cultural intimacy three thou-sand miles away. If in California I was sure that I was missing things, then in New Haven she was likewise sure that she was "missing out."

Missing out on the opportunity to date a variety of other men, for instance. Just twenty, she interpreted any degree of con-cession as lost opportunity. Although she had never been lack-ing in the attention of men, she continued to feel as if there remained some *types* of men who were still out of her grasp. And so, her love for me notwithstanding, there were conquests yet to be made and things yet to be proven to herself.

In a wider sense, her experience was typical of that of many women in elite colleges who had years earlier, in the shallow corridors of high school, been ignored by the captain of the football team. These were women who may have been quite attractive in their own right, but who were usually passed over the week of the senior prom as the most popular boys in school chased after the most popular pom-pom girl. These were women who were, in many cases, much smarter than the men they desired—men who paid attention to them only on the day of the chemistry test. These were strong, intelligent, motivated women who intimidated immature boys in high school and even, to some degree, immature young men in the Ivy League.

As with so much of our experience, there was, of course, an ethnic dimension to all this. As one of a handful of Mexican-Americans in an overwhelmingly white high school in Phoenix, she considered herself unattractive in adolescence. To her, attractive apparently meant blond, blue-eyed, and of light complexion. As a result, even in college, she was still disturbingly insecure despite her brunette, bronzed beauty. In high school, she had always wanted to date white boys. At Yale, she was suddenly immersed in an elite environment where she was most likely to meet and fall in love with someone who was white. Upon returning to the Southwest for vacation, she might have assumed that, given her association with an upstanding place like Yale, she had, in fact, discovered that thanks to the Ivy League, men she would encounter in Phoenix would find her more acceptable than if she were attending a local community college. And so, she may have assumed she would finally be attractive to the kind of men who had eluded her for so long and then, in their company, she might finally be considered genuinely attractive. Thus, her association with a pristine place like Yale could offer a physical, as well as an intellectual, reincarnation.

Apart from race, the very fact that one attended a school like Harvard seemed to affect men and women differently. My male friends and I would return home at Christmas to phone messages from women whom we hardly knew in high school, women who had tired of football players and were enticed by the idea of dating a Harvard Man. Amassing one-night stands, however sordid, could be like shooting fish in a barrel.

I remember, one spring break, dancing in a club in Florida with a pretty, young nurse. She asked where I went to college and I told her. She didn't believe me, so I showed her the Harvard ring on my finger. She promptly suggested that I was too drunk to get back to the hotel on my own and offered to drive me herself, after we went back to her apartment for a cup of coffee. When we stumbled into the room, I remember that there was no coffee machine in sight, only a queen-size bed. The next morning, she kept her promise and drove me back to my hotel.

I remember, during my summer in Sacramento, being lured to the banks of the Sacramento River by an attractive young girl whom I had met at work. After learning that I went to Harvard, *she* had asked me out. After kissing for hours in a parked car, she confessed to me, on our second date, that she felt compelled to go further or she would "never forgive" herself. With a trusting smile, she pulled me toward the darkness of the river bank.

I remember, one Christmas vacation, sitting in the bedroom of an old friend, talking about people we knew from high school and confessing feelings that we had never talked about in the seven years that we had known each other. Suddenly she was gone, having pulled herself from the perils of her bed and my backrub and leaving into the night. Though I was as attracted to her as she was to me, she left me alone, without a clue of what she wanted. Before long, I was pulled quietly into another bed in another room by her roommate, who had been flirting with me, her first Harvard Man, for much of the evening. A few hours later, I was in my friend's bathroom, washing my face and wondering why I do such things.

I remember also, will never forget, one bizarre night. I was back in Fresno, a twenty-year-old escorting two older women to some sort of Hispanic function. Before midnight, they began hinting that they would like to be taken home. We drove back to the apartment at which we had gathered. Someone excused herself into another room. Someone kissed me. Someone returned in a nightgown and took my hand. Someone followed us into the bedroom. Someone said something about how she couldn't believe that she was with a "fuckin' Harvard Man." All at once, I felt exploited; the power that I thought I had over my sexual escapades was missing. I resolved to never go to church again, because no priest could hear such a confession. Irrationally, on the drive home, I suddenly felt alone and unloved. As the road blurred ahead of me, I wiped my eyes.

But the boy does not always get the girl. Poetically, sometimes, instead of playing Cupid, Harvard plays spoiler.

At a party in Fresno, I was captivated by a pretty Latina in a tight dress. She was without a doubt the most attractive woman in the room, the type that I would have considered to be "out of my league" in high school. But at the time, with two years of Harvard under my belt and the confidence that suffering brings, I considered no one to be out of my league. I approached with a smile. We talked and danced. In the weeks that we would date, I knew and she knew that her mother and father loved the idea of a Harvard son-in-law. As *mexicanos*, they felt a certain pride for my accomplishments. As son-in-laws go, I seemed like a good investment, I suppose. They made it clear to me and to their daughter how proudly they gave their blessing. The only problem was that, given the rebellious stage that the young woman was going through, nothing displeased her more than pleasing her parents. Without tattoos, long hair, and a Harley, I was, she was convinced, all wrong for her. Amazingly, parental approval had been the kiss of death. Thank you, John Harvard.

Although naturally, Harvard women were not at all impressed with the singular fact of their male classmates' alma mater, the allure of Harvard men did sometimes extend to other campuses in the Ivy League. It is no exaggeration to say that, at Pachangas, for instance, Harvard Chicanos would be able to use their affiliation with the school as a way of luring curious women from Yale or Princeton or Brown back to their rooms.

Unfortunately (and unfairly, in a society that still labels strong women as "difficult" and "headstrong"), some Harvard women considered their well-earned distinction less of an attribute than a liability. I knew women who, when approached by men in a bar in Los Angeles, would actually lie about going to Harvard and tell them that they went to less competitive schools like Cal State LA or UCLA. I knew other women who pretended to be less intelligent in dinner conversations rather than frighten away men. If the conversation turned to minority rule in South Africa, for instance, a Harvard woman might decide it unwise to mention the in-depth research paper that she had recently completed on the subject, choosing instead to feign ignorance. That idea may seem incredible to some women. But those who have lived the experience of being a woman in an elite environment, or even those people of both genders who simply remember the insecurities of youth, may perhaps see the truth in this.

*   *   *

The road signs told me that I had entered the city limits. I had gone to spend a summer in Phoenix because I was in love. But I had gone also because, although two young lovers were desperate to spend time with each other, it was unthinkable that the young lady with whom I was in love would go to California instead. Owing to an unspoken Mexican protocol, a sacrifice of love was *my* responsibility. My duty, actually. The details of the courtship were mine to manage. If we had lived one hundred years earlier, I might have approached her father with two cows and some chickens and asked for his daughter's hand in marriage. Now, cows and chickens were no longer part of the process but the element of respect endured.

In the two years that we were together we often discussed the possibility of marriage. A few times, I flirted with proposals disguised in jest; always, she was receptive. Indeed, she seemed to be waiting for me to actually go through with it. The scenario that we played out in our talks invariably had my parents asking her parents for her hand on my behalf, another remnant of Mexican tradition. That was the way that it had always been in past generations and the way that we wanted it to be in our case. Although our association with institutions like Harvard and Yale arguably removed us from much of our culture, we both cherished the idea of a Mexican wedding. I imagined a flowing white gown, dollar dances, and mariachis.

While the wedding image was comforting to me, the more serious reality of marriage was not completely appealing to her. She seemed to vacillate between wanting to hear a proposal and fearing one. Part of the reason for her reluctance to accept a more sustained commitment was a lingering uncertainty that I was the right person for her in the first place. Although she admitted that she had grown to consider me attractive, she also confessed that, if she had not fallen in love with me, she would not have picked me out of a room crowded with blond, blue-eyed young men. It was those features, along with a light complexion, that she had consistently found so alluring in adolescence. It was those features that she had always hoped would be represented in the man who shared her wedding picture. It was those features that she envisioned in her children, remarkably put there by their father's gene pool. And for all the love letters and flowers in the world, it was those features that I lacked. Of all the things that I could offer her in a life filled with love and generous affection, blond, blue-eyed children was not one of them.

An even more frustrating source of her resistance to the idea of marriage revolved around her preoccupation with implied responsibility. Like me, she had been dropped into an intoxicating world of limitless opportunity. Unlike me, she felt compelled by circumstance to prove herself not once but twice. If being Mexican-American in the Ivy League made my head spin with restless ambition and implied obligation, then being both Mexican-American and female in such an environment made her head spin twice as fast. Whether the prize was good grades or admission to a good law school, she seemed even more hungry for approval and reward than I was.

Further, she had to contend with obstacles to which I was immune. For instance, no matter how sensitive I tried to be, we both knew that an unplanned pregnancy would affect our lives differently. I could walk away, at least theoretically. She could not. As a result, she was naturally protective of her future, guarding it as if it was a precious but fragile egg resting in a flimsy straw basket.

On the day that she had first left for Yale, her parents had told her not to forget her responsibilities, presumably those to family and to herself. But in a wider sense, they were speaking, as my father might have, of a responsibility not to squander a historic and hard-earned opportunity. A responsibility not to be ordinary, even at the price of delaying, or perhaps forgoing, ordinary pleasures like raising a family. For women of her generation, ordinary was not the corporate lawyer facilitating a multimillion dollar merger or the aspiring businesswoman boarding the commuter train to Connecticut with a briefcase and a stiff drink. Ordinary was the married woman, the bearer of children, the family chauffeur to Little League games and Girl Scout meetings.

In case I missed the subtlety, the message was delivered to me most clearly one evening in Phoenix during an impromptu discussion with my prospective mother-in-law. It was after din-

ner. My girlfriend had left the room and her mother had seized
the opportunity to speak to me alone. She seemed anxious, as
if primed to deliver a speech that she had been prepairing for
months. Given the way that her daughter and I looked at each
other, she may have feared that her educational investment—
complete with the sort of vicarious redemptive qualities so well
understood by my father—was in a great deal of danger. Her
worst case scenario? Pick 'em. Girl loves boy, drops out of Yale
to move to Cambridge to be with boy during his last year at
Harvard. Girl loves boy, graduates from college but forsakes
law school to follow boy to his graduate school. Girl loves boy,
gets pregnant, drops out of school; boy is killed by girl's horrified parents. It was those fears and more that I heard in this
woman's near-desperate tone.

"Well, you two have really blown it. . ."

"We two?"

"My daughter and you. Oh, you two had to go fall in love
with each other. At such a young age. The two of you at such
fine schools . . . Oh, your poor parents . . . They must be so worried. . ."

"Well, actually—"

"Well, I suppose now the two of you will get married and
have babies . . . She'll be like all her friends. She didn't have to
go to Yale for that! She could have done that staying here!"

Stunned, guilt-ridden, I said nothing to all this. Not a damn
thing! I have not often found myself left without words. Harvard
teaches that words are cheap, that one should never let a debate opponent have the last word.

For all my concession and sensitivity, I had been reduced to
a cultural caricature. My girlfriend reentered the room, completely unaware of the brief but pointed lecture that her mother
had delivered to me in her absence. I smiled at her somewhat
nervously and continued to clear the table. Silently.

In the weeks to come, in deference to the scolding I'd received,
I spent less time with my girlfriend and more time in the silence of my apartment.

It was that silence that enabled me to finish a piece of writing with which I had been wrestling for several months. It was

a confession of sorts, a wrenching personal account of the tragedy that had enveloped my former classmate, Joe Razo. It had been almost exactly two years since my father had interrupted the quiet of a summer afternoon in Sacramento with his disturbing phone call. In that time, Razo had been jailed for armed robbery, arraigned in court, released on bail, and brought to trial. Despite the deluge of press reports and news stories about the affair at the time of Razo's arrest and throughout the trial, I felt that there was still much that remained unsaid. Much that, among Chicanos in the Ivy League, been said only in a whisper. Ideas flowed through my head, calling out for release.

I had needed only an inspiration to start the process of writing it all down. It had come with a strong dose of irony. In June of 1989, in southern California, Joe Razo was convicted of six counts of armed robbery and held over for sentencing. The day before the verdict was announced, in Harvard Yard—three thousand miles and a world away from that courtroom—the remaining members of his class graduated. After Razo's conviction, I resolved to say out loud all that I had been thinking for two years and to say it in print. Even before I had written a single word of what would become a controversial editorial in a major newspaper, I knew that what I felt compelled to say would offend some. So I consulted an expert on the subject of offense. After hearing what I had in mind, Richard Rodriguez suggested that I forget the whole thing.

"My guess," he said at the end of a long phone conversation, "is that the kid's shoulders can't hold much metaphor."

Still, I persisted. I mailed Rodriguez the preliminary version of an essay that I had drafted about Razo's arrest and conviction. The thing that the author noticed first in the piece was a strong element of inhibition. The issue that had goaded me into writing the essay in the first place was the universal pressures endured by Mexican-American students at elite and predominantly white schools, pressures that I believed had swallowed Razo whole. After reading what I had written, Rodriguez suggested that I had been too diplomatic, too timid in my observations. He was right. I did not feel comfortable offering up for public consumption the intimacies of Razo's experience, or those of my own for that matter. Like a stone flying along the top of a pond, my words had skipped and glided across the soul of the Razo tragedy.

"You're being too careful," Rodriguez said. "Write it again . . . as if it is just for you, like no one is going to read it."

I returned to my computer. Over the course of one thousand words, I pulled and tugged at the drama. *Like no one is going to read it . . .* When pressed for easy answers, I gave none. Finally, on a scorching summer day in Phoenix, I finished the piece. I called *The Los Angeles Times* and asked if the editors there were interested in a personal perspective on the Razo tragedy from another Harvard Chicano. They were.

Completely unaware at the time of how profoundly those one thousand words would affect my life, I was motivated solely by a desire to clear my head and perhaps, in a sense, my conscience. Still, two weeks later, I was cashing a generous check from the newspaper and wondering, already, if I had done the right thing.

In August of 1989, on the actual day that the editorial, aptly entitled "Harvard Homeboy," appeared, I happened to be in Los Angeles. My girlfriend had flown in from Phoenix for a gathering of Chicano Yale students, and I had tagged along for the ride. That morning, after pulling myself from bed and pouring myself a cup of coffee, I calmly picked up a copy of the morning *Times* and turned to the editorial. After I found what I was looking for, the first thing that I noticed, oddly enough, was the editorial's byline. How curious it was for a twenty-two-year-old to see his own name in print and to know that the columns of print underneath it were his words. *RUBEN NAVARRETTE, JR.*

I allowed myself a proud smile, walked into the bedroom where my love was still sleeping and slipped the newspaper under her pillow. A few minutes later, as I sipped coffee in the living room, I heard a loud, joyous, and proud scream of approval coming from behind the bedroom door.

By the time we arrived at the hotel at which the alumni group was assembling, the newspaper had already begun floating through the crowd. The silent nodding of heads suggested to me that those who had, years earlier, endured in New Haven an experience presumably similar to mine saw some degree of truth in what I had written. And my girlfriend, a Yalie to the end, took special joy in announcing to the crowd that not only did she know the author of the editorial but that there I was, politely trailing behind her and carrying her bags as any good boyfriend should.

The immediate reaction to "Harvard Homeboy" was a mixed one. Some of those who had read the piece over their morning toast wrote letters complimenting me on my courage and candor in discussing such an emotional set of circumstances. Others congratulated me on weathering the trials of my college experience and urged me to press on.

My parents, of course, were extremely proud of what was perhaps a significant accomplishment for anyone, let alone a college student. And in an interesting appendix to the drama of Joe Razo, my father, after reading the observations presented in my essay, completely changed his opinion on the matter. The same man—the career cop living in a black and white world, who, two years earlier, was lamenting that one could take the kid out of the barrio but not the barrio out of the kid— was suddenly more compassionate. As a parent, he mourned the loss of a bright future and speculated about how difficult an experience it must be to attempt to bridge two worlds. Tell me about it.

As expected, though, there was also criticism of my editorial. Instead of being critical of the actual content of the piece, most critics were upset that I had written the editorial in the first place. And as expected, the most defensive forms of criticism came mostly from, for lack of a better phrase, intellectuals of color. An African-American professor of sociology was so incensed by my editorial that he took it upon himself to write one of his own in response. In his piece, after carefully introducing himself as a former minority graduate student at Harvard, the professor set forth his opinion that any pressures or unpleasantries encountered by minority students on elite and predominantly white campuses were not at all unique to them, but were experienced by students of all colors. Significantly, he did not deny that he himself had felt such pressure while at Harvard. Nor did he concede that, had he been a younger and more impressionable undergraduate there, he might have felt Razo's pain more acutely. Instead, he skirted the issue altogether, trying to downplay any cultural dimension to the stress associated with college.

As a kind of vindication, there were also a series of letters from minority college students on campuses throughout the country. Many of them wrote that they, too, had felt distinct cultural pressures evolving from the experience of being nonwhite in a largely white environment. "I thought that I was the only person who felt out of place in college, pushed into defending and accentuating my culture," a young Asian-American woman wrote. "Thank you for proving me wrong . . ." No, thank you.

What I was most struck by was the motivation behind much of the criticism. The African-American sociology professor was concerned that my frank and public discussion of the strains and pains quietly endured by many minority students on such campuses would hurt recruitment efforts by frightening away other minority aspirants from applying to schools such as Harvard. And it was then that I was reminded why the entire Razo drama had, at its conception, attracted so little attention among such intellectuals of color, those who were the usual vanguards of minority student concerns.

There were, it seemed, certain compromises and concessions that progressive intellectuals from the minority community were willing to make in the name of progress. I rejected that sentiment as completely unreasonable. After all, once the rhetoric and statistical data is wiped away, those asked to endure such compromises and concessions have human faces. They have worried parents, consumed with secret dreams and relentless fears. And, most of all, they often have extraordinary pressures that mercilessly push and pull at the fabric of their experience. Until intellectuals of color admit that those pressures exist, scores of bright young people will have a college experience more for others than for themselves.

As my girlfriend and I concluded our summer in Phoenix, our love affair was more intense than ever. She had always told me that she was captivated by my passion. When I believed in something, I defended it to the point of sometimes being arrogant and overbearing. I was growing impatient with elitism. I was more critical than ever of Ivy League intellectuals who remained so terribly far removed from what I considered to be the real world that I had revisited in California. Through it all, it was left to my loved one to soothe over hurt feelings, or if she could, to intercept my verbal assault.

On one autumn day, during our senior year, she was not nearly fast enough. We were together in New Haven, where I was strangely finding myself on many Monday mornings. She had taken me along with her to a seminar in Chicano studies, an Ivy League oddity that I would not have encountered at Harvard. Young people in sweatshirts and blue jeans sat around a long, rectangular table. My girlfriend's course syllabus told me that the professor was about to lead a discussion on a piece of Mexican-American literature. As the instructor cleared her throat, the students around the table reached into their backpacks and pulled out their copies of a familiar paperback book. I recognized the book as being the same one that lay scribbled and worn on my bookshelf back in Cambridge, Richard Rodriguez's controversial classic *Hunger of Memory*.

At that point, having known Rodriguez for over a year, I realized how unfair my initial judgments of him had been. Although I had not fully conceded to his theory that an elite education requires a loss of intimacy, my arduous experiment at home had at least taught me to respect his point. Certainly, I believed, those critics of Rodriguez who had viciously, if defensively, attacked his argument were living in a splendid dream world of denial, like the Mexican-American college professors who toasted farmworkers with champagne and professed solidarity with Mexican waiters before returning to their white spouses in expensive houses in the suburbs.

Seated around the table, I noticed two other Latinos and a young Asian-American woman. If there is criticism, I thought to myself, then these few will be the dissenters who attack the author most vehemently. These are the ones who hate him. Because these are the ones who hear his message most clearly. These are the ones, their Yale sweatshirts notwithstanding, carrying the baggage of less-educated parents with heavy accents. These are the ones with the lingering insecurities about having come to the Ivy League only by the grace of affirmative action. In short, these are the ones for whom the image cast in Rodriguez's literary mirror is most disconcerting.

What I did not expect, however, was that the discussion that was about to erupt in that ancient classroom would illuminate for me a major obstacle to the educational progress of Latinos and other ethnic minorities—that of trying to define yourself through excellence while others try to limit such definition through the assumptions of stereotype.

Sensing a combative mood in the room and well-aware of my stubborn loyalty to friends, my girlfriend squirmed in her seat in nervous anticipation of the storm brewing. *Please God, make Ruben behave himself...*

The book starts with an odd passage: "I have taken Caliban's advice. I have stolen their books." The reference, familiar to some readers and unfamiliar to others, alludes to a character in William Shakespeare's play, *The Tempest*. The professor was, for some reason, intrigued by the author's choice of words. She asked the class to probe its significance.

"Why did he use *these* words?" she asked. "Why mention *Caliban?*"

No response. Undaunted, she pressed on.

"Why not say, 'I have taken *Marquez's* advice...' or *Paz's* advice?" she asked. Then, a hint. "Could it be that by invoking a Shakespearean character, he is trying to tell the reader something about himself?"

Still nothing. A young woman held her head down and pretended to take notes, while one of her classmates cleared his throat.

Another hint. "Could it be that, by referring to Shakespeare, that Rodriguez is trying to be something that he's not...?"

Then, finally, the professor blurted out the idea around which she had been nibbling for several minutes. "Could it be," she asked, "that the author is trying to be... *white?*"

Hearing this, my eyes sprang open from the nap into which I was drifting and my girlfriend jumped up in her seat.

Oh shit! Here he goes. Please let him leave behind enough of her to grade my final...

Although I realized that, given my enrollment status at Harvard, my input might be put to better use in a classroom some two hundred miles to the north, I nonetheless raised my hand and asked for permission to speak.

Once permission was granted, I explained to the startled professor that I took exception to her suggestion that Rodriguez "wanted to be white"—something that I myself might have thought two years earlier. Moreover, I told her, I was offended by her implication that a more authentic Mexican-American author would have alluded to Paz or Marquez instead of Shakespeare, as if the world's great literature was somehow segregated. I asserted that, as another Mexican-American who had read Shakespeare, I neither "wanted to be white" or felt less authentically Mexican. I had tired of the vicious and childish games of freshman year, during which I had so eagerly passed judgment over the ethnic authenticity of my Chicano classmates. I had realized the hurt that I and others had caused, if only to make ourselves feel more authentic, and I was sorry for it. Finally, I told the professor that it was a sad state of affairs when a well-educated Latino intellectual and writer like Rodriguez could not mention Shakespeare without incurring hostile criticism that he wanted to be something that he was not.

Damn, right for the jugular! I wonder if I can transfer out of this class?

Rodriguez did not need reincarnation. He was a graduate of the same type of schools that had produced the professor who was criticizing him. And for her, as a white woman, to claim on behalf of her entire race an implied sovereignty over certain pieces of literature, or anything else, smacked of the intellectual exclusion of old. Her remark showed that she was unwilling to concede that Rodriguez, through his affiliation with pristine universities like Stanford, Berkeley, and Columbia— Did she know that years earlier, the author had himself been invited to teach at Yale?—had stolen her books. The same was true for me and the woman next to me. The books were ours now. They were ours to keep and yes, to quote.

Going on the attack, I then offered a question of my own. I asked, "If you think that an intellectual like Rodriguez—by a scholarly quoting of Shakespeare—wants to be *white*, then does that mean that in your mind, the more legitimate image of an authentic Mexican is some dark-skinned, Spanish-speaking farmworker who doesn't read Shakespeare? Don't you think that there should be enough room for diversity in my community as there is in yours?"

Embarrassed, the professor granted me the point and conceded the dangers of using intelligence as an indicator of ethnic authenticity. Meanwhile, my girlfriend's stomach was in knots and she was wondering why she loved me so much.

Along with passion and loyalty, I was constantly nurturing my own sensitivity. In matters of the heart, I hated being predictable or fitting into a preset pattern. Most of all, I hated being lumped together with other men, as if to assume that one set of characteristics could define an entire gender. I had heard somewhere the observation that men and women love differently, that while men love primarily with their bodies, women love mainly with their hearts. If that was at all true, then, I resolved, I wanted to make the way that I loved an exception. So, instead of consulting with male friends whose opinions were remarkably similar to one another, I more often sought out the opinions of women. I made a habit of anticipating what other men would typically do in a given situation and then I did the exact opposite. Maybe I had been taught well by the young feminists who, in my sophomore year, sat next to me in not one but two women's studies courses. Or maybe I was just trying to overcompensate as a personal repentance for my having sexually exploited my Harvard status years earlier.

In any case, I soon learned that the whole idea of male sensitivity was a bit of a generational novelty. I spoke to my girlfriend in ways that I could not imagine my father speaking to my mother. My parents both had a private fear that their sons would marry strong and domineering women who would leave them, in their words, "henpecked." Raised in an earlier age, they were somewhat suspicious of both *unmanly* men and *unladylike* women. As such, there was bound to be, eventually, a conflict between their image of the submissive, traditional woman that they had always imagined that I would marry and the reality of the types of strong, confident, intelligent women to whom I found myself drawn in the Ivy League.

That conflict had come, as I might have expected that it would, in a series of visits that my girlfriend paid to my parents' home in Sanger. Their reception of her, like that of me by her parents in Phoenix, had been kind and gracious. They had tried immediately to make her feel at home and, to a degree, like one of the family.

Still, there was a sense, a mood in the air, that my parents were somewhat startled by this strange creature, the likes of whom they had never seen. Here was an intelligent, articulate Mexican-American woman from Yale who had no intention of spending her life, a life as charmed as that of their son, in her husband's shadow. She would not be content to merely have children and stay home with them, and she was not willing to allow her husband, by sole virtue of gender, to be the family breadwinner. She might as well have been the Easter Bunny nibbling carrots at the table, the level of disbelief and apprehension was so high. When a dinner discussion turned to politics or to legal issues, my father and I would have our usual banter interrupted by our guest expressing her opinion. My father was a bit shocked at first. *Her* opinion? My father said nothing in response. No. A cop of twenty-five years who began his career at a time when there were no female police officers was, for instance, simply not ready to take seriously the perspective of a young woman on the legal ramifications of the Miranda warning.

My grandfather's generation had been conditioned to think of a woman as a successful man's ornament, someone to display proudly on his arm. My father's generation, which had been confronted in the 1970s with the economic reality that one wage could no longer feed a family, was forced to adapt to the idea of a woman as a successful man's helper, something to help him succeed and prosper. It was left to my generation to adapt yet again, this time to the most radical concept of all: a woman as a successful man's equal.

As I cleared the table of dishes or brought my girlfriend a pillow from the hall closet or whispered "I love you" in her ear only when I was sure that there was no one else around to hear me, I could feel the anxiety in my parents' stare as they directed it at me, their henpecked Harvard son. Ironically, in Phoenix, when the roles of host and houseguest had been reversed, I had sensed that her mother was just as apprehensive about her daughter clearing away my plate after dinner as my father was about my doing the same for her. She no more wanted a subservient daughter than my father wanted a henpecked son. Ap-

parently, unknown to the two of us, one of the fringe benefits
of going to a school like Harvard or Yale is that, once you go
there, you never have to clear your own place setting at dinner
again.

I could sense my grandfather's spirit hovering over my father's shoulder, both of them shaking their heads in concern.
Qué? A woman as an equal? It was up to me to reassert control
and uphold the family honor. The challenge was mine. What
would I do? I'll tell you what I did. One morning, I made breakfast. And then, as a thoughtful gesture intended to make her
feel special, I served it to her in bed. Looking back, it is a small
wonder that racing through the hallway toward the bedroom—
quietly so as to avoid my parents' notice and censure—all while
balancing a tray of eggs, bacon, toast, and orange juice, that I
did not stumble and scatter my sweet intentions all along the
floor.

And she returned those sweet intentions by caring for me and
supporting all of my endeavors. Without exception, she was my
biggest fan. After the publication of "Harvard Homeboy," I was
bombarded for several months with criticism from individuals
who accused me of exploiting the demise of a former classmate
for my own personal fame and profit. Not surprisingly, other
Mexican-American students at Harvard were the chief proponents of this allegation. In an extraordinary gesture, I received
an unexpected phone call from an old friend, a Chicano who
had entered Harvard with Joe Razo and me. The young man,
who had graduated the year before (on time), called from California to confront me directly. After two hours on the phone,
we smoothed things out. Yet I will never forget the anger in his
voice as he told me of a rumor that he had heard from yet
another former classmate of ours, a rumor that I was "selling
Razo down the river."

After three or four months of hearing such things, either in
whispers or in outright accusations, I began to believe them
myself. Before long, I considered myself a kind of Ivy League
undertaker. Depending on your perspective, what that meant
was either that I was the trustee of the legacy of my fallen
classmate or that I was merely an unscrupulous vulture shamelessly picking into his carcass.

For weeks, guilt knotted my stomach. Making matters worse,

there was, several months after the printing of my editorial, still positive attention being directed at me because of it. Someone from Williams College said that the piece had been included by a professor into a sourcebook of assigned reading for an ethnic studies course. A national magazine reprinted the article. A professor from Harvard Law School, who years earlier had me as the youngest of his students in a class into which I had cross-registered, invited me to contribute an original essay to a literary journal that he was publishing; my piece, he said, would appear after that of an esteemed law professor from Yale and before that of a federal judge. Most surprising of all, I was receiving a number of telephone calls from movie producers scrambling to tell the dual tale of the Harvard Hold-up Man and his undertaker, I mean caretaker.

The extra attention left me consumed by what I considered to be the arbitrary nature of what academia, and American society at large, deems success. Early on in life, Joe Razo had been singled out as different and better than his Mexican-American classmates; not surprisingly, there developed an immense gap between them. In trying to play the role of the gangster that he never was, he tried to bridge that gap. When he failed, he failed in a big way. Yet to most clearly appreciate the depth of tragedy, one needs to compare it to some form of success. And so the editors of newspapers and law professors and movie producers were grateful to have at their fingertips the example of a young man who had entered Harvard with Razo and had not only survived but had also prospered. In the ultimate irony, writing about Razo's tragedy had, in a sense, catapulted me into his shoes, as uncomfortable as they were.

I toyed with depression. I assumed a more private existence, dodging questions about whether I planned to do any more writing. I mumbled to myself about the fickle nature of those who search for and find success stories only to abandon them and replace them with others.

In that emotional time, it was my girlfriend who held my hand and comforted me when I needed it most. She listened to my mumblings and she tried to understand. But she could not understand, she said. She told me that she loved too much, was proud of me too much, and admired my developing writing talent too much to believe for one moment that I had not worked hard for, and thus deserved, any success that I might encounter. She convinced me that I should not feel guilty for Razo's demise, reminding me that I had done nothing wrong. *"Sweetheart, you didn't pull those robberies. . . . You didn't . . ."* I was her confidant, her lover, and her best friend. As such, I was, at least to her, wonderful. All in all, she was to me nothing less than my secret weapon against the madness of this world.

For my part, I was more deeply in love than I had ever been in my life. At the end of our final winter in New England, graduation was still months away. In addition to the filling out of graduate school applications, there was only the completion of our final courses that stood between us and commencement. Along with, of course, still unresolved questions about marriage and our future together. I had postponed and stalled and hesitated for months. In fact, I was so busy trying to avoid confronting the marriage issue that I did not notice, and should have, the calendar exhausting February. This time, as with Caesar, the Ides of March would deal their harshest blow.

We were approaching the conclusion of a drama that had defined the kind of people we would always be. The proverbial brass ring was closer than ever. But if we knew anything, then we knew that nothing we had accomplished up to that point would matter one bit if we were, for any reason, not able to seize it.

Not surprisingly, with graduation only a few months away, we felt increased pressure to tone down our relationship. By Christmas, amid our collective clutter of law school applications and debilitating standardized tests, she resented more than ever what she perceived to be the very real threat that our relationship would infringe upon her future. As what I considered an underhanded rhetorical weapon, she sometimes used our shared ethnicity against me by invoking the stereotype of dominant and overbearing macho Mexican man. She assumed that I was somehow culturally predisposed to assert control over her life. She assumed also, perhaps, that white men were genetically more supportive as husbands than were Latinos.

She accused me, wrongly, of expecting her to give up her dreams and be content with merely sharing mine. She mocked the women I had dated back home, without knowing them, assuming them to be mindless aspiring housewives with little education and even less ambition. She was convinced that such women were, first and foremost, concerned with landing a husband and that a Harvard husband would be a most coveted prize. She joked sarcastically that their education goals included not a JD or an MBA but simply a Mrs. degree.

I heard in my lover's words an angry resentment that, as a Mexican-American woman in the Ivy League, she might have to make sacrifices that would have seemed strange and unreasonable to her marrying-age cousins and friends back home. Not the least of which was her staunch refusal to let a common emotion like love, however compelling, interfere with the grandeur of destiny. She was not alone. Two of our closest friends, Latinas from Yale and Columbia, had each broken up with their boyfriends in their senior years rather than include them in their future plans. One told her boyfriend of two years that she wanted them each to decide on graduate school plans completely independent of each other, evidently afraid that love might interfere with ambition. And in the competitive environment of the Ivy League, when those two entities clash, love usually loses.

My girlfriend said that we had to have a talk. Whatever was bothering her was beginning to interfere with homework, grad school applications, everything. She told me that yet another friend back home had announced her engagement and that naturally the blessed event had prompted her into thinking of her own matrimonial future. She was tired of my excuses and my stalling. She wanted, needed, an answer. One way or another. Did I intend to marry her or not, she asked. I took a deep breath and realized that there was no more avoiding the question, the question in the back of my mind for over a year, the question that had lured us into jewelry stores in New Haven, the question with no answer.

Did I *want* to marry her? Yes, absolutely. More than anything. Without question. She was growing more beautiful to me each day; she was, in my mind, most lovely in those first few minutes out of bed, without makeup, her hair a disaster, and in her worn-out flannel pajamas. After two years, we still called each other every day, sometimes twice in one day. We were desperate for the sound of each other's voice, each other's touch. The thought of living a single day of my life without her was becoming more and more unbearable.

But all that said, did I *intend* to marry her? I had no idea. I was still unsure. I was unsure because I knew that, ultimately, that was not my decision to make. I could ask the question, but answering it would be up to her. And I had always assumed from our conversations that, at this point in our lives, the answer would be a polite no. There were two reasons or maybe two hundred.

First, there was the troubling sense I had that she would be happier and more content with someone else, a faceless blond, blue-eyed someone else who could give her children of a lighter complexion. Her professed love for me notwithstanding, I could not help but think that she would spend the rest of her life with me thinking that she had "missed out" on something better, better meaning less attainable. This feeling was even more frustrating because I was completely sure that no blond, blue-eyed man could love her and respect her as much as I did, that making me the best choice.

And then, there was also the exhaustive topic of responsibility. For two years, during the entirety of our relationship, it had always been me who had brought up the topic of marriage, if only as a romantic ploy, and it had always been she who had been sensible and practical and noncommittal. She had always argued that we should wait, that we should not let ourselves be distracted from our career goals. Like other young couples, we were likely to grow apart. It was highly doubtful that the two of us would end up at the same graduate school unless we planned it that way. I had heard all the lectures from my feminist friends about "modern women" not wanting men to saddle them with the traditional constraints of marriage. And I was, above all, still extremely sensitive to the lingering perception by some that marriage would amount to my stripping the woman I loved most of her own hard-earned success and asking her to settle for sharing mine. I was also well aware of our parents' fear that marriage would interfere with our goals. I envisioned forty years of Christmas dinners with in-laws, their resentful stares at me as the guy who made a wife and mother out of the woman who would have been, had I not interfered with destiny, history's first Latina Supreme Court justice.

Finally, I answered her question. "I don't think that we *can* get married..."

A week later, she called. The voice that used to wake me in the morning and comfort me in darkness was telling me that it was time to say good-bye.

"This isn't going to work ... we should see other people ... we're young ... we have to worry about law school and where we're going to be next year ... and I am not willing to stay with someone who is not prepared to marry me and help me sort through all these questions ... I hope that we can always be friends ... and yes, I still love you."

There would be no more messages that she had called "just to tell him that I miss him." As the calendar abandoned the darkness of March for the gray of April, I knew that I had never really been hurt before. This was hurt in its rawest and cruelest form. My eyes swollen with tears for weeks, a loss of appetite, an enduring dryness in my throat, and the helpless, hopeless sense of being completely alone and unwanted told me that my heart was not merely breaking. It was exploding. It was bursting inside of me, howling in a pain in my chest and begging to be put out of its misery. The romance that began, years earlier, with a single tear ended in a flood of them.

Now, two years after our last kiss, I can finally verbalize the main reason for my reluctance to marry someone with whom I felt so compatible and with whom I was so deeply in love. Simply: given the fact that my girlfriend had an array of responsibilities that were as compelling as mine and career prospects that were as bright, I considered a marriage proposal—however thoughtful and appropriate—to be a form of intervention in her life's path that I did not feel entitled to launch. Thus, in deference to her future, I assumed the role of a Shakespearean romantic, selflessly conceding my happiness for what I perceived to be my loved one's "own good."

And so, finally, I am left with an appreciation for a simple but important fact: No matter how strenuous and demanding the experience of a Harvard Chicano may be, there is another experience—distinguished not only by ethnicity but by gender as well—that is even more difficult.

CHAPTER 10

WISDOM

A MAN STUMBLES UPON A FISHERMAN WHO IS GATHERING
CRABS AND PLACING THEM IN A BUCKET WITH NO LID.
WHEN THE PASSERBY ASKS THE FISHERMAN WHETHER HE
IS CONCERNED THAT THE CRABS MIGHT CLIMB OUT OF THE
BUCKET AND CRAWL AWAY, THE FISHERMAN REPLIES THAT
THERE IS NO NEED FOR WORRY. "YOU SEE" HE SAYS,
"THESE ARE *MEXICAN* CRABS. WHENEVER ONE OF THEM
TRIES TO MOVE UP, THE OTHERS PULL HIM DOWN. . . ."

OLD MEXICAN FOLK TALE

Heartbroken and abandoned, I needed refuge from the cold winds of spring. Under normal circumstances, I might have sought out and found comfort in a familiar corner of the Harvard community that had offered me a kind of home away from home during my first three years in college. But the circumstances of my last ten weeks in school were anything but normal. There was no refuge. I was alone yet again, more completely than ever before, and I was left wondering how I had managed to isolate myself from so many people.

Months earlier, at the beginning of my senior year, I had been forsaken by another lover. A lover who had not only broken my heart but also shattered my idealism.

Through bruised egos and homesickness and failed courses and various addictions, the members of RAZA understood that supporting one another was not only encouraged, but expected. Acting as a "support system" for Chicanos on campus was not merely a function of the group; it was the explicit reason for its creation. In the beginning, when RAZA represented only a handful of students, that primary mission was easy to remember. But after twenty years, the Mexican-American student community at Harvard had seen not only an increase in the number of Chicano students but also an increase in the diversity of those students. The mission of peer support had been forgotten in the chaos of change.

Initially, RAZA members must have all looked alike. They were dark-skinned, lower-class males who had been reared speaking Spanish at home by parents who had come to the United States from Mexico. By the time I arrived at Harvard two decades later, that student profile had changed radically and in unforeseen ways. In the late 1980s, the Mexican-American students who I nodded to in Harvard Yard came not only from poor rural areas but also, more often, from cities. He and she were not just the children of farm workers, but also of college professors and engineers and, in my case, policemen. They were gay and straight, middle-class and upper-class. They came from mixed marriages and they had black girlfriends and white boyfriends. They defied stereotype. They were the young men and women who, during our freshman year, I had met and discounted as inauthentic "coconuts," those who I thought blurred and trivialized what I considered to be the important cultural distinctions of Mexican-Americans.

The change in the overall diversity of students mandated a change in RAZA's approach to them. The challenge was to greet them with a renewed respect and tolerance for difference. It was a challenge that was not met.

As a leader in the group, I had failed the test myself. I knew my own culpability. Maybe I was taught intolerance by my elders. Maybe I was inspired by the bizarre events unfolding among

Chicano students on other elite campuses. At Berkeley, an inter-campus conference of Chicanos had ended abruptly when delegates from UCLA became disgusted with the revolutionary tone of the meeting and stormed out into Sproul Plaza in protest. At Stanford, incredibly, an ideological split and power dispute had resulted in the existence of not one but two Chicano student organizations. And at Yale, in one of the most distasteful examples of ethnic infighting, the Chicano student group had been nearly torn apart by the issue of sexuality. During a group meeting, a member had hung a picture on the wall. A portrait of the typical Mexican family, he had said. Man, woman, and child. When one of the group's openly gay members had bravely objected to the characterization as not being "typical" to the life that he would lead, the mood got ugly. Fueled by defensiveness, the proceedings had fallen into a frenzy of division, intolerance, and outright bigotry. The president of the group had been so upset with what had happened that she contemplated disbanding the organization altogether. In each case, an ethnic organization that had promised support had delivered only judgment.

At Harvard, in the freshman exuberance of ethnic "Truth or Consequences," I had neatly divided up the Mexican-American student community into two camps. Us and Them. The assessment that separated the parties into these two camps was whether or not one was "ethnically correct."

To be ethnically correct was to be the "right kind" of Latino. Speaking English better than Spanish or questioning sacred programs like affirmative action was not ethnically correct. Being the offspring of an interracial marriage or dating white people was not ethnically correct. Wearing blue contact lenses, joining a white fraternity, or taking economics instead of Chicano studies was not ethnically correct. And being gay instead of straight, Republican instead of Democrat, or wealthy instead of poor was certainly not ethnically correct.

By the beginning of my senior year, I had realized my error. My enlightening experience at Fresno State had taught me that educationally privileged Chicanos at elite schools like Harvard, Yale, and Princeton were the last people on earth who were qualified to assess ethnic authenticity. It had taught me also that one's ethnicity is intimate and personal and not a matter of public discussion or dissection. A man realized the hurt that a younger and more foolish boy must have caused some of his classmates. And he wanted to make it right.

It had seemed appropriate that the apologies begin with one classmate in particular. Upon careful reflection, I realized that both RAZA's support for Joe Razo while he was at Harvard and its ass-covering reaction to the news of his arrest were woefully inadequate. From the beginning, he was shunned by many of his Chicano classmates. Many of us were intimidated by Razo's defiant style of dress. The bold imagery of his appearance was unsettling. Clad in the homeboy costume of bandanna and tattoos, he did not exactly fit our image of what a Harvard Chicano should look like. He embarrassed us. In a meeting with the Dean of Students, I doubt that a single member of RAZA would have taken Joe along.

There was, oddly, a delicate balance to being the "right kind" of Latino. If other Latino students were not ethnic enough, then Razo's image made him almost *too* ethnic. The truth was that, at Harvard, Joe was no more accepted by RAZA members than he was by the Harvard community at large. Before long, RAZA's rhetorical pledge of support for all Chicano students must have seemed a hollow gesture to such a scared and lonely young man.

In a move that would dramatically sever my ties with RAZA, I had included such observations in my editorial for *The Los Angeles Times*. I had written:

> Some of us know, and few will admit that Joe Razo experienced a kind of double alienation at Harvard. Confused and alone, he instinctively sought refuge in one corner of a foreign world that seemed familiar. The Mexican-American students' association at Harvard is called RAZA. Its professed goal has been to provide a support system for Chicano students...
>
> Yet those who know these types of student organizations best know also that sometimes they become as intolerant of individual differences as they accuse the campus community at large of being. Ethnic organizations sometimes develop an image deemed proper for minority students and shun those who contradict that image. To RAZA members awaiting ad-

mittance to the world of BMWs and designer suits, Joe Razo and his attire represented that sort of contradiction. . .

He was an embarrassment to some, a reminder of how close they still were to the world that they had left behind. He was dressed like the kid whose fate, we had been told, we could escape if we studied hard. So we did. And when, through all our efforts, we had arrived safely in the Ivy-covered world of cashmere and Kennedys, there he was— staring us in the face and forcing us to deal with the painful realization that we had not progressed nearly as far as we thought we had. He made us feel uncomfortable, and then guilty for feeling uncomfortable.

Needless to say, after the piece appeared, RAZA members were not pleased. Not only did they reaffirm the familiar accusation that I was exploiting our former classmate's tragedy for my own fame and fortune, but they also charged that I had no right to make what they considered unfair comments and to make them publicly. Indeed, they seemed most unnerved by the fact that, by being printed in a major newspaper, my remarks about their shabby treatment of one of their own had transcended the bounds of mere campus grumblings and reached a mass audience. Given that Latinos are a private people, I should not have been surprised. Besides, hadn't the whole Razo affair been cloaked in darkness?

I recalled the closed-door meeting in the semester that directly followed Razo's arrest, the panicked discussion of what to say publicly about the incident. I recalled the inane suggestion by one RAZA member that we not discuss it at all. I recalled the fear that other Chicanos in the Ivy League would mercilessly exploit the tragedy to serve their own recruitment ends. I recalled the overwhelming consensus, one to which I had never agreed: the least said, the better. Through their silence, they had followed Harvard's shameful example. *Ignore it and it will go away.*

RAZA members had been embarrassed once more, this time by me. And they were defensive again. They wanted to lash out, trusting that if they cut the messenger's throat, then they could avoid hearing the message. They wanted to isolate me. They wanted to assert to the campus community that, in the zeal of my passion and self-righteousness, I had lost all credibility.

They had precedent. The savaging of one Latino by another, whether over differences in appearance or opinion, is learned behavior, learned early. My ex-girlfriend told me once, with pain in her voice, of the events of a certain afternoon in her childhood. Her mother had gone to considerable expense to buy a pretty dress for her to wear to school. When she got there, she had been ruthlessly teased by a group of Mexican children. Considering her wardrobe to be too prim and proper, they had attacked.

Aw, look at her pretty dress. She must think that she's better than us. She must think that she's white or something . . . .

I remember my own experience in elementary school, the occasional taunts of Mexican classmates who accused me of trying to be white. My sin? Doing my homework, respecting our teacher, and correctly answering questions in class. All characteristics that, unfortunately for them, my classmates somehow equated with being white. The stories that I have heard, firsthand, of Latinos destroying and discrediting one another are too numerous to mention. There is the one about the Chicano law student scolded by her Chicano classmates because she wanted to forsake public interest law to practice the more ethnically incorrect corporate law. There is the one about the Chicano professor who was censured by his colleagues for teaching his students about the imperfection of affirmative action. There is the one, from UCLA, about the controversial Latina political figure who, after confronting a group of Chicano undergraduates in a class that she was teaching, returned to her car to find an unequivocal sign of displeasure in the form of excrement on her front seat. There is the one, from Harvard, about the same Latina being snidely scolded by a graduate student for the unspeakable offense of having a white husband. And there is, of course, the multitude of memories in my own father's quarter-century career in law enforcement that leads him to counsel young Mexican-Americans entering the profession to get used to the word *vendido*, sellout, because they will hear it often.

Some Mexican-Americans attribute the trait of ethnic infighting to heritage. *"Es el indio. . ."* my father jokes. His comment is a reference to what early Western historians portray as the aggressive character of Native Americans, who are, after all, our maternal ancestors.

Still, my experience straddling the separate worlds of Harvard and home has taught me that there is another reason for the discord among us, another log that feeds the fire separating Mexican-Americans from one another. It is ancient, grounded in five hundred years of Mexican history. We use it, among ourselves, not necessarily against those whom we despise, but against those whom we envy. Those of whom we are jealous. It is what the elders call *envidia*. Although envy is a part of every culture, when it appears among Mexicans, it assumes a special significance. It is most often directed at those with whom we would like to trade places. Those whom we consider too close to positions of power, wealth, and prestige. Richard Rodriguez has seen the green-eyed stare of *envidia*. So has Henry Cisneros.

I have seen it, too. With a shrug, I have acknowledged its presence in the voices of competitive parents who assure me that their daughter could have gone to a school like Harvard "if she wanted to." Or in the minds of RAZA members who wish each other luck in securing the summer internship in Washington while secretly hoping that, when all is divided, their proud plum will be the juiciest of all. Or in the minds of an old guard Latino leadership that is suspicious and resentful of younger, more well-educated political wannabes. Or even, closer to home, in the mind of a competitive aunt or cousin who assumes that the Harvard man in their familial ranks thinks himself better than them and who secretly hopes that he will ultimately fail. I have seen *envidia* fuel contempt for young people who attend elite schools such as Harvard or Yale, for authors who have sold too many books about "memory," and for elected officials who are popular and successful.

And as I would learn, *envidia* is no stranger to literary novices who have published their reflections in major newspapers. Already angered by my comments in *The Los Angeles Times*, my Chicano classmates needed only one more reason to turn against me. And one winter's night, I gave it to them.

There is one other thing that is never ethnically correct: publicly challenging an esteemed cultural icon. In a gesture that brought together the separate worlds of Harvard and the San Joaquin Valley, Cesar Chavez had come to campus to promote the United Farm Worker's aggressive grape boycott. He told horrible stories of babies born with birth defects caused by illegal pesticides and passed the collection plate, appealing (like no one else) to the sensibilities of eastern white liberals and amassing a good amount of financial support for the UFW in the process. The presentation is invariably effective; years earlier, when I had first seen an explicit UFW video with scenes of Mexican mothers holding their malformed infants, I had shed angry tears.

At Harvard, what the union president had certainly not expected to find amid the scratching of expensive fountain pens on checkbooks was an arrogant, passionate, and self-righteous young man who had just completed an unfruitful search for the UFW's influence in the lives of California farmworkers and who was determined not to be sold that easily again. I was seated in the last row alongside five or six other Chicanos who had no idea what was going through my mind. I had, through my experience in California, developed distinct inhibitions and doubts about the contemporary relevance of the UFW. Despite its populist rhetoric, I feared that the union had become as elite and as detached an institution as Harvard itself. With the UFW president standing twenty feet in front of me and with an opportunity that would never have been afforded me had I simply attended Fresno State, I had decided to take those doubts to the source. After Chavez's address, during the question and answer session, I had stood and asked the icon a brief and simple question.

Something like, "Señor Chavez, how do you respond to the perception by some that you have become more popular than the UFW itself? That you have become detached and distanced from the same farmworkers whom you claim to represent? In short, why is it we are more likely to find you speaking these days at Harvard or Yale than at Fresno State?"

I had resumed my seat to a distinct silence in the audience. I had heard the nervous clearing of throats. Caught off guard, the labor leader's response had come with obvious difficulty. The lost momentum, the stuttering repetition of phrases, the surrendering of the microphone to each of the two union vice-presidents who had accompanied him, and the angry, scornful look that penetrated the room like a loud silence had all told me that, perhaps this time, I had gone too far. My father had always said that one day, my big mouth would get me into serious trouble. Of course my father had also told me to speak my mind and defend my convictions.

After the abrupt ending of the presentation, I was approached by Chavez himself, who in a nose-to-nose shouting match, accused me of being a "grower plant." In what struck me as paranoia, he actually seemed to believe that I had been flown out from California by rich farmers, "growers," to embarrass him and thwart his fundraising. I responded, irreverently, that if he sought to embarrass himself, then he did not need my help. A childish tenacity seized us both, and neither one of us was ready to back down. Looking back, I suppose that I should have been more respectful of a man whose historical accomplishments were so significant. At least, respectful of an elder. But, respect is a two-way street. All the union leader had shown me was contempt. Besides, I knew that had the speaker been Richard Rodriguez or conservative commentator Linda Chavez or another ethnically incorrect Latino, RAZA members would have staged a feeding frenzy that would have been most disrespectful.

As an ironic twist to all this, I was also approached by someone else, a UFW supporter with curly blond hair, blue eyes, and prominent teeth. I had recognized those features even before she introduced herself as Robert Kennedy's daughter. She stood before me, shaking in anger over what she considered my misrepresention of the significance of an organization and a leader to which she and her family were fiercely loyal. Of course I knew the ties between Mexican-Americans and the Kennedys had always been strong. And if the two entities were married, then Cesar Chavez and the UFW had, thirty years earlier, helped perform the ceremony. At first, when confronted by a new generation, I considered deferring to that loyalty and to the legacy of a family that I respected nearly as much as my own. After all, the young woman's father and his affiliation with Harvard was one of the peculiar reasons why I had chosen to attend the school in the first place. Had Robert Kennedy gone to Yale, his daughter and I might have been having our little disagreement in New Haven. God forbid.

That is the way that I would have left it, politely excusing myself, had she not made an unfortunate remark about my "not knowing what I was talking about." Respect or not, I was unwilling to concede that a Kennedy knew more about Mexican farmworkers in the San Joaquin Valley than did the grandson of one. It was that simple. My ego kicked in and I resolved that, no matter what her name was, she was toast.

I reminded her, sternly, that twenty-two years earlier, her father had said of the UFW that it only wanted for the United States to be *better* in its protection of farmworkers' rights. I submitted that now, likewise, I was asking the same of the UFW, simply, for it to be *better* in its representation of farmworkers—those of the calloused hands and hollow stares who had, the year before, answered my questions about the UFW in the third person.

Stunned that someone who was in diapers when Robert Kennedy had gone to Delano to celebrate the breaking of Chavez's fast would have the audacity to quote her father back to her, the young woman stood speechless for a moment. Then she glared at me with a scornful look and asked, "Whose side are you on, anyway?" Whose side? Apparently in her mind, the fact that I shared Cesar Chavez's ethnicity implied that I also shared his politics. As a younger man, I might have believed that myself. No more. In the San Joaquin Valley, at Harvard, and in the world at large, I had learned that things were not that simple. After all, had I not met Mexican farmers in the Valley who had opposed the UFW agenda?

Later, over too many drinks in a Cambridge pub, a few friends allowed me to reflect privately on the consequences of publicly attacking a cultural saint. In his defensive ravings and accusations, I had not seen a saint. Only a scared little man, determined to have the last word with someone who had been taught, in the Harvard way, never to grant it.

"Do you know what you've just done . . . ?" someone asked. "You've just spit on the Virgin Mary."

I had done no such thing. I had only done exactly what Harvard and my family had taught me to do, to speak for those who were not in a position to speak for themselves. In this case, that meant Mexican farmworkers toiling in grape fields a world away from Harvard.

Any first semester student of Chicano studies could have predicted what had come next. As *chisme,* Mexican gossip, of my little performance had spread through campus and even through the Ivy League, RAZA members were once again forced to answer questions about one of their own. This time, not the Harvard Homeboy, but "the crazy guy who attacked Cesar Chavez."

The crazy guy who had always done RAZA's dirty work. As an arrogant underclassman, I had been the pitbull who would go to the *Crimson* with a provocative quote, or write the letter, or confront the dean—all of it uninhibited by the worries about public image that had stifled my cautious, ambitious classmates. I was very ethnically correct. Very down with brown, in RAZA terminology. In my senior year, after the Razo editorial and my "pissing contest" with Cesar Chavez, other Mexican-Americans on campus had had enough of my moralizing, my passion, my heaven and hell views of morality. They had had enough of embarrassment and defensiveness and blemishes on their public image. And they had had enough of me. I had come full circle, burned by the same judgment that I myself had employed years earlier. I was no longer *us;* I was finally part of *them.*

In my senior year, the months of January and February were much colder than usual. And within the Mexican-American community at Harvard, the icy temperature had nothing to do with the weather. I had been completely cut off socially. If I walked into a room in which a group of RAZA members were talking, the conversation would abruptly stop. If I sat at their table, they might all get up and leave in unison. If I passed them in the Square, they might cross the street to avoid me altogether. If there was a party, I was conspicuously not invited. Once, I jogged past two of them on the way to the gym. One whispered to the other and pointed in my direction. They said nothing. I ran by.

One day, a lunch companion who had listened to me relate some of this and who had not believed me, learned firsthand that I had not been exaggerating. As we sat down to lunch, the group of four or five Chicano students who had been sitting at the table before we arrived promptly got up and walked away.

"C'mon," he said incredulously. "They actually do this? What is this, the third grade?"

I smiled and shrugged. Never would I admit weakness. Never would I admit, even to myself, how lonely and hurt and embattled I felt. Instead, I told myself that alienation was the price of upholding my conviction.

This, I reasoned, was what Robert Kennedy must have meant when he talked about "moral courage [being] a rarer commodity than bravery in battle or great intelligence." One day, I quietly tacked that quotation on my bedroom door for both of my Chicano roommates to see, to see each morning as they walked past me to the bathroom that we shared, not saying a word. Incredibly, we did not speak for the last ten tension-filled weeks we lived together. I was a pariah, plain and simple. For much of winter, only weekend train trips to New Haven had kept me warm. Then, suddenly in March, there was no more sunshine in Connecticut. And no more weekend reprieves from my Chicano classmates.

These were the people who had once passed the shot glass of tequila. These were the people who I had helped through homesickness and insecurity and fear. The young man with the broken heart from a girlfriend back home. The young woman who hated Harvard and wanted out and cried to me until early morning. Those who needed advice on which classes to take or job contacts or a round of amateur therapy. My closest friends at Harvard were of no comfort to me against RAZA's silent attack. Because my closest friends were forging it. I had become an outcast from a group that I had nurtured and sustained for three years. In my final semester in college, they had betrayed me.

One person alone embodied the censure of my Chicano brethren. Poetically, he also symbolized the strongest connection between the opposing worlds of Harvard and the San Joaquin Valley. As a fellow Chicano at Harvard from the Valley, he was as close to being my alter ego as anyone.

We had met under the strangest of circumstances. The ultimate recruitment story. At the beginning of my freshman year, on the very day that I traveled from Fresno to Cambridge, I had read in the newspaper about a young man at a local high school who said he wanted to go to Harvard. Impulsively, I had picked up the phone and managed to contact him. We talked for a few minutes and I promised to send him an application and keep in touch through the school year. The next year, he had joined me in Cambridge as a bright-eyed, highly capable and motivated freshman whose only flaw was a touch of hero-worship for a classmate who was nowhere near ready for hero status.

We had been, during the first four years of our relationship, the absolute closest of friends. There had been a symmetry to our experiences. He used to joke to others that he was an extension of me and I was a reflection of him and vice versa. We were linked by past, present, and future. We had confessed intimacies. We had shared ambitions and weaknesses. We had trusted each other completely with our dreams and fears. In the Mexican way, our families, too, had been close. On one occasion, our mothers had flown together to Boston to see us. In fact, in time, we had become more like brothers than friends.

There was just one thing that separated us, and sadly, that one thing would drive us apart. As he grew increasingly ambitious, it seemed as if his every word, his every gesture was part of some careful campaign for the approval of others. Futhermore, he seemed to be not only concerned with his own image, but also with the image of Harvard Chicanos in general; he worried, in particular, about the ramifications of my public behavior. What did the Dean of Admissions, in whose office he worked, think of my editorial? Would his favorite professor think less of all Mexican-American students due to my revelations of disloyalty in our ranks? And of course, what were other Chicano students from Yale and Princeton and Columbia whispering about us at Pachanga? Consequently, no one in RAZA was more horror-struck than my old friend by the reckless, self-destructive trip on which, it was said, I had embarked. No one felt more profoundly the glare of the spotlight that I had brought to bear on RAZA. He must have wondered how would what I had written about the group reflect on *him* as a member?

Certainly, the experience of rekindling intimacy in California had changed me, making me more suspect of educational privilege and more mindful of Richard Rodriguez's theory that education takes an inevitable toll on cultural intimacy. But my friend and I had spent that year apart. While I was in Fresno becoming skeptical of Harvard's elitism, he was in Cambridge still bathing in it.

At the end of the year, upon my return to Harvard, we were more different than alike. I had seen and felt things that I could only tell him about. I challenged him to recognize the liabilities, as well as the benefits, of his Harvard experience; he resisted. I challenged the ambitious, complacent Mexican-Americans around me to be better, to be more connected to the world that we all purported to represent to the Harvard Admissions Office; he considered me to be consumed with self-righteousness and "out of control." Rather than stand with me against the criticism of our colleagues, he apparently found it more expedient to turn his back on me with the others.

And so it was that, just two months from graduation, I found myself nursing a broken heart and surrounded by people who wanted to break my spirit as well. I should have realized the seriousness of their intention. And I should have listened to Richard Rodriguez's ominous warning over the phone late one spring night.

"Be careful, child..."

My old RAZA colleagues wanted me out, not just out of the group but out of their lives. That meant out of Harvard. A friend from freshman year had done it. Packed his bags, flipped off John Harvard's statue, and hailed a taxi to Logan Airport, all just four months before graduation. To him, those must have seemed like four horribly punishing and imposing months; looking at the weeks on my calendar, I felt his fear. I was sure that most of RAZA would relish nothing as much as the sight of me packing up and dropping out of school in the eleventh hour of my college experience. They would have considered my departure not only an absolute relief, but also a kind of victory of good over evil.

Because I am not a good loser, I was not eager to grant my old partners such a clean and easy divorce. Still, alone and exhausted from the struggle and more homesick than I had been since freshman year, I considered giving in. Yes, I could leave. No diploma, no finals, no graduation, no nothing. Just go. After all, wasn't my sanity more important than any of this shit?

I knew full well the consequences of such a decision. I knew that quitting was just another form of being beaten, of failing. I thought of my parents, the disappointed and confused expressions on their faces as they stared helplessly at the unused plane tickets in their hands. I thought of my hometown and the sad precedent that would be set if the first Mexican-American student to attend Harvard was also the first to drop out of it. I could hear the people back home along Seventh Street, "And he was so close, too." The smirk of smug relatives, "I knew it . . ." I stared at my suitcase near the door.

If I left, the hard work and sacrifice and pain of four years in Cambridge and one in Fresno would be wasted. It would be like I had never gone to college in the first place. I would be reduced to nothingness, except, perhaps, a statistic buried in some foundations' report on the low retention of minority students on Ivy League campuses.

Moreover, because I was fleeing such an elite school, I knew that I could expect to experience an exaggerated sense of failure. That is one way that elitism sustains itself, by convincing those who indulge in its excesses that they cannot live without them. I remembered talking to an old friend from elementary school who had been suspended from the Naval Academy in his senior year. He was beyond depressed; he was devastated. More than a mere diploma, he appeared to have lost a part of his soul. Why?

For four years, every dimension of Academy life emphasized that through their association with Annapolis, midshipmen were *better*. Better than those at West Point. Better than those who had enlisted in the navy. Better than other officer candidates in college ROTC corps. Better, in fact, than the vast majority of American people that they were sworn to protect. He had been taught that his association with Annapolis made him special and he had believed it. And so, when that association was temporarily severed, he was left with nothing but a sense of unspeakable shame and irreparable loss.

And of course, there was nothing that Annapolis could teach Harvard about elitism or terms like "better than." I knew that if I left without a diploma, I would be, dare I say it, ordinary.

I probably would have left had it not been for the loyal support and comfort of two very special people, two classmates who stumbled across my tormented soul in the first days of May, just one month before a graduation ceremony that seemed like it would never arrive.

One was a strong and beautiful young woman, a Mexican-American who crossed over the RAZA picket line to be at my side. Through her personal dealings with the group she, too, had come to consider it to be little more than a narrow-minded purveyor of self-serving judgment. And she understood judgment. Given the fact that she came from a mixed marriage and did not speak Spanish, some RAZA members considered her inauthentic. In any case, she remained a true friend who re-affirmed my faith in the goodness of the human spirit. For the loyalty she gave me at a time when I needed it most, she will always have a piece of my heart.

My other savior affected my life in an even more profound way. Though he would help salvage my future, he had actually come from my past. He was the same young man from the Norman Rockwell town in Connecticut who had, a lifetime earlier, suffered the misfortune of being my freshman roommate. Striving for the assurances of firmer ground, we had challenged each other constantly in our year together. We had argued ruthlessly with each other about politics and especially about ethnicity and race.

I had been unable, and unwilling, to see any complexity behind his white face. Only later, when I had met his parents, did I remember that he was Italian-American. There were distinct similarities between the two of us to which I had been completely blind. He had the same difficulty communicating with his immigrant grandmother as I did with mine. His father's life, like that of my father, had been a tribute to the ethic of hard work and determination being a conquering force over ethnic prejudice. And in that context, his acceptance to Harvard had been no less extraordinary or monumental to his family than mine had been to my own.

Still, consumed with simple definition, I had instinctively and unfairly associated my old roommate with what I had perceived to be the country's racist and oppressive white ruling class. *White ruling class?* What did that mean? From digesting and regurgitating radical rhetoric from the Chicano student movement of the 1960s and from observing contemporary efforts to promote "minority issues" on college campuses, a foolish young man was sure that he knew. In my mind, the population of the United States was succinctly divided up into the same five categories that were listed under the heading of "ethnicity" on the Harvard undergraduate application. There were Latinos, African-Americans, Asian-Americans, and Native-Americans. Everyone else was simply white. Only later would I question the simplicity of those distinctions and admit to myself that, in humankind, no group of people was completely exempt from bigotry and prejudice just as no group could claim a monopoly on it.

I remember the exact moment when that fact, an obvious one, had first occurred to me. I was sitting in a Chicano studies class at Fresno State. A group of Mexican-American students had reached a consensus that "white people" could not possibly understand discrimination because they had never felt it. It was completely impossible for those young people to conceive of a pecking order that did not place Latinos and African-Americans at the bottom. Separate childhoods spent in a rural environment with limited opportunity for social mobility had reinforced that black and white view of the world.

In their opinion, everyone had their place. On campus, students flocked to various ethnic groups or to largely white fraternities and sororities. Off campus, they drank and danced and associated with their own in clubs along Shaw Avenue that were distinguished from one another by the skin color of their patrons. In popular stereotype, farmworkers were usually Mexican; Harvard students were usually not. Mexican parents, it was said, underemphasized the importance of education. And so, not surprisingly, what many parents considered the "best" school district in the area was coincidentally the one with the most number of white students and the least number of minorities.

But given my exposure to other ethnic groups at Harvard, I no longer found that argument very compelling. I thought back to the Jewish student in my dorm who mentioned the well-established fact that, immediately before World War II, Harvard had instituted admission quotas to keep the numbers of Jewish undergraduates at an "acceptable" level. I remembered the exhibits at the blessed John F. Kennedy Presidential Library in Boston, including a help-wanted ad from the 1920s that stipulated "Irish Need Not Apply." I recalled conversations with the descendants of Italian immigrants, whose recollections of the stories told them by their grandparents mirrored those told to me by mine. And of course I remembered what I had learned about the historical indignities suffered by Armenian-Americans in my own beloved San Joaquin Valley. Slowly, I learned that bigotry and prejudice and ugliness are not the sole province of Mexican-Americans or any other ethnic group. Rather, at various points in American history, the cancer of those unpleasantries has directly or indirectly infected us all.

And then there are other groups, similarly oppressed in our society, which are defined not by ethnicity or race at all. That would be my final, most important lesson at Harvard. And, it was graciously imparted to me by my old roommate. Always when I had pompously accused him of not knowing what it felt like to be an outsider or to suffer through prejudice or to ex-perience alienation, his response had been simple and ominous.

There's shit that you don't know about me...

The shit had been a well-kept secret during the entirety of our freshman year together. One night, at the beginning of our sophomore year, in the protection of a dark room, he had shaken and stammered with courageous fear in pulling that secret from his pocket and sharing it with me. The reality was that my old friend knew full well the definition of prejudice and oppression and alienation. He knew exactly what being the outsider felt like, even within his own family. And none of this had anything to do with his ethnicity. Instead, it stemmed from something that was just as intimate and just as personal and just as worthy of respect: his sexual identity. He had trusted me, and initially only a few others, with a bold and liberating admission that marked for him, in his twenties, nothing short of the beginning of life itself.

And so, I can say that in the darkness and loneliness of what should have been my joyous final days in college, I learned infinitely more about the values of integrity and friendship from a gay young man than I did from a group of petty, defen-sive, and self-consumed Mexican-Americans who professed a support based on an assumed commonality of experience.

Had it not been for pints of chocolate Häagen-Dazs and throwing baseballs along the banks of the Charles and trips to Fenway Park and eating frozen ravioli in his living room when things got way too hot in mine, I doubt that I would have made it through. A fellow Kennedy fanatic, he shared with me the literature of Greek tragedy that helped Robert Kennedy recover from his brother's death. As I searched desperately for some sort of meaning in all that I had endured in my time at Harvard, Aeschylus soon became my favorite.

He who learns must suffer. In our sleep, pain that cannot forget falls drop by drop upon the heart and in our despair, against our will, comes wisdom through the awful grace of God.

It is likely that without the support and compassion of my two dear friends, I would have left before graduation. I will never forget the fierce loyalty and comfort they offered me, enabling me to focus on my responsibilities. Page by page, papers were completed. One by one, finals passed.

As June finally arrived, I cleaned out my room and awaited my parents' arrival so that we all might hail a blessed taxi and leave that place—together. On the day of commencement, I greedily absorbed the final images of an experience that had irreparably changed my life. I savored the ceremony of colored flags and the long procession of students through Harvard Yard and the speeches peppered with pompous Latin and the old clichés at the traditional morning service in Memorial Church.

You know, you can always tell a Harvard man but you can't tell him much. And . . . never anything on commencement morning.

I even smiled through inspirational speeches from Harvard administrators whom I hardly recognized. Where was their inspiration when I had really needed it? Those who had greeted me from the same spot in the Yard five years earlier, promising a world of limitless opportunity. Those invisible men who had, since that time, represented to me mere names on letterhead. Those who had abided by an implicit code of conduct of not coddling students or accommodating ethnic difference, even through the most innocuous of concessions. Those who had instead created an environment in which the ground rules were primal: sink or swim. Those who had helped make Harvard, in the words of a beleaguered freshman, so impossible to love but strangely still worthy of respect. Those who, I was sure, would have not cared one bit if I had left their school in shame, and who would have cared even less had I never attended in the first place.

And now, at the podium, they began the process of ingratiating themselves back into the hearts of young people who were, with every tick of the clock, being magically transformed from lowly undergraduates to respected alumni who might one day, it was hoped, give generously to their beloved alma mater.

I did not hear the pitch. I was too busy trying to light a cigar with my right hand and pop the cork off a bottle of champagne with my left. As the speaker's words faded into a chorus of applause, and hundreds of tassled caps filled the air, I smiled. I had made it.

After the ceremony, I was immediately surrounded by the scattering of family members and friends who had, that same morning, flown in for the event. For weeks, they had been concerned with the most meaningless of details. What would they wear? It took much doing but I had finally convinced them that we had earned the right to go to the thing as ourselves, dressed our own way. And, I had told them, I would accept nothing less. And so, it was with a warmth in my heart that I noticed my father and uncle, as ambassadors of the Southwest, casually dressed in expensive cowboy boots, turquoise, and Stetsons.

Appropriately in the group, accompanied by his wife, was the same Irish policeman who had, years earlier, given my father directions in Harvard Square. He had remained a family friend since that chance encounter, staying in touch through holiday phone calls. He, too, was beaming with pride, explaining that although a Boston native, ours was the first Harvard graduation to which he had ever been invited.

At one point, my uncle pulled me aside and whispered congratulations in a way that seemed to explain why he had felt compelled to travel three thousand miles to attend the graduation ceremony.

"What you have done here, nephew, is, I think, good for the family."

And so, my graduation from Harvard, like the achievements that led me there, assumed a distinctly public dimension. Fittingly, immediately, my diploma slipped through my hands and onto a shelf in my parents' trophy case. No matter. Stripped of its ancient trappings and pretensions, the experience of attending Harvard is significant in and of itself. In truth, the act of having endured the place just long enough to graduate was more empowering than the scroll in my hand, the congratulatory tears of Mexican strangers back home and the impressed looks on the faces of prospective employers.

As I watched the images of familiar buildings get smaller and smaller through the car window, I made a private peace with my old school. In pushing me to my absolute limits and redefining the boundaries of my own capability, Harvard had taught me that only when the human spirit is at risk is it most alive. And, as Aeschylus promised, it rewarded a young man's endurance of that most punishing ordeal by bestowing a modest dose of wisdom. As with a lover who, through the sharing of joy and pain, becomes a part of your very soul and so cannot be forgotten, or a trusted friend who leaves your life but is always welcome in it, so it was that as Harvard embraced me, finally, as one of its own, the last trace of my resentment faded away and all was forgiven.

By midafternoon, the bright colored flags came down, the ground crews moved into the Yard, and the restaurants in Harvard Square filled up with proud parents buying their children a well-earned lunch.

As my classmates passed for the last time through a familiar gate, some of them may have noticed overhead, the second line of that ancient inscription carved in the stone. I did. And it is as a gesture of appreciation to a school that left me better than it found me that I consider myself bound to honor the dictates of John Harvard's final command.

Enter to Grow in Wisdom . . .
Depart to Serve Better Thy Country and Thy Kind.

RECONCILIATION

"The problem of education must first of all deal with the Talented Tenth."

W. E. B. DuBois

Ph.D., Harvard University, Class of 1895

"For those to whom much is given, much is required. And when at some future date the high court of history sits in judgment on each of us, recording whether in our brief span of service we fulfilled our responsibilities . . . our success or failure . . . will be measured by the answers to four questions: First, were we truly men of courage . . . Second, were we truly men of judgment . . . Third, were we truly men of integrity . . . Finally, were we truly men of dedication?"

John F. Kennedy

Harvard College, Class of 1940

Even after making my private peace with Harvard, there still remained the delicate task of making peace with home.

Reconciliation would, I knew, require confrontation.

It takes place in a familiar setting.

With more courage than common sense, I have come as a guest speaker to a government class in my old high school. It is the spring of 1991, the first thawing of winter since my graduation from college. The season is appropriate given my own experience within these walls, six years earlier, as a younger and more fragile being. In the San Joaquin Valley, a gentle winter should yield a gentle spring. But sometimes circumstances will not allow it. I have been invited by a teacher to weather a familiar firestorm. I have been asked to defend affirmative action policies in college admissions to a group of high school seniors, some of whom will, in a few days, find disappointment waiting for them in their parents' mailbox. In a sense, I have come to settle an old score with the spirit of an old adversary. One named Allan Bakke.

The role of lecturer is becoming familiar to me. For five years, I have routinely visited the rural high schools of the San Joaquin Valley, recruiting applicant prospects for Harvard. Initially, my efforts were sponsored by the university, which, in my sophomore year, subsidized a trip home so that I might visit a handful of Valley schools. I was not alone. Along with a dozen or so other Mexican-American students, the university's Undergraduate Minority Recruitment Program, each fall, sponsored similar efforts involving African-American, Asian-American, and Puerto Rican students.

Given the consistently high drop-out rate of Hispanic students from American public schools, the distressingly low number of Hispanics at schools such as Harvard, and the generally dismal state of what former president George Bush once called "the crisis in Hispanic education," I will admit that I went searching primarily for Mexican-American recruits. As a Chicano "success story," Harvard hoped that my background might allow me to serve as a role model and possibly counter the effect of the low expectation that so many young people confront in their educational life. However, because I never turned away an interested student because of their ethnicity, my recruitment efforts ultimately produced a distinctly multiracial pool of outstanding young people.

I visited well-funded, predominantly white high schools with Olympic-size swimming pools. The only annoyance would be an occasional sarcastic question, from a guidance counselor trying to make me squirm, about the role that a student's race plays in their admission to a school like Harvard. Looking around the room at rows of all white faces, I wondered for whose benefit that peculiar question had been asked.

I also visited remote, overwhelmingly Mexican schools where most students had never before even heard the word "Harvard." There, among cracking walls and worn out textbooks, I offered these young people their first glimpse into an elite world that they had never been taught existed. I did so only after sidestepping still more guidance counselors, these intent on assuring me that there was no "Harvard material" to be found there.

Through the 1980s and 1990s, politicians, syndicated columnists, and television commentators have tantalized the scandal-thrilled American public by presenting affirmative action as the newest and, in the minds of white people, most insidious form of racial injustice. Realizing that human beings are always most afraid of those things that we understand least, Republican political strategists have relentlessly exploited the fears that many Americans have about the preferential treatment of minority applicants in employment and education. The tactic, a shrewd one, is to motivate support for a conservative agenda by scaring lower and middle-class white people into believing that hordes of "less-qualified" minorities are scheming with socialist Democrats to steal their jobs or rob their children of the college education to which they feel entitled.

Sadly, too often, the politics of fear work. In 1990, Jesse Helms was reelected to the United States Senate against a black opponent; he was helped in that effort by his use of a brilliant television commercial in which a white South Carolinian loses his job because of affirmative action. Early in 1991, former Education Secretary William Bennett had already stated his intention to make "reverse discrimination" a fiery lightning rod of the following year's presidential race; ultimately, his plan would be thwarted not by a lack of will but by the embarrassing fact that, by the time the election rolled around, his party's candidate had already mooted the issue by signing the 1991 Civil Rights Act, which conservatives labeled a "quota bill."

Mr. Bennett's exuberance not withstanding, my own experience getting into and staying at Harvard, along with my stint as one of its recruiters and as an assistant clerk in the file room of its undergraduate admissions office has taught me that at Harvard and too many schools that emulate it, affirmative action is not at all revolutionary. In fact, in most cases, the practice degenerates into mostly posturing and piecemeal efforts. In reality, its modest results are hardly the heralded fall of the academy, the darkening of higher education, the abandonment of meritocracy, and the destruction of our society's delicate racial equilibrium as conservatives would have the public believe.

Shh . . . a secret. Yes, in the admissions process at Harvard an applicant's ethnicity is considered—along with academic excellence—as one of a variety of factors that may positively influence his or her chance for admission. Other factors might include home state, athletic ability, leadership skill, extracurricular activity, and whether or not an alumni relative donated a library to the university. It is all these things together, interlocked and inseparable, that substantiates Harvard's professed "commitment to diversity," diversity being the only thing about Harvard that is worth $25,000 a year.

Curiously, though, only in the case of minority students does preferential treatment bring with it implicit suspicions of one's qualifications. That is, although the application of a white student from Minnesota may be given special attention because of a lack of applicants from that part of the country, that student will not be dogged by innuendo that he received special treatment because his home state was underrepresented. However, a Latino from East Los Angeles will probably not be so lucky.

Moreover, I have seen the play-it-safe reality of affirmative action, Ivy League–style, consistently result in the rejection of superb Latino candidates whom the admissions committee deemed "unqualified." Those not good enough. Those whose grade point average was not 4.0, only 3.89. Those who did not take calculus because their high school did not offer calculus. Those whose verbal score on the SAT was considered "too low," even though they grew up in a Spanish-speaking household and only recently arrived from Mexico. Those too authentic, too scarred. Those, in a sense, "too Hispanic" for Harvard.

On one occasion, I asked the only Latina on the Harvard admissions committee why it seemed that incoming Chicano freshmen were, each year, sporting better and better high school records. She responded that the reason revolved around the fact that, while the overall educational condition of Latinos remained dismal, the caliber of individual students had improved dramatically since the advent of affirmative action programs. I remember her casual response amid the shuffling of papers.

Schools like ours are simply not taking the amount of risk that we used to. Given the quality of students today, we don't have to . . .

In truth, Harvard loved me. Such elite schools have the luxury of being able to use a small number of "safe," conventionally well-qualified minority students like me to lightly diversify their campuses without raising eyebrows, tinkering with their espoused standards, or provoking the legal fiasco of a second coming of Allan Bakke. Some might call it caution. Others, progress.

I have come to call this practice something else: skimming the cream. In the Ivy League, what passes for racial progress and greater access is often nothing more than the perpetuation of a tradition of rewarding excellence. In any given admissions season, Harvard, Yale, and Princeton all fight for the same 1 percent of minority students. The result is the pointless heaping of praise primarily on those who are accustomed to it, those who need it least.

Each spring, hopeful young Latino men and women anxiously check the mail in search of affirmation that they are "good enough" to attend schools like Harvard. Reading words on letterhead that they will never see again, they are forced to accept a stranger's judgment that they are not "good enough."

In those days, I have anguished over what I had not even realized was my duplicity in a charade brimming with dishonesty and deception.

I had traveled at my own expense and with no personal gain to dusty, remote country high schools where I asked young people with tired eyes to disregard their own skepticism and believe in the incredible possibility that a school like Harvard was interested in them. The students rolled their tired eyes. Snickered. Maybe tapped a pencil on their desk in boredom. Was I lost? Didn't I know that kids from a school like this did not go to schools like Harvard?

I persisted and convinced a few, only a few, to apply. Cautiously they had taken the application from my hand and had spent a substantial amount of time completing it during Christmas vacation. Time that, ultimately, would have been less wasted waiting for Santa to come down the chimney.

Months later, after the rejection letters went out, I had dreaded making difficult phone calls to those for whom Santa did not appear, those less-than-perfect minority students who would take their place in the natural order by taking their place at state college. Although they tried to hide their disappointment, it comes over the phone line.

"Well, thanks anyway . . . for all your help, I mean."

All my help.

In my own cynicism, I imagine myself telling the young people on the phone that it is their own fault.

You see, you should have been born to an upper-class family with parents who spoke to you only in English and read classics to you and enrolled you in an expensive SAT prep course . . .

But I do not have the strength to say such things. I merely wish them well and hang up the phone. A fraction of my idealism dies with the click. When a reporter asked him what he thought of western civilization, Mahatma Gandhi replied: "I think it would be a good idea." With what I know about skimming, I could say the same of affirmative action at Harvard.

And so I have returned to my old high school. I have come to set the record straight, and perhaps, in a sense, to find my idealism again. In confronting a familiar spirit, I have come to say to a new crop of accusers what I did not have the words to say to their predecessors years earlier. Among other things, that while I do not expect those who have been rejected to college to throw congratulatory parties for those who have been accepted, that I do expect an honest admission, finally, that white people do not hold a monopoly on words like "qualified."

As I stepped on campus and walked up familiar steps, I shivered slightly. The place still had, even to a Harvard man returning in triumph, an unnerving feel to it. This was, I remembered, the stage for the difficult and painful drama of my adolescence. These walls had always prompted worry, exploiting the constant feeling that I was not _____ enough. Not cute enough to date cheerleaders. Not athletic enough to play sports. And according to some, not smart enough to go to Harvard were it not for the grace of affirmative action. Now in my return, I sensed those insecurities still lingering in the air around me like a thick fog of self-doubt.

It was here, as a junior, that I first experienced what might loosely be termed racism. In an election for student body president, my opponents were two white students, young men who might loosely be termed friends. We spoke in the boy's gymnasium to a hundred or so student delegates who were entrusted with ousting one of the candidates. By a narrow vote, they decreed that my name should not be placed on the ballot with the other two for the general election. Then a delegate stood up and asked for a separate vote, majority rule, on the suggestion that I be allowed to remain on the ballot anyway. That suggestion was overwhelmingly approved. My opponents were horrified. They gathered on the bleachers, whispering and shaking their heads. A few minutes later, they appealed the second vote to the faculty adviser to student government, who overturned it and removed me from the ballot once again. The next day, the general election proceeded and students were offered a choice between two, but not three, candidates.

As word of what had happened in the gym spread throughout campus, students of all races who were looking forward to voting for me grumbled at having been denied the chance to do so. Faculty members complained. Parents called the school to voice concern. The local chapter of the Mexican-American Political Association (MAPA) worried that the whole affair was too neatly contrived; of the three candidates, the one who was removed, then reinstated, then removed again happened to be the only Mexican-American.

A child, I was not so cynical. It could have been, I told myself, that my opponents' decision to challenge the delegates' second vote had nothing to do with race. I may have convinced myself, too, had it not been for what a friend overheard as being my opponents' chief motivation. In whispers, they had agreed that, the student body demographics being what they were, they faced defeat with me on the ballot. They worried, one had said, that they would "split the vote" and allow me to win.

The vote? What exactly did that mean? They understood it to mean the white vote, assuming that young people might follow the example of some adults and vote along racial lines. If that was true, then vote-splitting or not, with a student body that was over sixty percent Latino, they had reason to worry. They were afraid of losing. And that fear caused them to submit me to treatment to which I would not have been submitted had I not been Latino.

In the final and messy analysis, I am confident that, had I been Irish or Italian or Armenian or Chinese, my opponents would not have been as afraid of losing the general election and would not have whispered about something like "splitting the vote." That, I am afraid, is racism. On the day of the assembly in the gym, I left my high school campus feeling more than defeated. I felt violated and disillusioned. I was no longer a virgin to racism. My idealism had been taken by force and without remorse.

Now, as I stare out across the fresh, young faces before me, I am astonished by the realization that these young people, born after Watergate, have memories that go back only as far as President Ronald Reagan. Things like outright racial exclusion and discrimination are foreign to them, as they are to many in my generation. The idea that one's race can be an impediment to their success and happiness is to them, perhaps, incomprehensible. Children of the 1980s, they know Bill Cosby and not Jim Crow.

After my speech, there are questions. "Granted, racial discrimination was wrong back then [presumably pre-civil rights movement]," a student concedes. "But now that that's over with, shouldn't we get rid of affirmative action? And, if we don't, aren't we just creating new victims?"

Hello Allan.

The first time that I heard this argument was from Nathan Glazer, one of my professors at Harvard. Professor Glazer, who some say originally coined the phrase "reverse discrimination," argues that once any society has completely liberated its educational and employment opportunities and fully met the burden of its democratic principles, then any further tampering with the laws of appropriation through race-conscious preference programs from that point on constitutes impermissible "reverse discrimination."

Fair enough.

My dispute with my old professor and those other critics of affirmative action is that, from my vantage point, American society has not yet reached the wonderful window in time where the burden of equal opportunity has been fully met. In fact, as we near the year 2000, being Mexican-American or a member of another racial minority in the United States is arguably more burden than blessing.

I suggested to the students in the government class that they need only look at their immediate surroundings to examine the degree of racial progress in our hometown, a small town nestled in the center of California.

According to the 1990 Census, Sanger is, I reminded them, 72.8 percent Latino. The fire chief, the police chief, the mayor, the city attorney, the city manager, and the majority of city council members elected by (the constitutionally suspect practice of) at-large elections are, I pointed out, all white. In both the private and public sector, the unemployment rate of Latinos is significantly higher than of whites.

The dropout rate for Latino students from the school district that produced me and far too few students like me is consistent with the distressing national figure of 50 percent. The overall dropout rate purported by the district is deflated by the existence of a continuation high school which absorbs those considered most difficult to teach, the overwhelming majority of whom are coincidentally Latino. On average, only about 29 percent of the senior class of a public school system that is over 70 percent Latino is considered academically "eligible" to enter the University of California after graduation; on average, less than 5 percent do so. Of the nearly two hundred teachers employed by the Sanger Unified School District, an estimated less than 10 percent are Latino. At the threshold of the twenty-first century, there has never been, in the one-hundred-year history of the district, a Latino principal of its only high school or a Mexican-American superintendent of schools. As for the hiring body responsible for most of these personnel issues, the local school board (also elected at-large) is, not surprisingly, all white.

I suggested that, nationally, dozens of towns like Sanger peppered across the American Southwest, with bigger cities often not faring much better, have left distressing economic gaps between Latinos and non-Latinos. Again, the 1990 Census reported that 23.4 percent of Latino families live in poverty, compared to 9.2 percent of white families. About 30 percent of male Latino workers are concentrated in lower-paying jobs such as assembly-line workers, compared with 19.5 percent of non-Latino workers. Finally, the median income of Latino families is $23,400, compared to $35,200 for non-Latino families. At every stage of life, the odds for prosperity are slim. The Latino child is more likely to live in poverty, the Latino adolescent more likely to drop out of school, and the Latino adult more likely to be unemployed or incarcerated than their white counterparts.

It should be no surprise, I told them, that a 1990 survey by Korn/Ferry International found that 95 percent of the real power positions in corporate America were then still held by white males.

Clearly, I argued, no matter how slick and seductive the rhetoric about the suffering of "new victims," the harsh reality is that, even as we approach a new millennium, American society has not yet ended the suffering of its old victims. Certainly the students were no more anxious to hear that there was work yet to be done than might be journalists or academics or politicians. Nevertheless, I submitted, it is only against a more realistic backdrop of the continued economic disempowerment and educational neglect of the nation's Latino population, along with tragically similar statistics for African-Americans that charges of "reverse discrimination" are best and most honestly considered.

After all, I concluded, for Mexican-Americans, along with occupying a modest 2.5 percent of the student population at Harvard comes a long list of far less glamorous statistics that must first be endured.

The questions ended. Some of the students nodded on their way out the door. One young man confessed confusion, saying that he was no longer so sure that affirmative action was all bad. That is something, I suppose.

As I walked off campus, I realized that defending affirmative action is new for me. In the past, when I have written or lectured about affirmative action, my intention has been to criticize the program and the halfhearted, fast-food way in which, I believe, it is currently implemented on many college campuses.

I am painfully aware of the program's shortcomings. I know the insecurity in one's ability that invariably baptizes what Yale Law Professor Stephen L. Carter calls, an "affirmative action baby." I have worried, with columnist William Raspberry of *The Washington Post*, that the greedy exploitation of affirmative action benefits by an elite few amounts to little more than merely replacing white pigs at the opportunity trough with black and brown ones, those who shamelessly feast on scraps from a guilt-ridden table in the name of others who go hungry. Most of all, recalling my own experience with Harvard, I have seen the most timid forms of affirmative action do little more than perpetuate the status quo by benefiting only those who need special consideration the least.

Although we share the same target, the crucial difference between my inhibitions about affirmative action and that of most of its critics is that, while they attack the preferential treatment of minority college applicants because they believe that it goes too far toward addressing the racial inequality that still exists in our society, I have attacked it because I continue to believe that it does not nearly go *far enough* toward meeting that end.

The door of educational opportunity, opened only a crack by two decades of professed preferential treatment, is letting in a draft that is already giving many Americans a bit of a cold and they are seeking to close it before their condition worsens. That is unfortunate, given the fact that a new generation of Americans is determined to knock down that archaic barrier once and for all. Now that we have entered your libraries and found your books, it is impossible for us to forget what we have learned. Like the English language, these opportunities are mine now and I will not give them back.

More than a year after my graduation from college, it is opportunity that has brought me to the gentle climate of Westwood. After spending a semester working as an instructor at Fresno State and another as a substitute teacher in the elementary and secondary schools of Sanger Unified, I have enrolled as a doctoral student in education at the University of California, Los Angeles. I have arrived with a new optimism and a pocketful of promises. Los Angeles promises a milder winter than that to which I have grown accustomed. UCLA promises the anonymity of a large state university. And the degree program itself promises an advanced credential to join the framed Harvard degree collecting a thick layer of dust on the shelf in my parents' living room.

By going on to graduate school almost immediately after college, I have, to an extent, succumbed to peer pressure from those Harvard classmates of mine whose ambition was not tempered with a mere undergraduate degree, however prestigious. I remembered the audacity, the sense of immortality that engulfed a Latino classmate who once, while contemplating his academic ambitions, spouted off a succession of graduate degrees like so much alphabet soup. *Let's see, I want an M.B.A., a Ph.D., and a J.D. to go with my B.A.* Somewhere in all those letters, he was sure, lay happiness and, hopefully, respect.

But there is a more personal motivation behind my arrival at UCLA. I have by now finally realized that, in the high-powered professional circles to which I have been exposed throughout my association with Harvard, elite credentials like a Ph.D. bring with them a certain amount of legitimacy. And that legitimacy brings access to power, the sort of power needed to affect the social change that I have begun to envision myself, one day, creating. These are lessons that I learned not at Harvard but at home in the San Joaquin Valley, where as a young man I basked in the access to local government and business leaders that my Harvard affiliation provided me. They are lessons that were learned much earlier by a classmate, now imprisoned, who once professed to me in the same breath a distaste for Harvard College and also a desire to go to Harvard Law School in pursuit of some wonderful blessing which would leave him immune to the skepticism and criticism of others.

Still, for Latino students concerned not only with legitimacy but also with broader access, a lingering paradox is the tiny numbers of their colleagues who are ever afforded the chance to dine at elite tables. At UCLA, on orientation day, I survey the roomful of several dozen fellow doctoral students and, with no real surprise, notice only a handful of other Latinos.

As I search in vain for a parking space and walk off to class surrounded by baby-faced undergraduates, I realize that I am not supposed to be here. My plan had always been to become a lawyer. Inspired in part by my father's law enforcement background, I decided early in my childhood to use a career in law to seek out some measure of that elusive entity called justice.

My mother and father had always approved of and taken comfort from my career decision. For Mexican parents, the idea of a lawyer in the family is at once warm and reassuring. *Un abogado.* It is said, among gossiping aunts, that a lawyer is a professional worthy of respect and deserving of a high wage. It is said that a lawyer protects people's rights. That simple concept is especially appealing to groups of people, like Mexican-Americans, who feel, often not without cause, that their rights are constantly in jeopardy.

In my lifetime, the term "rights" had already progressed from access to toilet facilities to access to colleges and universities. Still, even as I graduated from perhaps the best university in the country, I knew that my experience was anything but typical. Dire statistics on the evening news reminded me that the overwhelming majority of Latino young people in the United States were being denied their birthright to an equal and quality education. I had seen the evidence firsthand. I had been a student at Harvard and I had been a student at Fresno State. The stark differences that I observed in the quality of education afforded young people in each of those two worlds told me in no uncertain terms that if Americans were ever to have a fully-educated citizenry, the education system had to be radically reformed. At first, it seemed to me the courtroom might well be the arena for the reformation. In college, a course at Harvard Law School into which I cross-registered and in which I excelled inspired me to use my planned legal training as a tool for educational reform.

Appropriately, comically, the only obstacle in my path was admission to law school. The rejection letters came in a funeral procession of thin white envelopes, each thanking me for my interest in their schools and wishing me well in my future—that is, as long as I spent it somewhere else. Granted, I had applied to an elite bunch of law schools. In fact, many of them were affiliated with the same universities to which I had applied for undergraduate study years earlier. I could attribute my inability to repeat history to several glaring blemishes on my college transcript, or to a mediocre score on the LSAT, or to any number of other unknown factors. It didn't matter. What did matter was that, for some reason, fate was interceding into my carefully conceived plans to alter my life's path in another direction.

Shielded by John Harvard's graduation present—exaggerated sense of self—I was not discouraged by the small stack of thin envelopes in my hand. Although, I will admit that I recognized them as heralding not only rejection but also, at least in one case, a sense of outright abandonment. Perhaps understandably, no letter stung more profoundly than the one from Harvard Law School. The concept was poetic. The school that had courted me years earlier, the place that had robbed me of my idealism but left me with unyielding confidence and a sense of limitless possibility, the institution that had neglected me, embraced me, humbled me, enriched me, and left me better than it found me now wanted nothing to do with me.

My ambition curtailed for the first time by rejection, I resolved that I would attend graduate school in education not en route to a career as a school superintendent or a university professor but instead as an entrée into law school in subsequent years. Then, armed with not one but two professional degrees, I would rejoin my Harvard brethren in the professional world. Maybe, I told myself, my destiny lay in "the power triangle" of Boston, New York, and Washington or in the major cities of the west coast. No matter. A true Son of Harvard, I imagined no limits. Anything was possible.

UCLA was most accommodating. In an exception to protocol, I had been admitted to the doctoral program of the school of education without the usual prerequisite of a masters' degree. Along with admission, the school had offered me an embarrassingly large fellowship to facilitate my graduate work, then subsequently raised the amount to an even more embarrassing level. In another exception, the school had also allowed me to defer enrollment and fellowship for one year so that I might accept an offer to teach at Fresno State. As pre-enrollment registration approached, there was an unexpected phone call from a concerned professor ("Just checking to see if everything is all right...") and another from a vice chancellor ("Looking forward to meeting you...").

Upon arrival, I was welcomed by staff, faculty, and fellow students. I had, since the Razo editorial, continued to write opinion pieces in *The Los Angeles Times*, and someone mentioned having seen my byline a few times. Taken by the arm, I was introduced to person after person who, it was said, would be valuable to me in my graduate work. I was allowed to override the mountains of bureaucratic red tape that my fellow students encountered in obtaining comfortable housing, high-paying campus employment, and even the most priceless commodity in Los Angeles, a parking permit.

All of this conspicuous, bend-over-backward effort to honor their novelty, to make their Harvard Chicano feel comfortable. Odd, then, that it would all make me feel so uncomfortable.

Even with the discomfort over the fawning that introduced me to my doctoral program, I did not expect that, in that program, I would learn the single most important and most painful lesson of my academic career. What I learned would be so personal and so disturbing that, consumed with the force of the revelation, I would be unable to complete the power journey. Overwhelmed with guilt, I would eventually find relief only in the complete surrendering of ambition and with the dramatic, and what some might consider self-destructive, renunciation of academic privilege.

The defining lesson comes to me in memory, a childhood memory prompted in large part by the curriculum of my graduate program; specifically, a series of classroom lectures, class discussions, and assigned reading about the educational practice commonly known as ability-grouping, or "tracking."

Memory takes me back to Madison Elementary School, an inconspicuous assortment of gray buildings in my brown and white hometown. The place where, during recess, I first played with my Mexican-American friends. The place where, in the classroom, I was first set apart from them.

Set apart by teachers. Not demons, but teachers—well-intentioned men and women searching for more efficient ways of teaching roomfuls of students of different aptitude. Teachers convinced that, for any number of reasons, they could not teach us all. Teachers making private concessions, content to educate at least some with a blind eye toward the rest.

My educational journey began in the early 1970s. Richard M. Nixon had just been re-elected president and the term "Watergate" signified no more than the name of an obscure office complex in Washington. The images of the Vietnam War still permeated the evening news. There was violence and division everywhere, from Kent State to Munich. And a wounded country began its delicate recovery from the social upheaval of the 1960s.

In Cambridge, a handful of Mexican-American students, pioneers who had endured and survived an exploratory expedition, graduated from Harvard College and began the precarious journey home. Meanwhile, three thousand miles away, a five-year-old Mexican-American boy in a kindergarten classroom nibbled graham crackers and milk and, by excitedly answering his teacher's questions, unknowingly began an equally precarious journey away from home.

One fateful day, in the second grade, my teacher decided to teach her class more efficiently by dividing it into six groups of five students each. Each group was assigned a geometric symbol to differentiate it from the others. There were the Circles. There were the Squares. There were the Triangles and Rectangles.

I remember being a Hexagon.

I remember something else, an odd coincidence. The Hexagons were the smartest kids in the class. These distinctions are not lost on a child of seven. Child psychologists suggest that children usually conclude their first year of schooling already well aware of which of their classmates are smart and which are not so smart. Even in second grade, my classmates and I knew who was smarter than whom. And on the day on which we were assigned our respective shapes, we knew that our teacher knew, too.

As Hexagons, we would wait for her to call to us, then answer by hurrying to her with books and pencils in hand. We sat around a table in our "reading group," chattering excitedly to one another and basking in the intoxication of positive learning. We did not notice, did not care to notice, over our shoulders, the frustrated looks on the faces of Circles and Squares and Triangles who sat quietly at their desks, doodling on scratch paper or mumbling to one another. Obediently, they waited their turn at the reading table, anticipating their few minutes of attention. Occasionally, the teacher would look up from our lesson and command order to the rest of the class.

"Could I have all my Circles be quiet..."

We knew also that, along with our geometric shapes, our books were different and that each group had different amounts of work to do. The textbook company maximized profit by printing not one but a series of six different reading books, each one more difficult than the one preceding it in the series. The Circles had the easiest books and were assigned to read only a few pages at a time. The Triangles had books that were a little more difficult than those of the Circles, and they were expected to read a few more pages in them. Not surprisingly, the Hexagons had the most difficult books of all, those with the biggest words and the fewest pictures, and we were expected to read the most pages.

The result of all this education by separation was exactly what the teacher had imagined that it would be: Students could, and did, learn at their own pace without being encumbered by one another. Some learned faster than others. Some, I realized only as a doctoral student at a pristine university, did not learn at all.

What I had been exposed to, and in truth had benefited from, in that dusty elementary school was the educational practice of ability-grouping, or tracking. And if my classmates and I were being tracked by teachers and guidance counselors, then I was certainly on the right one. Fourth grade honors led to fifth grade honors which led to sixth grade honors. At the brink of entering junior high school, a crucial point in my educational development, my sixth grade teacher recommended to junior high officials that I be placed in a pre-algebra class instead of one for general math. That simple distinction enabled me to take, in subsequent years, courses in algebra, geometry, advanced algebra, trigonometry, math analysis, and finally calculus—that elite course that winked approvingly from my transcript at the Harvard admissions officer.

From grade school to high school, teachers and counselors and principals understood that I was intelligent. Not one of them was brave enough to question my ability, to second-guess the scribblings of their colleagues on my cumulative file.

So, in truth, it was tracking, along with the support of my family and my own effort and talent, that had ultimately carried me from a small farming town to the most prestigious university in the country. And now, it was tracking that was responsible for the new assortment of "goodies"—the doctoral program, the administrative policy exceptions, and, of course, the excessive fellowship that filled my bank account. It was no accident, no quirk of fate that I now found myself in such elite company. In essence, my ascension to the heights of academic privilege was orchestrated almost twenty years earlier by well-intentioned grade school teachers and an assortment of odd geometric shapes.

Confronted with this new, old reality, I initially thought of writing my old second grade teacher, then retired, a thank you note for indirectly saving my academic life. Still, the more that I learned about the insidious nature and harmful consequences of tracking, consequences even for its benefactors, the less I felt like thanking anyone.

For me, the most distressing lesson about ability grouping was the disparate effect that it seems to have on certain students.

In the 1980s, a number of studies examining tracking in an array of elementary and secondary schools found that African-American, Latino, and Native-American students were typically among those most adversely affected by the practice. Researchers invariably found that, in racially integrated learning environments, disproportionate numbers of minority students were relegated by teachers and guidance counselors to slow-learner, low-achieving, and vocational classes than were their Asian-American and white classmates.

The findings were not unlike those of a subsequent 1992 report by the American Association of University Women that concluded, among other things, that elementary and secondary school teachers typically track their female students away from careers in math and science. Encompassing twenty years of research, the report also found that teachers give significantly less classroom attention to girls than to boys, call upon them for answers to questions much less frequently than they do boys, and sometimes even chastise girls for calling out the correct answers while rewarding boys for the same type of behavior.

Whether disparate academic treatment is predicated upon racial or gender differences, researchers agree, an inevitable consequence of teachers differentiating between children based on perceived academic ability is that, within the classroom, less-favored groups of students receive an implicit label of inferiority and are considered less intelligent than more-favored groups.

Squares and Circles, we knew, were not as smart as Hexagons.

More troublesome still, the research suggests, is that less-favored students themselves eventually realize that they carry such a label and that, understandably, such a realization proves detrimental to their fragile and developing notions of self-esteem.

Even at seven, Circles knew *why* they were Circles, as well as what was expected, and not expected, from them.

All of this, researchers conclude, eventually results in a damaging loss of self-confidence and self-respect in impacted students and consequently, in staggering statistics of meagre educational performance like drop-out rates and low test scores for Latino students.

Hexagons answered the teacher's command by excitedly running to her with books and papers in hand . . . Not much was expected from Circles, Squares, and Triangles, so not much was received from them either.

As autumn yields to winter in Los Angeles, the memory of my early academic life is becoming clearer and clearer.

I see myself as a little boy. I am in the second grade. I am lucky. I am a Hexagon. I will be cared for. I call out the right answer. My teacher smiles her approval and I smile back. I do not notice the others, the Circles and Squares and Triangles daydreaming in their boredom. I do not notice something else—a curious observation that will ultimately define the character of my life. I am an oddity.

Yes, I am a Hexagon. I am also the only Mexican-American Hexagon.

In a classroom, in a school, and in a town which were all over half Mexican-American, I was the only one. The lucky one. The lonely one. For the next ten years in public school, I will occasionally be taunted by some of the same Mexican friends with whom I was once intimate, those with whom I shared harmless elementary school vices. They will view me with a mixture of suspicion and respect and awe. They will call me "Brain" as I walk through hallways in junior high school. Mimicking adults, some of them will even practice ethnic division. They will accuse me, by virtue of my academic success, of "trying to be white." Whatever that means.

Above all, they will recognize early on that, similar skin color and a familiar surname notwithstanding, we are *not* the same. They will know, in their hearts, that we have not been given the same education and they will resent me and others like me for conspicuously gorging on opportunity while they go hungry. And they will be right to feel that way. All that I will understand at the time is that I feel embarrassed for having been set aside from those friends so similar to me. And because we all know that what initially fueled the separation was one teacher's assessment that I was not only different but smarter than them, that sense of embarrassment will gradually be compounded with a bitter dose of guilt.

It is the exact same guilt that now finds me in Los Angeles, a twenty-four-year-old graduate student in education examining for the first time the road that took me there. The guilt returns to me with a vengeance. It reaches out from my textbook and strangles me with my own complicity in a tragic drama that has spanned nearly twenty years. A drama of win some, lose some.

Finally I face the truth: I have, in my academic lifetime, experienced a form of racial injustice reminiscent of the sort of outright discrimination that, years ago, crippled the lives of so many members of my parents' and grandparents' generations. It is newer and more subtle, and so more insidious. Let the academics call it "intraracial differentiation." Let the rest of us understand it to simply mean teachers, particularly elementary school teachers, passing an early judgment about the learning ability of their students with regard to race. And while this sort of thing is not historically unique, what is new is that, in this case, teachers are distinguishing between students of the same race.

The phenomenon revolves around the frustrated concession by educators that since they cannot teach them all, they should settle for a few success stories. The new educational mission drifts away from the romantic ideal of enlightening the masses and toward the more manageable, more cynical, goal of merely searching out a few bright stars to pierce the darkness of racial stereotype. Teachers' lounge distinctions takes on a new dimension: *Smart Mexican, Dumb Mexican.*

In that scenario, I was always the Smart Mexican. For twelve years of public schooling, I was groomed to take college-prep courses and apply for academic scholarships by the very same people who were telling the dark-skinned Mexican boy sitting next to me that he would be lucky to graduate from high school. Maybe the boy did graduate. Eventually. Barely. Restrained by his own low self-esteem, he struggled helplessly in the same schoolwork in which I excelled. Ironically, given our shared ethnicity, my classmate's difficulty only made my academic success seem even more extraordinary by comparison. Again I was praised.

To the bureaucrats in the Harvard admissions office who studied my college application, I was a most alluring novelty— a Mexican-American valedictorian in a school system with a 50 percent drop-out rate for Hispanic students. Graciously, they invited me to join their elite family. Shamelessly, I did. Unknowingly, I went to Harvard in the name of the less fortunate, in place of the educational casualties embodied by the dire statistics on the evening news. I went to "represent" them to the America's elite ruling class, to upper-class children of privilege who would foolishly view me as being typical of the millions of Latinos in the United States.

And so, truth be known, I am not a victim of the injustice of intraracial differentiation. I am actually its beneficiary. I have benefited from the very sort of educational inequity that I went to graduate school with the hope of eliminating. I was allowed to excel in the American educational system by virtue of the same form of ability-grouping that had undermined the educational progress of so many other Mexican-American students like me.

This realization comes to me only now, as a doctoral student lost on the final leg of my educational trek. As I run along the Pacific shoreline and feel warmth of the southern California sun on my skin before my afternoon class, the tranquillity of the moment fades. Only discomfort remains.

Making matters worse, by now my complicity in the drama has thickened. My fellow doctoral students, most of them white teachers who are much older than me, have warmly accepted me into their ranks. One day, in a class discussion of the possible reasons for the academic difficulties of minority students, someone suggests that Latinos cannot learn at the same pace as many of their classmates. Someone else agrees, blaming the parents. "Didn't former Secretary of Education Lauro Cavazos once say as much?" Someone else blames economics. "Poor students from high schools in East Los Angeles can't be expected to compete with the kids at Beverly Hills High." Someone else blames bilingualism. "Isn't having to keep both Spanish and English in their heads confusing for Mexican kids?" And a home environment devoid of hope. "What do you expect given where they come from?" And, of course, being teachers as well as students, they all blame low salaries for educators.

What they do not blame, not one of them, is an educational system implicated in three generations of racial discrimination. What they do not blame are teachers who are content with educating only a few of the young people with whose conception of self they have been entrusted. What they do not blame is tracking, the insidious practice of subtle and not-so-subtle differentiation that makes their admittedly difficult jobs much easier.

I am one of them. Their classmate, colleague, and confidant. More than that, I am what I am *because* of them. They smile at me as they tell me, implicitly, that people like my parents, like my old friends, like the new girlfriend back home whose immeasurable love is sustaining me, are incompetent and unintelligent and unmotivated and hopeless. They wink and nod at me, perhaps taking comfort from the assumption that I am different from the cultural caricature that they envision when they hear the word "Chicano." In a sense, they are right. In adolescence, I did not gang-bang, smoke pot, impregnate my girlfriend, or drop out of high school.

I am a Chicano, but a *Harvard* Chicano. The cultural influence of Harvard has followed me to graduate school; indeed, it has paved my way to graduate study. As a young man studying in Los Angeles, I read *The New York Times* over cappuccino in Hollywood and attend the symphony at the Dorothy Chandler Pavilion. I argue with my professors, confidently and without deference. I recognize that, ironically, I am in many ways more like my white doctoral colleagues than I am like the Latino freshmen who are, at that moment, enrolled in a general math class across town at Garfield High School. That distinction has brought me reward, a lavish fellowship that pays for my symphony tickets. Suddenly I feel dirty.

By Christmas vacation, I am not merely uncomfortable with my degree program, I am, in truth, at war with it. I seem determined to self-destruct. I have skipped classes. I have missed reading assignments. I am drinking again. My regular jogging has once again become therapeutic. Wrapped in the familiar security of a battered Harvard sweatshirt, I run on the sand at Venice Beach. I run deliberately, against the ocean waves. Each day, the pace becomes faster, more desperate. I am running out of energy. I am running out of breath. I am running out.

My girlfriend calls. She thinks it curious that, in recent weeks, I have written three pensive newspaper editorials but, at the same time, I have not started any of the term papers that are due in a few weeks. I explain that I have no desire to spend hours buried deep in the quiet crevices of university libraries.

I am more skeptical than ever of elitism, skeptical of the idea that Ph.D.s have a monopoly on intelligence. I like the newspapers, I say. I like the feeling that my written words are being digested, not only by an elite self-serving few, but by the literate masses. I have become convinced that dry, abstract term papers with dozens of footnotes will not have the societal impact of editorials in the morning paper baptized by coffee stains. I have begun to think that, in the ambitious zeal of jumping through one hoop after another, I have somehow ended up in entirely the wrong place.

The woman I love hears my confused mumbles over the phone and she worries. As I spit out what is troubling me—this abstract stuff about Hexagons and Triangles, the tight grasp of guilt clutching at my throat, the sense that my admission and fellowship is nothing but blood money buying my silence—she tries to be sympathetic. But like her predecessor—now studying law in Arizona—she cannot understand.

She is the pretty and popular girl from my hometown, the one who was never encouraged to be intelligent by the adults who taught her or the boys who dated her. Perhaps a Circle in early life, school has always been something for her to endure and not enjoy. She has no idea what damage was done to her back then or how I indirectly benefited from it. She cries and admits that she misses me. When will I be coming home again? When can she come to see me? Lately, we have discussed marriage, discussed it to death really.

Being a wife and mother are not only at the top of her priority list, they seem to be every item on the list. She is the nightmare that my last girlfriend, the Yale cheerleader, envisioned in our most heated arguments in New Haven.

Ultimately, though, in a stream of tears, this new love will also fade. We will be driven apart not by the intellectual canyon that admittedly separates us, but by, among other things, the strain of maintaining separate and incompatible beliefs. Our argument, like our love, is passionate.

Her fiercest convictions are born of a recent conversion to Christian fundamentalism; mine can be traced to progressive politics, enduring liberal vestiges of my Harvard experience. She believes, has been taught, that—according to Scripture— homosexuality is an abnormal sin against God and women are intended to be subservient to men.

I think of my two last and best friends at Harvard, those who saved my emotional life as I dangled helplessly in my own despair. Those to whom I owe more than I can ever repay. Those to whom I have pledged my undying loyalty. A gay man and a feminist. They will likely be bookends at my wedding. As I sit, nervously, next to my girlfriend in her church, I notice that Christian politicians and political Christians are methodically spewing forth a judgment and a hatred and an intolerance toward those who are different. I am different. My skin is darker than that of every other member of the congregation, including my light-skinned girlfriend. I wonder if, when they are done punishing the gays and the feminists, I will be next. Gradually, in her zealous obedience to such sentiment, the young woman so beautiful in my arms as we made love in the innocence of night becomes much less appealing to me. About the same time, she reaches a similar conclusion. She says we have to have a talk. A familiar refrain by now.

I am alone again. But this time, I am left with resolution. I will not join the popular chorus of condemnation for those who want only the dignity and self-definition for which I have fought for so long. I will honor the private pledge of loyalty that I made in those final, most horrid, days at Harvard. And in the remainder of my friends' lifetimes, as it was in college, if bigotry and intolerance and hatred overcome the strength of our idealism, then we will all go down together.

At UCLA, I continue to stew over the unpleasant facts of educational life. Then one day, appropriately in the familiar and menacing month of March, the contradictions of my life's experience all at once become too loud to ignore. They explode in my ear. I am exiting a class which has just endured a heated and emotional discussion about racial inequality in education. In the hallway, a fellow doctoral student who has been my ally in numerous class discussions is arguing with a middle-aged blond woman. A Native-American, his hair is restrained in an authentic ponytail. Uncomfortable with the hard lessons of the day, he is pleading with the woman for consensus.

"It's just not right. Indian kids don't have a chance. Public schools don't teach them anything. No one believes in them. And the reservations are even worse. They'll never end up in a place like this. . . ."

The woman, visibly bored with the conversation, offers up a careless quip to end it as she walks away.

"Oh, calm down," she says with a smile. "You'll get *your* Ph.D."

With that, my friend is caught in midsentence, his mouth left open in embarrassment. He says nothing else. What could he say? He only lowers his head and walks away. I want to catch up to him and say something reassuring. But what? What could I say to him that he does not already know?

He knows that, as a Native-American doctoral student, he is a valuable commodity that helps the American educational system live with itself. He knows that he is a pacifier, an excuse for the system not to try harder to educate others like him. As long as he continues to succeed, the educational crisis facing the vast majority of Native-Americans can be overlooked. Ignored. Above all, he knows that he is expected to be nothing but grateful for all that he has been "given" by an educational system that plays favorites, a system that parades him out for colleagues to view with condescending nods of approval. The woman had won the argument. She had done it surgically, and yet viciously, with an insincere smile and a casual but eviscerating remark.

I proceed to the parking lot at a quick pace. Young people, college students, pass before me in a blur. Smiling, laughing. By the time that I reach my car, my heart is racing. As I drive away from campus—fast, then faster—the images of bright lights pass before my eyes. By the time that I reach my apartment, I am filled with contempt for the whole charade that passes itself off as the American educational system. To think that it would be so easily satisfied to educate a few in the name of the many!

My Native-American colleague's brutal encounter leaves me to wonder: Is that the way that it is going to be for the few and the fortunate? Are academia's concessions to affirmative action never really forgiven, only invoked at indelicate moments to help keep "minority students" (that dubious distinction) humble and in our place? Are we, as dissidents of two worlds, expected to sacrifice our dignity at the altar of opportunity? Is access to pristine schools, beautiful libraries, and rare books so much easier for academia to grant us than simple respect? Most of all, are we to keep completely silent about the demise of our fallen brethren? And if we embarrass or disobey our benefactor, as did my imprisoned Harvard classmate, will it leave us humiliated, naked and weeping in the university courtyard?

As I pace the floor of my apartment, I consider the consequences of leaving an old, familiar lover who has always sustained me with nurturing, positive attention. I know at least one thing: If I burn the bridge that I have constructed between the worlds of academia and home, there will be no room for second thoughts.

I pack one bag, then another. I call a few friends from college and from home. Some suggest continuing in the doctoral program, maybe becoming a school superintendent and eliminating injustices like tracking from "within" the system. But no. I will not crawl into the mouth of the lion to clean its teeth. Someone asks if I am "burned out," then quickly retracts the question as she realizes that the concept of burn out is a simplification of a torment that is, for me, anything but simple. My friends all express concern, even worry. What will I do? Where will I go?

An old and trusted friend from Yale is blunt in his assessment

of the consequences of walking away from the warmth of privilege and into the cold darkness of the unknown. "I don't know
about you," he says. "But, given the depressed economy out
there and the outright worthlessness of a bachelor's degree—
even one like ours—I would be scared shitless. . ."

As I load my car and drive into the LA traffic, heading for the
freeway, I realize that I *am* scared. The one thing that I fear
most is that my abrupt departure in the night will bring disappointment to others. The good student. The good son. My
ambitions have always honored the promises of an elite education. But it is not elitism that is important to me now, but
conviction and truth and some semblance of equality. It is those
forces that push me north along the interstate, propelling me
away from prestige and privilege and once again toward the
honest simplicity of the San Joaquin Valley.

As I approach the familiar exit on the highway, I start to feel
safe. The reassuring smell of grapevines and freshly plowed
earth floats through the open car window. I am returning, once
again, to a good and decent place. A simple place of compassion and wisdom, those elusive qualities that are more rare and
valuable than simple intelligence. Compassion like the kind in-
grained in my mother's smile and in her moral absolutes, her
unyielding sense of right and wrong. Wisdom like the kind embodied in the majesty of my grandfather's storytelling or in the
tenacity of my father's argument. The place of my birth. The
place that withstood a boy's ungrateful departure and still, in
forgiveness, welcomes a young man's return. The place where
I *belong.*

It is here, in my hometown, far away from Harvard, that I
seek my own private reconciliation with the faces of the past.
I remember the labels that defined their early existence. Triangles, Squares, Circles. I run into them in the routine of daily
errands, at the post office, at the bank, at the grocery store. I
almost feel compelled to apologize to them for the broken
promises that they have, unknowingly, endured. They push
baby carriages and carry diaper bags and seem old for their
young age. Referring to a flattering article about me in the local
newspaper, they ask about my life. With a smile, I avoid the
question and search for polite ways to ask about theirs.

Some are still in college, in the seventh year of a four-year program. Some work at monotonous jobs that make them hate getting up in the morning. They hear about places like New York and London, but they will never visit them. They smile broadly and tell me that they are proud of all that I am doing— and at our age! We exchange good-byes. Maybe we will see each other at the upcoming high school reunion. Maybe not. They push their baby carriages through the door and eventually pass from view. I know that I am watching the deferment of the American dream from one generation to the next, a young parent's solemn hope that perhaps a child will, one day, navigate better than they the important, but treacherous, waters of the American educational system.

That is my parents' concession. That is the hope of the two young, old people who taught me my earliest lessons. Those who taught me how to count to ten in English and Spanish and played memory games with a deck of playing cards, all before I entered my first classroom. My parents, who wallowed, along with so many of their contemporaries, in the despair of low expectation. My parents, whose experiences in public school were much harder, and whose stories much sadder, than mine.

One night, not long after my return, my father listened intently as I rambled on at the dinner table about tracking and less subtle forms of educational discrimination. After a few moments adrift in memory, he allows himself a well-earned complaint forty years after the fact.

"Come to think of it," he says. "That wasn't right . . . what they did to us."

It is ultimately that simple. The educational neglect of young people—especially in those years in which they are most susceptible to its negative effects—is not right. And no amount of feeble attempts to educate the few in place of the many can make it right.

Some will consider this ungrateful. The biting of a hand that has fed me so well for so long. But there are too many others who still go hungry. I will apologize no more.

This Hexagon has had enough.

ACKNOWLEDGMENTS

Undeniably, I am indebted to those educators who, over two decades, had such a positive impact on my life as a student. Those of the Sanger Unified School District, especially high-school teachers Larry Powell, whose defense of me to colleagues was an inspiration, and the late Janet Mabray, whose praise for my writing nurtured my earliest literary instincts; yes, I believe Mrs. Mabray would have liked this. Those at Harvard, especially Marshall Hyatt at the College, Randall Kennedy at the Law School, and Jay Heubert at the Graduate School of Education—each of whom validated the worth of an elite education. And, finally, at UCLA, I appreciate the extraordinary kindness of Dr. Raymond Paredes, Dr. Kris Gutierrez, and Ms. Brenda Woods. I would also like to specifically thank two of my professors there—Dr. Daniel Solorzano, who reminded me what a real teacher was, and Dr. Amy Wells, who heard a disillusioned young man's cry for help and mercifully rescued him from his own ambition.

For sustaining me through difficult times—both in the writing of this manuscript and throughout the experiences embodied in it—I am grateful for an array of special relationships that a man twice my age would be fortunate to claim as his own. From Harvard, I treasure my association with Jay Stewart, Douglas Cerasoli, Greg Bell, Jennifer Dargan, David Carney, Suzette Malveaux, Jerry McDowell, Frank Huerta, John Metzger, and Michael Camunez. From home, I cherish my enduring friendships with, among others, Jerry Padron, Anthony Monreal, Sandy Herrera, Joe Hinojosa, Melissa Huerta, Larry Lopez, and Rebecca Richens. I am also grateful for the continued friendship of Michael Quintana, who—as a student at MIT—touched both worlds with me and was never far along the Charles River when I needed a sympathetic ear.

I was also blessed, in my college years, with membership in a small, intimate band of very special young people—an informal Ivy League alliance that was bound together in mutual love, shared misery, and the taste of Long Island Iced Teas. I am grateful to Anna Maria Chavez, Rene Cantu, Monica Byrne-Jimenez, Beatriz Ponce de Leon, and Raul Perez for allowing me, as part of the SAC-PAC, to share such a precious time in their lives.

And, of course, I am indebted beyond my repayment to Joseph Henry Cice and Kedron McDonald for their compassion and loyalty and most of all for standing by me in the final days of an experience so painful that I may not have survived it without them.

I am also appreciative of those older and wiser individuals who, during my education, provided warm and supportive words when I needed to hear them. I am especially grateful for the encouragement, at fateful moments, of Isa Rodriguez, Steve White, Donald M. Stewart, Drs. William Flores, Jesus Luna, and Lea Ybarra at California State University, Fresno, the Honorable Alex Kozinski of the Ninth Circuit Court of Appeals, Gary Spiecker of *The Los Angeles Times*, William A. Tinsley of Tinsley Communications, and the Honorable Henry G. Cisneros, United States Secretary of Housing and Urban Development.

And, of course, I owe a special word of thanks to Richard Rodriguez, whose advice, critique, and friendship reminds me how much more poetic words can be and how far I still have to go.

In the completion of this work, I am especially grateful for the faith, initiative, and hard work of my agents, Lori Perkins in New York and Judy Coppage in Hollywood. And, more than words can express, I appreciate the incredible talents, patience, and vision of Becky Cabaza, my editor at Bantam, who along with her assistant Jennifer Steinbach, orchestrated a skillful and sensitive edit of personal and often cumbersome material. Blessed with the invaluable empathy of our shared culture, Becky saw the value of this story immediately. From the beginning, she commanded that I "bleed"; and, so, on these pages I have bled.

Most of all, I appreciate the consistent and immeasurable love, patience, and encouragement of my family. Without the blessing of the quarter century of moral support bestowed upon me by my parents, my sister Cindy, and my brother Roman, none of this adventure would have ever been possible.